A DO-IT-YO[

SUBMACHINE GUN

A DO-IT-YOURSELF

SUBMACHINE GUN

Gérard Métral

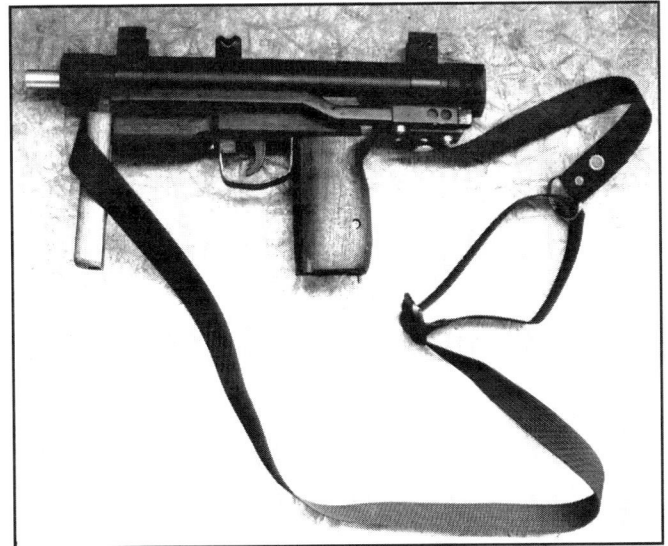

It's Homemade, 9mm, Lightweight, Durable—and It'll Never Be on Any Import Ban Lists!

Paladin Press
Boulder, Colorado

A Do-It-Yourself Submachine Gun:
It's Homemade, 9mm, Lightweight, Durable—
and It'll Never Be on Any Import Ban List!
by Gérard Métral

Copyright © 1995 by Gérard Métral

ISBN 13: 978-0-87364-840-0
Printed in the United States of America

Published by Paladin Press, a division of
Paladin Enterprises, Inc.
Gunbarrel Tech Center
7077 Winchester Circle
Boulder, Colorado 80301 USA
+1.303.443.7250

Direct inquiries and/or orders to the above address.

PALADIN, PALADIN PRESS, and the "horse head" design
are trademarks belonging to Paladin Enterprises and
registered in United States Patent and Trademark Office.

Visit our Web site at www.paladin-press.com

CONTENTS

WARNING

In most countries it is against the law to do the following:

1.   Manufacture a firearm without an official license from the government.
2.   Own a fully automatic weapon.
3.   Possess a silencer for a firearm.

In the United States, the appropriate licenses must be secured from (and taxes paid to) the Bureau of Alcohol, Tobacco, and Firearms before manufacturing any firearm, taking possession of any fully automatic weapon, or building or owning a silencer for a firearm. Many states and municipalities also restrict firearm ownership and use. Severe penalties are prescribed for violations of these laws.

People who choose to build this Métral submachine gun do so at their own risk. Neither the author nor the publisher can be responsible for any use or misuse of the information contained in this book. This material is presented for academic study only.

PREFACE

The uprising of the Warsaw ghetto in April 1943 came as a complete surprise to the Nazis. A small number of young Jews armed mostly with pistols and a few rifles, hand grenades, and fire bombs offered a strong and desperate resistance to crack SS troops. Many German soldiers were killed or wounded, and only after days of hard fighting and the use of heavy weapons did the Nazis take control of the ghetto. Only a few Jews escaped through the canals; the others, many hundreds, either died during the fighting or were executed in concentration camps. Militarily, it was a defeat for the Jews, but it is also a wonderful lesson in honor: it is better to die standing and fighting than to be driven without resistance like sheep to the slaughterhouse.

Years later, during a TV show commemorating the uprising, one of the few Jewish survivors remarked, "There is one thing I regret very much: I didn't have a submachine gun."

To resist tyranny or to make a contribution to the liberation of his own occupied country, a human being, as courageous as he may be, is helpless without weapons. In some favorable circumstances it is possible to rely on foreign help, but in many others, especially at the beginning of an uprising, one must only rely on one's own forces. To face a well-armed oppressor, a freedom fighter needs firepower. In such circumstances submachine guns are the best choice: they aren't as powerful as assault rifles, but they are much easier to conceal, making them ideal for clandestine operations.

Even in countries where there is little danger of invasion or foreign occupation and oppression, a new threat is escalating: that of violent crime. In many towns and countries in the most advanced parts of the world, ordinary citizens are at risk of being assaulted, raped, and often killed. In many regions the police are no longer able to protect the people. Worst of all, many countries forbid ordinary citizens from owning firearms. Criminals, who by definition don't respect laws, have no problem

Two generations of resistance weapons: my homemade submachine gun and a Viet Minh copy of a STEN used by the Vietnamese against the French.

arming themselves and can therefore act with the abandon of a fox in an unguarded henhouse.

This book was written for those who don't want to be passive victims of oppression or criminals and who have no other ways of obtaining weapons.

As can be seen in the Bibliography, other books exist about weapons designed with the same purpose, but the Métral gun presented in this book has some unique features that make it uniquely suitable for self-defense. Small and handy, it can be disassembled quickly into a limited number of easy-to-conceal parts. It was also specially designed for clandestine manufacture, even on a large scale.

The author made prototypes, tested them, and got rid of all the bugs that occurred during development. The result is an efficient and reliable weapon that you can count on.

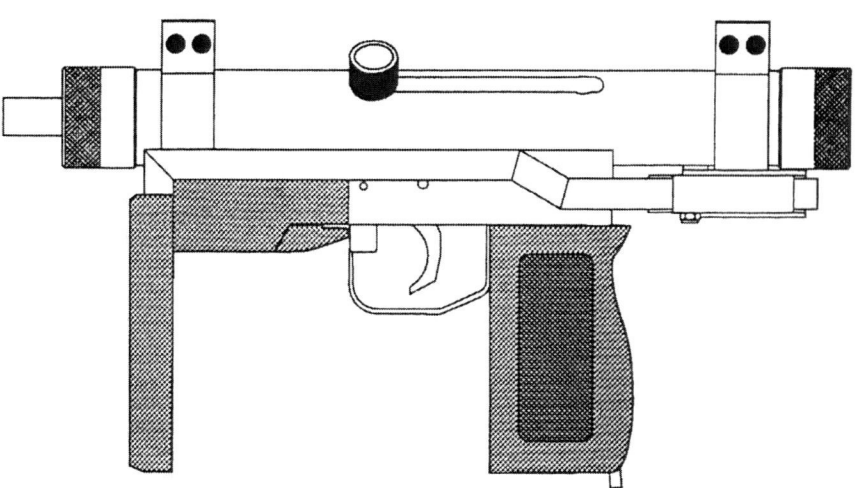

Illustration of the Métral submachine gun described in this book.

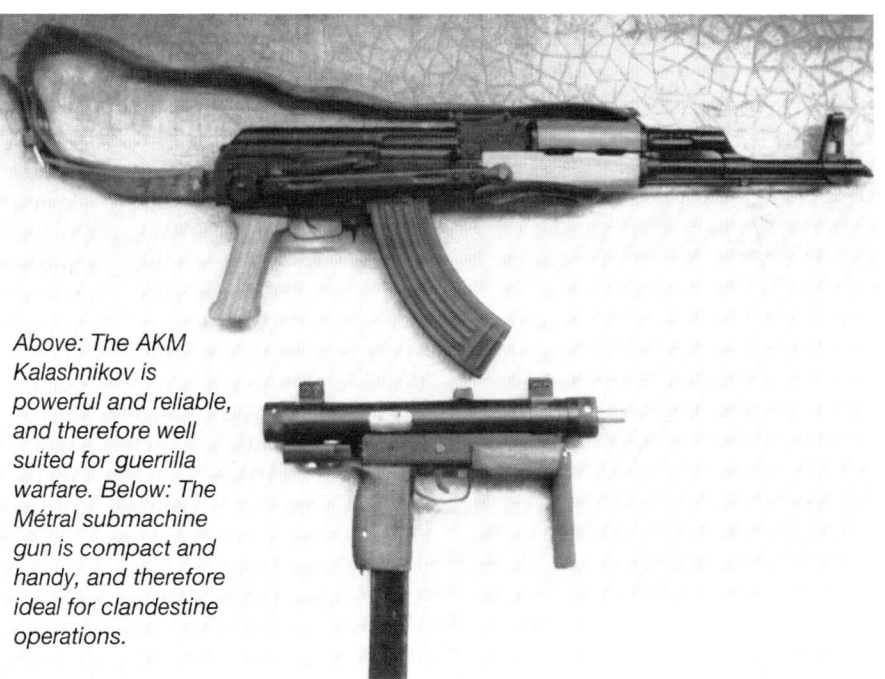

Above: The AKM Kalashnikov is powerful and reliable, and therefore well suited for guerrilla warfare. Below: The Métral submachine gun is compact and handy, and therefore ideal for clandestine operations.

PRESENTATION

SPECIFICATIONS

The Métral gun was designed according to the following specifications:

1. It must be able to be built by people or groups with limited equipment. It should be feasible for an individual to produce the entire weapon in a small workshop.
2. Decentralization of large-scale production of the various parts is possible.
3. Most parts should appear innocuous, looking like pieces of ordinary civilian machines or tools.
4. Taken down, the gun should be able to be concealed easily; for example in a car, if a couple of components are found, it should not be obvious without a complete search of the vehicle that they are submachine gun parts.
5. The size of the weapon facilitates its use from a car.
6. Users should meet, on equal terms, opponents armed with such submachine guns as the Uzi, Beretta Model 12, Heckler & Koch MP5, or similar weapons found in most parts of the world.
7. The gun has an attractive appearance.

DESCRIPTION

The Métral gun is a 9mm Parabellum (called also 9mm Luger, 9x19, or other local designations). Its design is based on known principles and solutions found in other guns, put together with the aim of reliability and ease of manufacture under clandestine conditions. The general shape of the weapon is similar to the Czech CZ 25 and the Uzi. The selector of the trigger mechanism comes from the Suomi M1931 and the bolt security from the Ingram M10. I claim as my own inventions the bolt construction and the way the weapon is assembled. The folding stock adopted is also my brainchild.

A very critical part of a submachine gun is the magazine. I decided to use the STEN magazine because originals are easy to find at low prices. It is also possible to build usable fiberglass versions of this magazine.

With small modifications in the pistol grip's dimensions, magazine latch, and perhaps the loading ramp and underside of the bolt, it is possible to use magazines designed for other weapons.

I kept the number of different parts to a minimum to ease decentralized production. For example, all symmetrical parts such as plugs, support rings, and sights are almost identical. I also tried to make them look like ordinary mechanical components to conceal their final function.

Data for Métral Gun
Cartridge: 9mmx19
Operation: blowback, selective fire
Feed: 32-round box magazine (from British World War II STEN gun)
Weight, empty: 2.9 kg
Length: (butt extended) 600 mm; (butt folded) 360 mm
Barrel: 200 mm
Rifling: 4 grooves, rh, one turn in 254 mm
Muzzle velocity: 390 m/s
Rate of fire (cyclic): 600 rounds per minute

Data for Uzi
Cartridge: 9mmx19
Operation: blowback, selective fire
Feed: 25- and 32-round box magazine
Weight, empty: 3.7 kg
Length: (metal stock extended) 640 mm; (stock folded) 455 mm
Barrel: 260 mm
Rifling: 4 grooves, rh, one turn in 254 mm
Muzzle velocity: 390 m/s
Rate of fire (cyclic): 600 rounds per minute

OPERATING INSTRUCTIONS

How to Load and Fire the Métral

1. Pull the selector to the rear safe position.
2. Pull the cocking handle to the rear. The weapon fires from an open bolt, and therefore the bolt will remain to the rear. Rotate the cocking handle 90° clockwise or counterclockwise as a safety measure.
3. Insert a loaded magazine into the magazine well, located in the pistol grip, and push in until it locks with a click. Try to pull it out to be sure it is firmly locked in. Rotate the cocking handle 90° back to its firing position.

Caution: Many people are used to inserting the magazine first and then pulling the bolt back, which is the usual way to load an automatic pistol. With a

This gun is easy to hide, e.g., in the tire of the spare wheel. With adequate filling, a tubeless tire may be inflated and the loaded spare wheel used for a short distance.

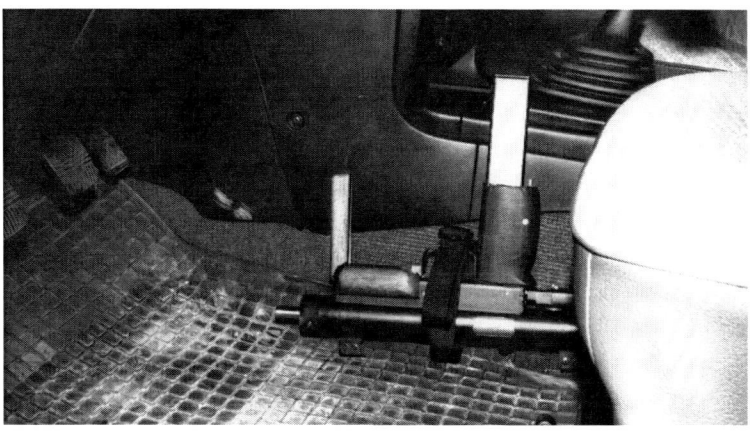
The small size of the Métral gun makes it ideal to carry in a car in an unsafe country. (In a small car use a short 15-round magazine, which is sufficient for a first reaction and easier to handle in a cramped space).

Author's daughter with Métral submachine gun in car.

A comparison of the CZ 25 (top) and the Métral gun (bottom).

Comparison of Uzi (top) and Métral (bottom).

submachine gun, if you fire from an open bolt position, there is a danger of releasing the bolt accidentally before it is caught by the sear; the bolt will then ram the first cartridge into the chamber and fire! The order of operation given above is much safer.

To fire single shots, push the selector to the middle position. When you squeeze the trigger, the gun will fire one shot, eject the empty case, and then the bolt will remain to the rear. To fire another shot, you must release the trigger and pull it again.

To fire full auto, push the selector completely forward. The gun will fire automatically until the ammunition is exhausted or until the trigger is released.

The position of the selector is easy to feel at night because of its relation to the trigger guard.

To remove the magazine, push the magazine latch at the bottom rear of the pistol grip, and pull the magazine out of the weapon.

To unload the gun: remove the magazine. Then squeeze the trigger while retaining the bolt handle. Let the bolt go slowly forward and ensure by looking through the ejection port that the chamber is empty.

Safety Measures

1. Store the gun unloaded, without a magazine, bolt forward locked by the bolt handle rotated 90°, and with the selector set at "safe."

    In situations where there in no immediate danger keep the gun with magazine inserted, bolt rearward and locked by the bolt handle, and selector set at "safe."

2. In a hostile environment carry the gun loaded, bolt rearward with handle unlocked and selector set at "safe." To fire, just push the selector forward with the back of your forefinger and squeeze the trigger.

3. If the gun is ready to fire, with bolt open and magazine inserted, and you have to move quickly to another position, lock the bolt by rotating the bolt handle. This will prevent an accidental firing while you are crawling, jumping, or making any other movement. Unlock the bolt once you are ready to fire again.

4. Never carry the gun with a loaded magazine inserted and bolt forward unlocked by the bolt handle: it may fire accidentally if dropped.

    If you're going to store the gun, ensure that the chamber is empty and then pull the bolt rearward until you can see the chamber through the ejection slot. In case of ejection failure or misfire, you will see a cartridge held to the bolt face by the extractor. In that case, pull the bolt rearward until it falls either through the ejection port or the pistol grip.

Stripping

1. Remove the magazine.
2. Unfold the stock.
3. Push the selector to the "single shot" position. Holding the bolt handle with your left hand, let the bolt go slowly forward by pressing the trigger.
4. With the tip of a bullet, push down the stud on the side of the front plug, unscrew the plug, and remove it.
5. Separate the trigger mechanism housing from the upper part of the gun.
6. Pull the operating handle out and remove the barrel and bolt together from the front end of the gun.
7. Take the barrel out of the bolt extension.
8. Reassemble the gun in the reverse order.
9. Take care to insert the ejector in its hole on the rear face of the bolt; use a finger inserted through the ejection port to guide it while you push the bolt assembly and barrel rearward with the other hand.
10. Push the barrel to align the bolt handle location of the bolt with the opening in the receiver and insert the bolt handle.

Folding Stock

To fold the stock, pull it to the rear and to the left. Fold it forward until it comes along the trigger mechanism housing. Push the handle forward and to the right until the stud is engaged in its slot. Then release the handle: spring pressure pushes the stock back to lock it.

To unfold the stock, push it forward and then to the left. Once unfolded let it go forward under spring pressure and lock. If necessary, push it forward to help the locking operation.

Inserting the magazine. Note the cocking handle locked in the rear position.

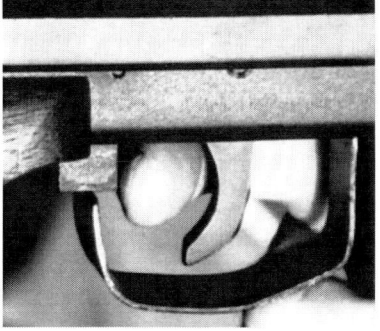

Push the selector with your forefinger.

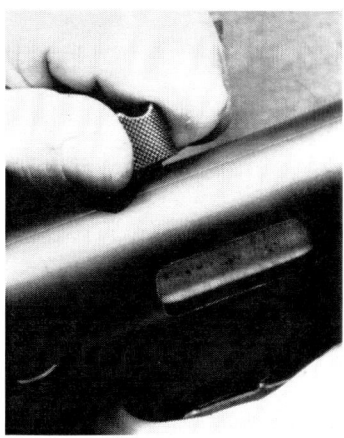

Rotating the bolt handle.

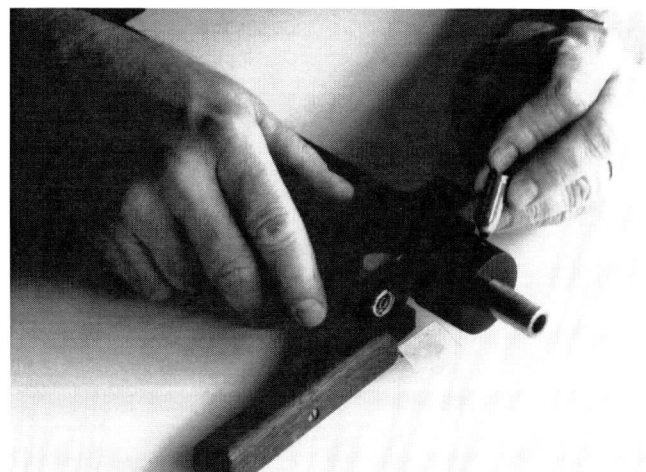

Use the tip of a bullet to release the front plug.

HOW THE GUN WORKS

Field-stripped Métral.

Unfolding the stock.

With the bolt in rearward position, pull the trigger. This depresses the sear, releasing the bolt. The main spring drives the bolt forward. The lower edge of the bolt face strips a round from the magazine and forces it forward into the chamber.

Firing occurs when the fixed firing pin strikes the primer of the chambered round. Simultaneously, the extractor engages in the extraction groove of the cartridge case. The cartridge case is forced back by gas pressure and drives the bolt rearward.

The cartridge case, held onto the bolt face by the extractor, clears the chamber, strikes the tip of the stationary ejector rod, and pivots to the right. At the same time, the ejection ports of the bolt carrier and the receiver move into alignment, allowing the spent case to be thrown clear of the weapon.

The spring and the rear cap of the body bring the bolt to rest. If the selector is set to "single shot" the sear will have risen to hold the bolt to the rear until the trigger is operated again. If the selector is set to "auto," the bolt will move forward again, driven by the spring, and the cycle will be repeated.

The bolt carrier's weight and length of travel help to reduce the cyclic rate of fire.

Warning: This weapon was designed to fire 9x19mm NATO standard ammunition (115-grains = 7.45 g bullet, with a muzzle velocity of 1,320 fps = 396 m/s). There are many other loads for the 9mm Luger ammunition, some weaker than the NATO standard. If you want to use these weaker loads, be warned: there is a risk that the bolt will have sufficient energy to travel backward far enough to pick a fresh cartridge, but not enough to be caught by the sear; the gun will then fire the entire magazine automatically.

To prevent such accidents from happening, test the gun with the ammunition you are going to use. Load only one shot in the magazine, put the selector at single shot, and fire. If the gun does eject correctly and the bolt is caught by the sear, you may use this kind of ammunition without any transformation of the gun. If the bolt isn't held back, your bolt is too heavy or your spring too strong. You can then choose another brand of ammunition, purchase a weaker spring, or lighten the bolt by drilling holes in the left side of the bolt carrier.

UNITS AND STANDARDS

All drawings are made according to the International Standards Organization (ISO) standards, and dimensions are expressed in the metric system. The following reasons dictated these choices:

1. Most parts of the world use these systems. Even in the United States there is a scheduled gradual transition to the metric system.
2. For any mechanical system a prototype must be built and tested, and remedies must be found for the inevitable teething troubles. My submachine gun was built in Europe, using locally available supplies; it was therefore necessary to use the metric system.

A conversion will be necessary to build the gun in the United States or in countries using British standards. Values for this conversion are given in Appendix C.

People who are used to working with drawings made according the ANSI system should be warned: the ISO system doesn't present the views in the same order. The ISO representation system is shown here.

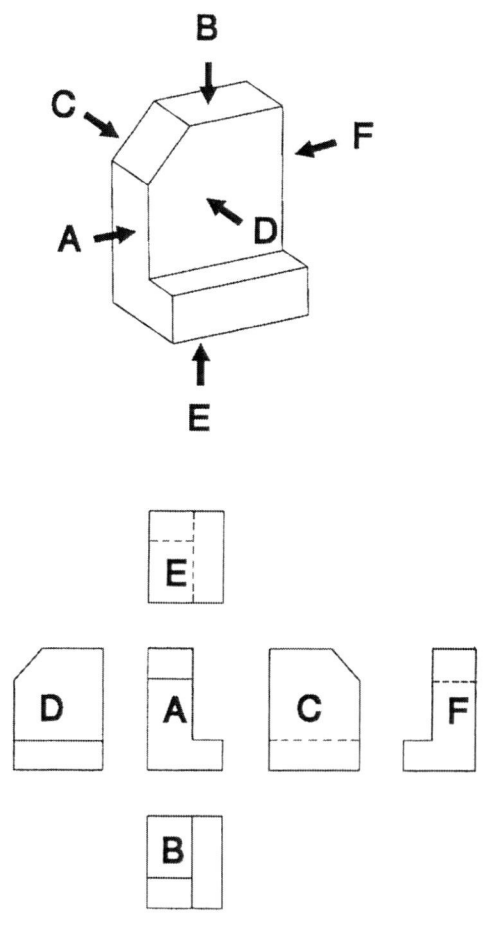

HOW TO BUILD THE GUN

SKILLS REQUIRED

This book isn't a manual for beginners in mechanics. I presume that the reader already has basic knowledge and skills. Therefore the following instructions are restricted to the minimum. I will only present the general order of operations I used to build the prototype and give some tips to help avoid common pitfalls.

EQUIPMENT

To build the Métral you need access to the following equipment:

- a lathe big enough to turn the longer parts (350 mm = 14 inches)
- a drill press
- a good heavy vise
- a vertical milling machine (helpful, but not absolutely necessary)
- tools to thread the body and plugs (it may be done on the lathe or with equipment for threading gas pipes)
- welding sets (electrical or acetylene)
- a grinding wheel
- files, drill, taps, hacksaw, and other basic hand tools

You may not have all the needed machine tools, but a lathe and a drill press are fairly common in automotive shops. One way to get these parts built may be to contact a local vocational or trade school that has courses in mechanics; teachers and students often need new models for practice.

MATERIALS

Steel tube, sheet, and bar stock are easy to obtain in industrial countries. You may use ordinary steel for most parts of the gun; a few pieces need to be hardened. Automobile and truck scrap yards are good sources for high-quality steel; look for axles and suspension components.

Purchase the main spring, barrel, and magazine from industrial manufacturers, because the are difficult to build. Try doing it yourself only if you have no other choice.

A lathe is indispensable to the construction of this gun.

A milling machine is recommended but not essential.

You must have access to a drill press to complete this gun.

List of Materials Used to Build the Prototype

- Seamless steel tube, diameter 38/34 mm
- Steel bar diameter 40 mm
- Steel tube diameter 34/18 mm
- Heat-treatable steel bar diameter 34 mm
- Heat-treatable steel bar diameter 18 mm
- Steel bar diameter 20 mm
- Very tough steel diameter 6 mm (for example, 980-1,180N/mm2 DIN 34 CrNiMo 6)
- Commercial special steel barrel rifled for 9mm Luger
- Heat-treatable steel bars diameter 8, 6, 5, 4, 3, and 2 mm
- U or square 30 mm x 30 mm steel profile, 2 mm thick
- 10 mm x 15 mm heat-treatable steel bar
- Steel tube diameter 6/4 mm
- 8 mm x 20 mm heat-treatable steel bar
- 8 mm x 6 mm heat-treatable steel bar
- 6 mm x 16 mm aluminum bar (for the front sight support)
- 5 mm x 12 mm steel bar
- 5 mm x 30 mm steel bar
- 3 mm x 15 mm heat-treatable steel bar
- 20 mm x 20 mm steel tube, 2 mm thick
- 15 mm x 15 mm steel tube, 1.5 mm thick
- 12 mm x 12 mm steel tube, 1.5 mm thick
- 2 mm steel sheet
- 1.5 mm steel sheet
- 2 mm x 10 mm heat-treatable steel bar
- Industrial coil springs (see drawings)
- 0.5 mm diameter piano wire
- Standard commercial screws and nuts M5, M4, and M3
- Surplus STEN gun magazines

BUILDING INSTRUCTIONS

Warning: Before beginning to work on any piece, read the description and study all the drawings completely and carefully. Be sure to have all tools at hand. You may sometimes find that the order of operations given here does not fit your particular working conditions; in such cases you may, of course, adapt it, but be careful. I highly recommend that you go over the entire engineering process mentally before you act with your hands.

Group 1: Receiver with Barrel and Main Spring

Receiver (Drawings 001 and 002)
Use seamless steel tube. The prototype was made from 38/34 mm diameter tubing. Cut the tube the desired length. Cut the openings with a milling machine or with a drill press and files.

The only tricky part is the threading for the plugs. You can either use a threading tool or do it on the lathe. Thread to metric M38 x 1.5, as shown in the drawing.

If you are building a single gun, thread it on the lathe. If you want to make several, purchase appropriate threading tools.

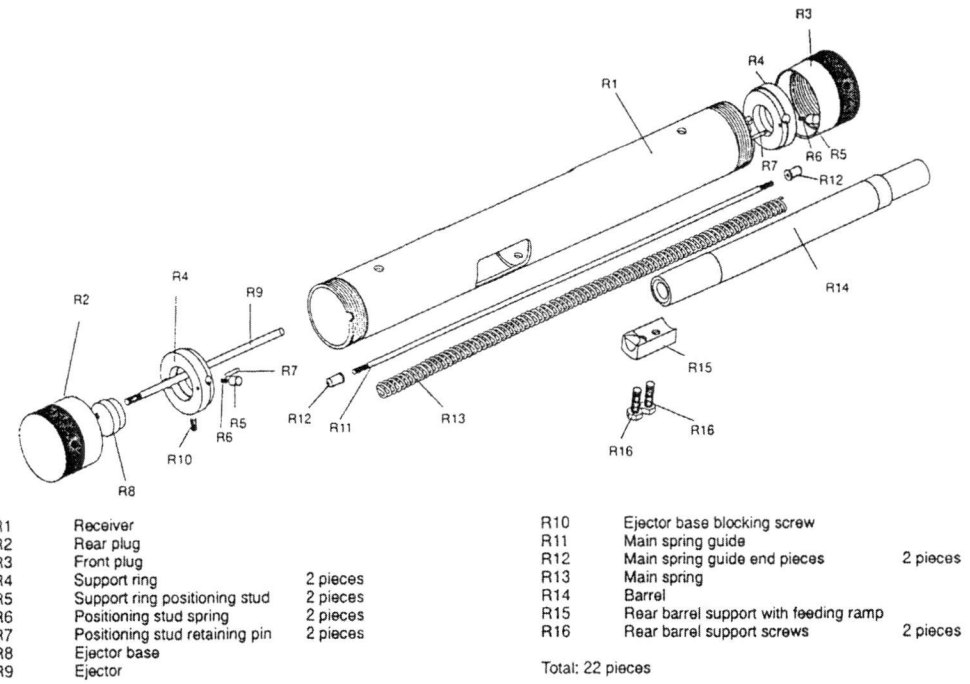

R1	Receiver			R10	Ejector base blocking screw	
R2	Rear plug			R11	Main spring guide	
R3	Front plug			R12	Main spring guide end pieces	2 pieces
R4	Support ring	2 pieces		R13	Main spring	
R5	Support ring positioning stud	2 pieces		R14	Barrel	
R6	Positioning stud spring	2 pieces		R15	Rear barrel support with feeding ramp	
R7	Positioning stud retaining pin	2 pieces		R16	Rear barrel support screws	2 pieces
R8	Ejector base					
R9	Ejector			Total: 22 pieces		

Receiver with barrel and main spring.

Plugs (Drawing 003)

The only difference between the front and the back plug is the opening for the barrel in the former. Both are machined out of solid 40 mm diameter round stock. All of the work is done on the lathe.

First cut the stock to the desired length, and bore out the inside to a 36.5 mm diameter (or the diameter needed for the threading you have chosen).

Next, thread the inside with an appropriate tool.

Next, carve knurls over a 15 mm space on the outside surface.

Then turn the inside to a diameter of 38 mm for 10 mm. Use a soft metal sheet between the mandrel's jaws and the piece to protect the knurled part.

The hole for the positioning stud is drilled during the final adjustment.

Front and Rear Support Rings (Drawings 004 and 005)

These two pieces are identical and therefore interchangeable. You must drill the hole for the positioning stud before turning the shoulder.

With the help of tool #1 (see page 19), drill the hole for the main spring's rod. This hole, once drilled, is reamed with a rat-tail file to allow easy removal of the rod.

Ejector Base (Drawing 007)

This piece is easily made on the lathe. The only difficulty is in finding the ejector's position, especially if the ejector's channel in the bolt wasn't bored straight. To do this, insert the bolt in the bolt carrier and mount the ejector's base in the rear support ring. Insert the bolt assembly in the receiver (or a tube of the same inner diameter) and put the ring on its rear end. Insert a pointed and hardened 4 mm diameter steel rod into the ejector's channel and, holding the assembly vertically, hit it with a small hammer to mark the ejector's position on the base.

Rotate the ejector base to adjust the rod's position and block it with the rear ring's M4 screw. When you have found the correct position during the final assembly, mark the screw position on the ejector base. Take it apart and file a small recess in it to ensure a positive locking by the screw.

Ejector (Drawing 007)

The ejector is a simple hardened 4 mm rod threaded at its rear extremity. The length of the ejector is critical. If its position is not correct the gun will fail to eject and will therefore jam. Therefore, after the final assembly, test the function with empty cases and dummy cartridges. When the bolt is retracted with enough speed, the empty case should fly away through the ejection opening. If it fails to do so, adjust the ejector's position by screwing or unscrewing it.

Once the correct position is found, fix the ejector on its base with soft solder.

Barrel (Drawing 009)

The barrel is the heart of the gun. It is very difficult for an amateur to make it by himself starting from a plain bar. I do not recommend it, but if you have no other choice, try it, as described in the Expedient Solutions section of this book.

An easier way is to purchase barrel blanks already rifled from industrial manufacturers. Bore diameter must be 8.8 mm to 8.9 mm (.346 to .350 inch), and groove diameter should be 9 mm to 9.1 mm (.354 to .358 inch). The rifling twist should be one turn in 250 mm but may be quite different: the Métral is a fighting instrument and not a precision weapon designed for competition shooting.

The chamber dimensions are critical. I suggest that you use a special reamer (indispensable for large- or even small-scale production). Once cut to the correct dimensions, the chamber must be thoroughly polished.

The conical recess on the rear face helps feed the rounds. It should not go deeper than indicated. If you don't attain these dimensions, the unsupported cartridge wall will split as pressure rises. Fortunately the shooter is well protected from the escaping gases and brass particles, but the weapon will jam with the broken cartridge case stuck in the barrel.

The exterior dimensions are easily turned on a lathe, but pay special attention to the critical length given in the drawing.

You may want to use a longer barrel, to obtain a higher muzzle velocity and greater penetration; you may if you wish.

Barrel Rear Support with Feeding Ramp (Drawing 010)

First, turn and cut a heat-treatable steel bar to the preliminary shape shown in the drawing.

Then, with a milling machine or hacksaw and files, remove the sides of this cylinder.

Drill the two holes for the retaining screws and tap them to M5.

Cut the feeding ramp with a milling machine or a round file.

After the final adjustment, polish the ramp.

Main Spring Assembly (Drawing 008)

The coil spring must be industrially made; therefore, you must purchase this part. If you have difficulties in obtaining a spring of the desired length, you can use a shorter one assembled with the help of the joining ring shown in the drawing.

The main spring guide rod is made out of piano-wire-quality steel. Harden it to prevent accidental bending.

Both end pieces are identical, made out of steel and hardened. I suggest fixing them to the rod with soft solder to prevent unscrewing. You may also deform the extremities slightly by hammering, to obtain the same result more quickly.

Group 2: Bolt

Tools

First, make the different tools needed as guides to drill the holes and hold the piece.

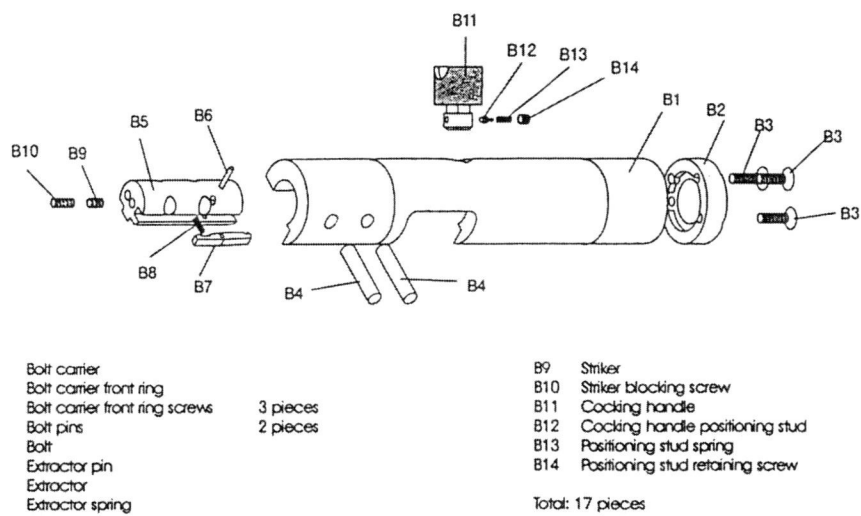

B1	Bolt carrier		
B2	Bolt carrier front ring		
B3	Bolt carrier front ring screws	3 pieces	
B4	Bolt pins	2 pieces	
B5	Bolt		
B6	Extractor pin		
B7	Extractor		
B8	Extractor spring		

B9	Striker
B10	Striker blocking screw
B11	Cocking handle
B12	Cocking handle positioning stud
B13	Positioning stud spring
B14	Positioning stud retaining screw

Total: 17 pieces

Bolt.

Bolt Carrier (Drawing 001 through 014)

I suggest that you build this part in four steps:

Step 1

You need a steel tube of 34/18 mm diameter. It is also possible to bore an 18-mm-diameter hole lengthwise through a 34-mm-diameter plain bar, but it requires a pretty big lathe. You may also choose to make the bolt carrier in three parts, as shown in the Expedient Solutions section of this book.

Cut the lower part away, according to the drawing. To do it, a milling machine is the easiest solution. If you have none, refer to Expedient Solutions.

The next step is to drill the main pin holes. I recommend drilling the carrier and the bolt together in the same operation. To do it, carefully position the bolt to make sure it is horizontal and fix it provisionally to the carrier with a small drop of cyanacrylate glue. Since the axis of the pin is not exactly above the diameter of the bolt carrier, you must prevent the drill from slipping to the side. The surest way is to mill the place flat. If you can't, use a centering drill of 6 mm diameter: slowly guide the fast-rotating drill and penetrate deeply enough to ensure that the full diameter of the drill is enclosed in the metal. Once done you can then use a conventional helical (twist) drill. Another way is to use a wooden drilling guide with a metallic tube liner (tool #2).

Step 2

You must now drill the cocking handle hole with its positioning cuts. Mark the position of the hole, by tracing layout lines with the help of the lathe. Then place the piece on the drill press. To hold the piece in the vise, I recommend inserting it into a tube of 34 mm inner diameter, which may be the future receiver itself. First, drill the 10 mm hole and then enlarge it to 12 mm as shown in the drawing.

With a round file, cut the cocking handle's positioning slots.

Step 3

Cut the ejection opening with a milling machine. If you have none, you can first cut the sides of the opening with a hacksaw. After that, you drill a series of adjacent holes along the length of the opening. You can then cut most of the metal away with a chisel. Finish the opening with hand files or with the help of a small grinder driven by a flexible shaft (flexade).

With the help of the positioning tool (tool #1), mark and drill the three front screw holes and then tap them.

Step 4

Fix the carrier on the lathe with the help of tool #3. You can then turn the recess for the front ring and diminish the diameter of the bolt carrier as shown in the drawing to reduce friction.

Bolt Carrier Front Ring (Drawing 015)

This part of the bolt requires a heat-treatable steel and must be hardened. The easiest way is to purchase a bar of 34 mm diameter and then cut it to length.

Next locate and drill the four holes with the help of the guiding tool (tool #1). Then drill the countersink for the three screw heads.

Take the ring on the lathe and turn the inner 24 mm diameter recess.

Cut the main spring abutment place either with an appropriate tool or file it off.

Finally cut the opening for the main spring guide rod.

Bolt (Drawing 017)

If you have access to a milling machine, I suggest that you first mill a 18-mm-diameter steel bar to the preliminary shape shown in the drawing. The bar should be long enough to make four to five pieces or more. If you don't have access to the right equipment to do this, refer to Expedient Solutions.

Take the piece on the lathe and drill the firing pin hole all the way through.

Mark the ejector hole position on the lathe (layout lines) and drill it on the drill press. Because the drill may wander, begin from the front face.

Next drill the holes for the extractor axis pin and spring.

Put the bolt back on the lathe and turn the cartridge head recess out. Then tap the firing pin hole.

I suggest that you drill the main pin's locations together with the bolt carrier, as described above.

Main Pins (Drawing 016)

Make these parts out the toughest steel you can obtain. For the prototype I used DIN 34 CrNiMo 6 steel heat treated to 980-1,180 N/mm² resistance.

You must take care to work according to close tolerances because these pins should not move freely in their locations, but rather should be hammered in place (a press fit).

Extractor (Drawing 018)

This small piece is made out of tough heat-treatable steel. If you are building a single gun, or just a few, you will have to adjust it by hand-filing. The extractor should engage the cartridge head smoothly to prevent losing too much energy from the slamming bolt. Therefore, keep the lower angle of the hook under 45°.

The extractor's axis pin is made out a 2-mm-diameter piano wire. The axis pin is inserted from above, and its superior end deformed by hammering to prevent it from falling.

The coil spring is made out of standard commercial stock.

Firing Pin (Drawing 018)

Use a headless M4 Allen screw and turn it to shape. This piece must be hardened. A commercial M4 Allen screw located just behind blocks it in the correct position.

Cocking Handle (Drawing 019)

This part is easy to make on a lathe and does not require special instructions. Take special care to cut the flat sides exactly parallel with the positioning stud hole.

The only function of the two cuts on the superior (fatter) part is to indicate the cocking handle position ("safe" or "fire") at night. You can choose another solution if you want; for example, you can file one side flat. You may also use a steel ball in place of the positioning stud. In this case crimp the opening with an appropriate tool.

Group 3: Trigger Mechanism Housing

Housing (Drawings 020 and 021)

If possible, use a 30/30 mm U steel profile, 2 mm thick. You may also work from a square 30/30 mm tube and remove the side with the seam.

Cut the openings with either a file or a milling machine and drill the holes on the drill press.

You may want to build a semiauto-only version of the gun. To do so, just limit the length of the selectors cut to 46 mm, instead of 51.5 mm for the full-auto version.

Front and Back Plates (Drawing 022)

The front and back plates are made out of 5-mm-thick soft steel. Take care to correctly adjust the rounded cut to the gun's body. The plates are then welded to the housing.

Hooks (Drawing 023)

These two parts have the very important task of holding the upper and lower parts of the gun together. They must be hard enough to resist deformation in spite of many repetitions of assembly and disassembly. Therefore, do not use soft steel sheet; choose a tough alloyed brand. Forge and control the adjustment by assembling the trigger mechanism housing to the receiver.

After this, the hooks are hardened and tempered.

Welded Brackets (Optional) (Drawing 064)

If the quality of the steel you are using for the hooks isn't high enough, use the welded bracket solution, described in Expedient Solutions.

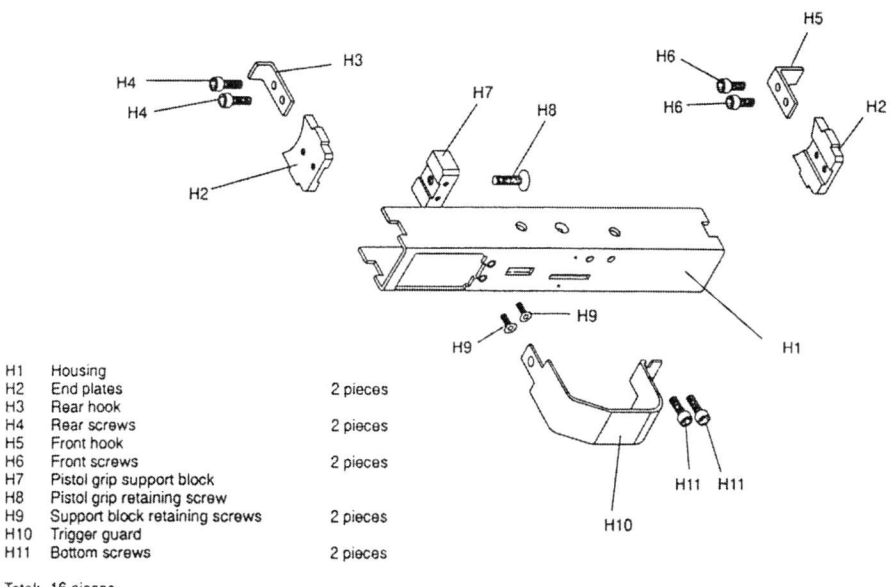

H1	Housing	
H2	End plates	2 pieces
H3	Rear hook	
H4	Rear screws	2 pieces
H5	Front hook	
H6	Front screws	2 pieces
H7	Pistol grip support block	
H8	Pistol grip retaining screw	
H9	Support block retaining screws	2 pieces
H10	Trigger guard	
H11	Bottom screws	2 pieces

Total: 16 pieces

Trigger mechanism housing.

Trigger Guard (Drawing 025)

The trigger guard is made out of 1.5 mm steel sheet and must be bent with the help of a vise.

If you're building a series of guns, I recommend making a male forming die out of hardwood or any suitable material and bending the sheet around it.

Group 4: Trigger Mechanism (Drawing 026 through 032)

Small Parts

Make the sear, sear plunger, disconnector, selector, and axis pin (T6) out of tough heat-treatable steel. The trigger arm can be made out soft steel, as can the trigger itself and the rivets (T3). These parts are relatively easy to build with files, a drill press, and a lathe.

The front side of the trigger should be rounded to make it more comfortable for the finger.

Adjust the disconnector hook and the sear. For small- or large-scale production use the test bed shown in drawing 052 at the back of the book. The length of the sear's arm shown in the drawing is intentionally oversized (but just a little bit) to allow fine adjustment with a file.

Trigger and Sear Axis Pin

These two pieces are interchangeable and made out of heat-treatable steel. They are held in place by a small spring engaged in their groove, as shown in illustrations. This spring is made out of 0.5-mm-diameter piano wire. It is held in place between the side of the housing and a self-locking nut, on the transverse screw limiting the movement of the sear. This screw should be hardened if possible.

The trigger and the sear are maintained in place on the other side by the small cylindrical spacer (T8).

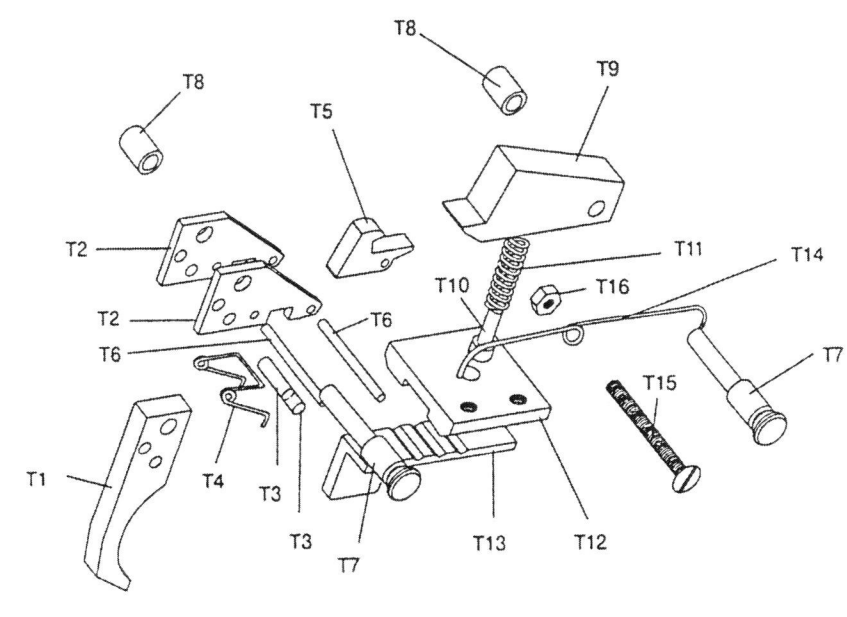

T1	Trigger	
T2	Trigger arm	2 pieces
T3	Rivets	2 pieces
T4	Trigger spring	
T5	Disconnector	
T6	Disconnector and spring axis pin	2 pieces
T7	Trigger and sear axis pin	2 pieces
T8	Trigger and sear spacer	2 pieces
T9	Sear	

T10	Plunger
T11	Sear spring
T12	Selector guide
T13	Selector
T14	**Axis pin retaining spring**
T15	Sear positioning screw
T16	M3 self locking nut

Total: 21 pieces

Trigger mechanism.

Group 5: Pistol Grip (Drawing 024)

You can either build the pistol grip with a folded steel sheet and wooden or plastic side plates, or make it completely out of plastic.

For mass production the best solution is, of course, a molded hard plastic grip, with or without metal inserts depending of the kind of plastic used. An injection mold requires special equipment and a large investment in the mold's design and construction. Since this gun isn't designed for industrial mass production, directions for molded plastic grips are not given here.

You may choose either to cast a resin and fiberglass grip or build a conventional steel sheet one, with wooden side plates. The steel sheet version will be described here; for the resin and fiberglass version see Appendix A.

Construction

First cut a 1.5 mm steel sheet to the correct dimensions. Inside dimensions are critical; therefore, you must first make a form block corresponding to the magazine you are going to use. Drawing 033 gives the dimensions for a STEN magazine.

To build a single piece, use the form block of drawing 033 and a vise. For small-scale production use the forming die shown in drawing 051.

According to the equipment you have available, braze or weld the rear lips together.

With a hammer and an anvil, with (better) or without the help of a torch, deform the small bridges at the lower end of the magazine housing to build the passage for the magazine depth stops.

Then make the small U-shaped piece to support the magazine catch. Drill the holes for the magazine catch's axis pin. Weld or braze it to the grip.

Try to insert the grip in the trigger housing; some adjustment with a file may be necessary.

Try to insert the magazine; adjust as needed with a file. The magazine should be able to be inserted and removed without force.

At this point verify the position of the magazine on the gun, but take care: it is the most essential adjustment to ensure a smooth feeding and positive ignition of the cartridge. The magazine's lips must not touch the bottom of the bolt but should be as high as possible. The bolt must strip the round from the magazine to push it into the chamber. Try it with a dummy cartridge. You may adjust to get the correct position by filing the top of the side slots. If you have already gone too far, pull the pistol grip out. Once you have found the correct position, mark the locations of the retaining screw's holes, and drill them.

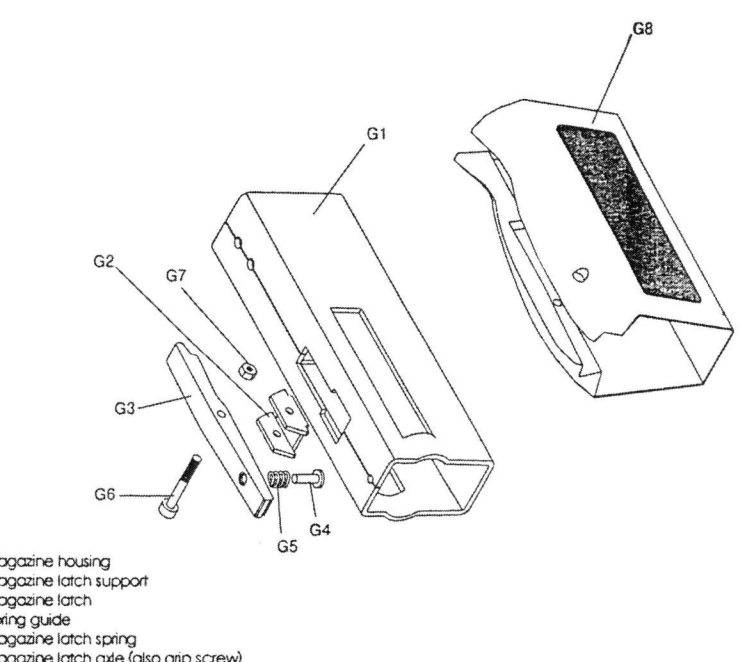

G1	Magazine housing
G2	Magazine latch support
G3	Magazine latch
G4	Spring guide
G5	Magazine latch spring
G6	Magazine latch axle (also grip screw)
G7	M3 self locking nut
G8	Pistol grip shell

Total: 8 pieces

Pistol grip.

Magazine Latch (Drawing 035)

The magazine latch is made out of a square heat-treatable steel bar. I recommend that you file the top part during the final adjustment operation, because the magazine position is critical to prevent jamming while feeding the rounds.

Magazine Latch Spring (Drawing 035)

The spring is a conventional commercial compression coil spring. You may use the same brand as the main spring.

The spring guide is maintained in place on the magazine latch by a small deformation of its end formed by hammering. It should be done only after the magazine latch has been hardened.

Side Plates (Drawing 036)

Both should be made out the same hardwood. Walnut is the best choice, but you may use another.

You should first machine the wood to the preliminary L-shape shown in the drawing. The piece is then formed with a saw and the help of a template.

For the prototype, I used the following solution. Resin-impregnated glass fabric formed the front and inner sides of the grip, and the wooden side plates were epoxied onto it. The separation between the two wooden halves was left free, so the finished grip could open like an oyster at its rear side (see Illustration G). Finish it with a rasp and a buffer.

The retainer screw acts also as axis pin for the magazine latch. To drill its location, put the wooden left side plate in place on the pistol grip and use the axis pin holes as guides. Proceed the same way for the right side. Now you have to drill the recesses for the screw head on the right half and for the nut on the left half. I suggest using a self-locking nut.

Group 6: Sights (Drawing 037 through 039)

The front and rear sights are both made out of the same basic module. To build the basic module you need a U-shaped steel profile 20 x 20 mm, 2 mm thick. You can also make it out of 20 x 20 mm square steel tube.

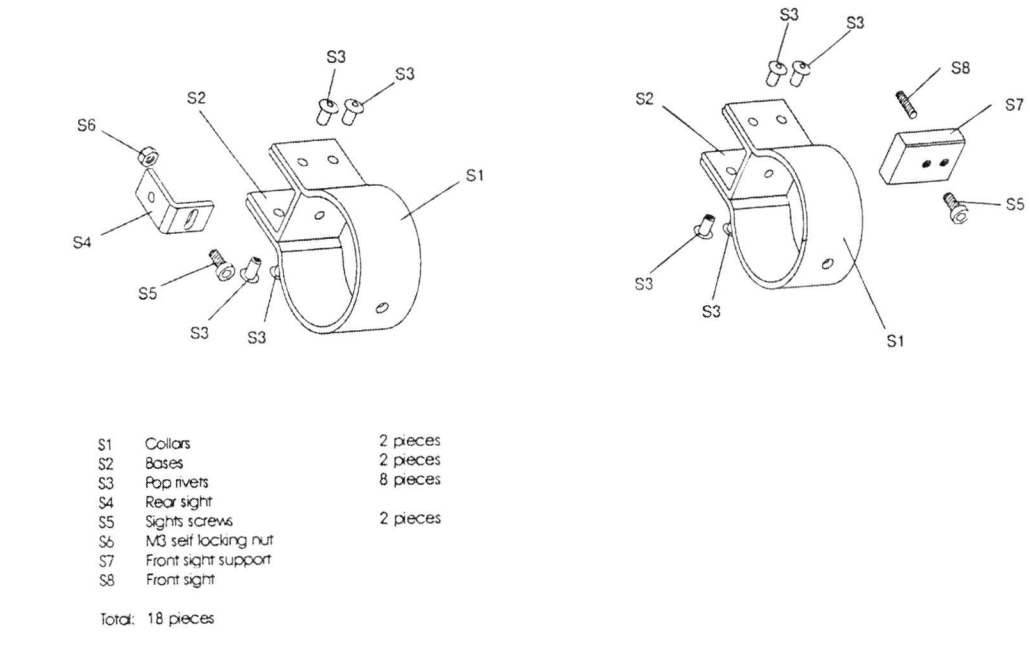

S1	Collars	2 pieces
S2	Bases	2 pieces
S3	Pop rivets	8 pieces
S4	Rear sight	
S5	Sights screws	2 pieces
S6	M3 self locking nut	
S7	Front sight support	
S8	Front sight	
	Total: 18 pieces	

Sights.

Drill the holes for the rivets in the U profile and one extremity of the strip.

Bend the metal strip with the help of tool #4.

Mark the position for the rivets on the strip and drill them. You must ensure a tight adjustment around the tube. Then rivet the two pieces together.

The parts specific to the front and rear sights are very simple and are self-explanatory.

The front sight is assembled on the gun, with a screw inserted through the gun's receiver. Caution: This screw should not protrude inside the receiver.

The rear sight assembly is made according the same principles.

Group 7: Folding Stock (Drawing 040 through 043)

The folding stock is made out of commercial square tubes. The only difficulty is that the stock itself must slide smoothly into the rear tube, but not be loose. You have to be careful if you're going to adjust it with a file.

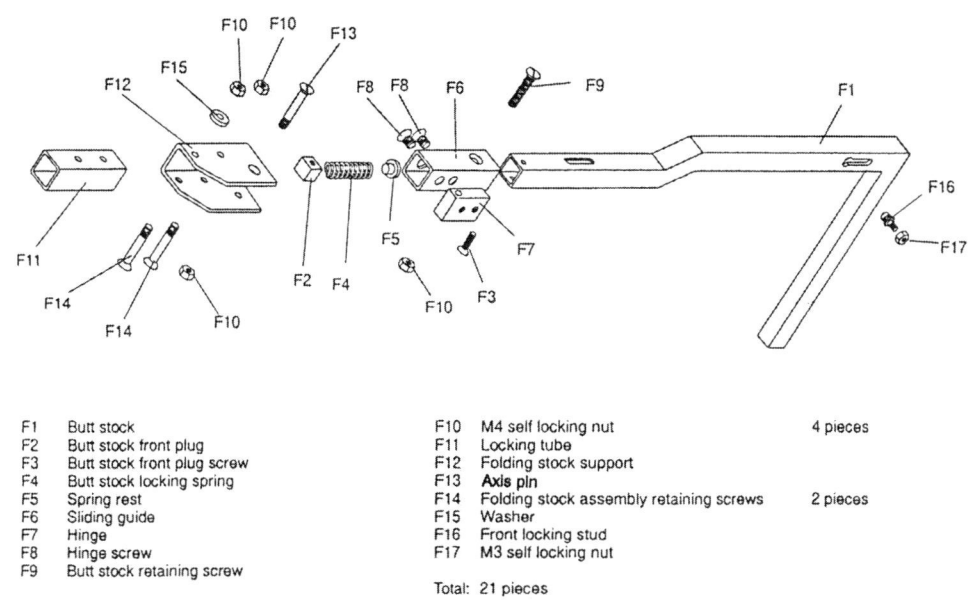

F1	Butt stock		
F2	Butt stock front plug		
F3	Butt stock front plug screw		
F4	Butt stock locking spring		
F5	Spring rest		
F6	Sliding guide		
F7	Hinge		
F8	Hinge screw		
F9	Butt stock retaining screw		
F10	M4 self locking nut	4 pieces	
F11	Locking tube		
F12	Folding stock support		
F13	**Axis pin**		
F14	Folding stock assembly retaining screws	2 pieces	
F15	Washer		
F16	Front locking stud		
F17	M3 self locking nut		
	Total: 21 pieces		

Folding stock.

I suggest that you wait to install the retaining stud on the trigger mechanism housing until the final step. The stock should engage the retaining stud when pushed in its foremost position. Releasing it will let it return under spring pressure and be locked.

When firing at the hip, the shooter uses the stock butt as a foregrip. Since the grip is located to the left of the gun's axis, pulling on it will counteract the tendency of the weapon to climb to the right during automatic fire.

Group 8: Handguard and Front Grip (Drawing 044 and 045)

These parts may be made either from hardwood or some kind of plastic material.

Drawing 044 shows one of the simplest and easiest wooden solutions. You may, of course, choose another better-looking one, which would require more time to manufacture.

As for the pistol grip, I suggest reinforcing the inner surfaces with glass bedding.

Group Tools

Tool 1 (Drawing 046)

This template doesn't require special comments.

Tool 2 (Drawing 047)

This tool is only necessary if you have no milling machine. Use hard plastic, as indicated, or hardwood for the block. Fasten the steel liner to the block with epoxy or similar adhesive.

Tool 3 (Drawing 048)

This device is useful for the fourth construction step of the bolt carrier. You may use brass instead of steel.

Tool 4 (Drawing 049)

This device is very useful to bend the sights' collars, with the help of a hammer and a vise.

Dummy Round (Drawing 050)

These dummy rounds are used first without primer to test feeding, extracting, and ejecting operations. You will test the ignition with primer. Use a fired cartridge case resized with an appropriate reloading tool. Primers are commercial reloading components.

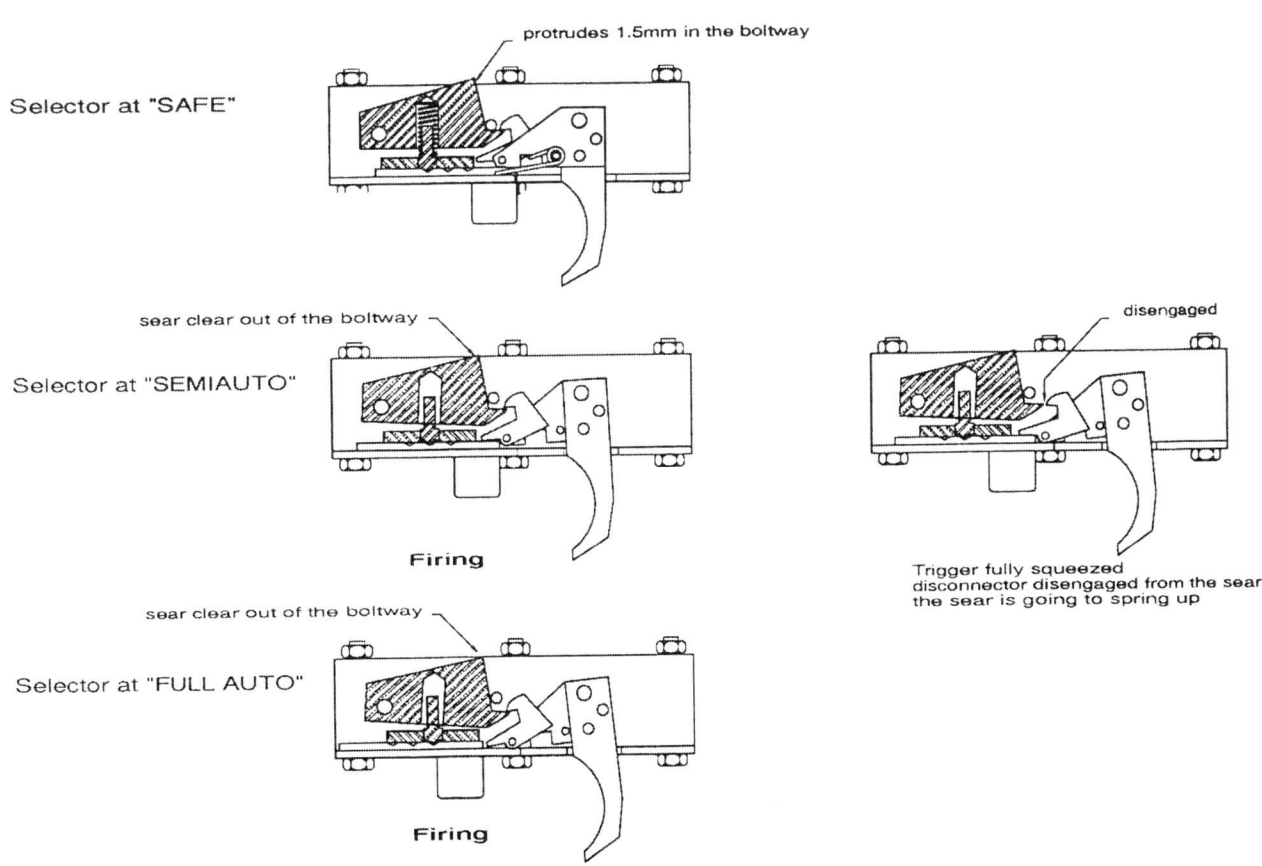

Functioning of the trigger mechanism, shown on the test fixture.

Tool 5 (Drawing 051)

This tool is designed for small-scale production of the magazine housing. It is to be used with the help of a heavy vise.

Trigger Mechanism Test Bed (Drawing 052)

The test bed is useful for small-scale production. Use the spacers (T8) to position the sear and trigger assembly.

TESTING

TRIGGER MECHANISM

First adjust the trigger mechanism on the trigger mechanism test fixture (Drawing 052). When the mechanism works correctly, assemble it in the trigger mechanism housing and pistol grip assembly.

With the selector at the rear position, it should be impossible to move the trigger. With the selector at the middle position, you pull the trigger and the disconnector lowers the sear until it is brought back out of engagement; the sear then springs up. Once the trigger is released it springs forward and the disconnector snaps on the sear's arm. With the selector at the foremost position, you pull the trigger all the way back. The disconnector remains engaged to the sear. If things don't work that way, adjust with a file.

Now assemble the trigger mechanism housing to the receiver without the bolt and barrel. Don't use the front plug and hold the two parts together with your hand. Looking from the front of the body, observe the sear. As you pull the trigger with the selector (in both semiauto or full-auto position) the sear should completely clear the bolt way, but return high enough to catch the bolt once the trigger is released or the disconnector disengaged. If necessary, adjust the sear. Then assemble the gun completely, with bolt and barrel.

Retract the bolt to its firing position. With the selector set at semiauto, pull the trigger to let the bolt fly forward and, without releasing it, pull the bolt handle all the way back. The bolt should remain to the rear. If you release the trigger, it will return to the firing position, and, if you pull it again, the bolt will fly forward. If the selector is set at full auto, the bolt will not remain at the rear during that operation. If your gun doesn't work that way, you will have to adjust the point of contact between the sear and the bolt.

FEEDING AND FIRING OPERATIONS

I recommend first using inert dummy rounds to test the feeding and firing operations. Load one inert dummy cartridge in the magazine and fire. The gun should chamber the round smoothly. Sharply pull the bolt handle all the way back, and the round should fly away through the ejection port. Inspect the case for any abnormal sign of wear; for example, on the rear face where the extractor snaps on the cartridge head. If necessary, adjust the magazine position; next check the feeding ramp or extractor's angle. You may also have to correct the ejector's position by screwing or unscrewing it.

Once the gun feeds and ejects inert rounds correctly, test it with primer-only dummy rounds. These rounds are useful to test the ignition process in the workshop, without necessitating a trip to the shooting range. But be careful: primer projections can be dangerous; don't fire in the direction of any

Above: Firing at full auto.

Top right: Accuracy testing at the shooting range.

Right: Testing at 25 meters at the range.

Above: Results of five shots shoulder-fired on semiauto in 10 seconds at a distance of 25 meters.

living being. If you can't purchase primers, you will have to test with live rounds.

When selecting a place to test the gun with live rounds, you must pay attention to the ordinary security measures usual with handgun shooting. Keep in mind also that any submachine gun recoils during full-auto fire and that the bullets tend to go to the right and up.

There is only one danger when you fire the gun for the first time, but it is serious: if the cartridge chamber in the barrel hasn't been reamed to the correct dimensions, there is a possibility of premature ignition. The cap will be crushed by the firing pin before the round is fully chambered, and the unsupported rear part of the cartridge case will split. Small brass particles will fly through the ejection port, which is dangerous to the eyes. You must wear protective goggles and keep any bystanders away from the right side of the gun.

First load only one round, set the selector at semiauto, aim, and fire. If all works correctly, the gun will fire, the empty case will be ejected, and the bolt will remain to the rear. Check the ejected case for any abnormal deformation.

If the gun fails to eject, modify the ejector's position.

If the gun fails to fire, check and eventually modify the firing pin or the extractor.

If the bolt is not caught by the sear, check the trigger mechanism again (see above). If all seems correct there, the problem may come from weak ammunition, a stiff main spring, or too much friction during the bolt's travel. Determine what is causing the malfunction and make the necessary modifications.

If everything worked correctly with a single round, load three cartridges. Fire them on semiauto. Try with five rounds and then a full magazine. Be careful: there is a small risk that the amount of friction generated by the magazine spring under full pressure will not allow the bolt to travel far enough to the rear to be caught by the sear; the gun will then fire some rounds at full auto. If that happens, modify the gun by thoroughly polishing the underpart of the bolt and the contact surfaces of the bolt carrier. The moving parts should be well lubricated.

When the gun functions correctly at semiauto, test it at full auto, first with a few rounds and then with a full magazine.

MAGAZINE

Because magazines may come from various manufacturers and may be in questionable condition, test the gun with many of them and discard those that cause problems.

SIGHTS

Zeroing the sights should be done at the shooting range. The elevation is corrected by screwing or unscrewing the Allen screw that acts as front sight. Side deviation is corrected by laterally displacing the L-shaped back sight.

I suggest a rough adjustment at 10 meters and a fine tuning at 25 or 50 meters. Once adjusted, the back sight is secured by the self-locking nut, and the front one by a drop of epoxy.

FINISHING

PLUGS

With the help of a micrometer, find and mark the location of the hole for the positioning stud on the front and rear plugs.

HARDENING

Harden the following pieces:

- sear
- trigger and sear axis pins
- disconnector
- bolt front ring
- extractor
- ejector
- striker
- feeding ramp
- magazine latch

After being hardened these parts must be tempered.

POLISHING

Giving a gun a good-looking finish can take a lot of time, primarily because of the polishing operations.

This submachine gun isn't a decorative item to be hung on the wall of your living room. In fact, it is probably an illegal fighting weapon that should be hidden most of the time. Therefore, don't spend too much time on the finishing.

The only thing that you must do is to treat the metal and wooden parts to protect them against humidity and rust.

WOODEN PARTS

The wood is first well polished. Unless the wood is very dense, a filler should be use to fill the pores. After drying, the excess filler is removed with fine sandpaper. To treat the wood, then apply protective oil or another currently available high-quality product according to the manufacturer's directions.

METAL PARTS

You may choose between a conversion coating (such as bluing or Parkerizing) and a paint coating. Until recently, paint was seldom used for firearms, but now more and more military weapons are protected with new very resistant synthetic coatings. I highly recommend using paint because of the wide availability of high-quality and relatively cheap commercial products.

For the prototypes I used a black high-temperature-resistant paint designed for automobile exhaust pipes. The paint was also resistant to the lubricating grease and oil used on the gun.

The traditional finish used in the small-arms industry is a conversion coating, by which the surface of steel is converted to a rust-resistant iron compound. You may choose between the bluing process, which creates a microscopic sheet of black ferrous oxide, and phosphatization, which gives gray iron-phosphate. If you prefer a conversion coating, please refer to Appendix B.

SLING

You can easily make a sling to carry Métral submachine gun around if you like. There are any number of books that tell how to fashion a sling, so there is no need to provide instructions here.

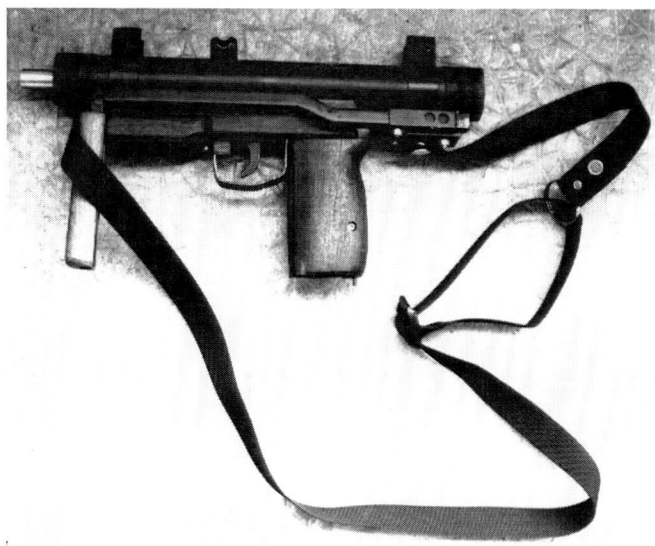

A leather or nylon sling may be added.

EXPEDIENT SOLUTIONS

PLUGS WITHOUT THREADING

The solution shown in drawing 053 was tested, and it is usable but not recommended. The removal of these plugs is not as easy as with threaded ones. To do it you will need the takedown tools shown in the drawing. Use them to push the retaining studs inside and jerk the plug slightly until the studs are disengaged from the holes in the receiver walls. Then pull the plug out with a gentle jerking motion, alternatively clockwise and counterclockwise. Be careful to avoid a too wide rotation that could distort the main spring rod.

Because threading on a lathe is no more difficult than correctly drilling the holes for the studs, use the latter solution only if you absolutely cannot thread the plugs and gun receiver.

Improvised prototype, including plugs without threading, welded bracket, and plastic pistol grip (top) compared with the standard prototype (bottom).

BOLT CARRIER: HOW TO BUILD IT IN THREE PARTS

If you can't find a 34/18 steel tube and can't bore it in one operation, you can make it in three parts and append them, as shown in Drawings 059 through 062.

I used screws to assemble the parts for the prototype, but you can weld or rivet them together. If no milling machine is available, use the preliminary shape shown on drawing 059. Use tool #3 to turn the bolt carrier diameter down to 34 mm.

Three-part bolt carrier, with bolt and handle.

BOLT

Drawing 063 gives a solution for cutting the preliminary shape if no milling machine is available.

WELDED BRACKETS

If the steel quality you are using for the hooks isn't good enough, use the welded bracket solution, given in drawing 064. Be careful to prevent any deformation of the receiver during the welding operation.

HOW TO RIFLE A BARREL

You will find a complete description of the process in *Home Workshop Guns for Defense and Resistance Volume 1: The Submachine Gun* by Bill Holmes (available from Paladin Press). For those who don't have access to this book, I will recap the main steps.

Start with a plain bar. The first and perhaps biggest difficulty is to drill it straight. Then you have to ream it to a diameter of 8.80 mm.

Then rifle it, cutting two or four grooves with a twist of one turn in about 254 mm (10 inches). Military barrels during World War II were often made with only two grooves, which proved to be sufficient.

To rifle the barrel you have to build a rifling bank (bench), as shown in the accompanying photo.

The author operating the rifling bank (bench).

As a guide, use an old rifle barrel. To drive the cutting tool, I cast a lead slug around the notched part of a rifle cleaning rod inside the bore of the guide barrel.

After testing the hook-type rifling head described in the above-mentioned book, I made an improved rifling head, shown in drawing 065, that is easier to build and operate.

To use it, begin with the depth-controlling nut screwed into its foremost position, which brings the cutting tool into its lowest position. Unscrew the nut until the cutter comes in contact with the barrel wall. Then pull the cutter completely through the barrel and push it back. Remove the cutter from the upper slot and insert it in the lower slot. Pull the cutter through the barrel again and push it back. Then unscrew the nut one-quarter of a turn; this will allow the cutter to go 0.01 mm higher. Pull the cutter through the barrel again and push it back. Then remove the cutter from the lower slot and insert it in the upper one. Repeat these operations until the desired groove depth is obtained. For a 9mm Parabellum barrel, the groove diameter will be 9 mm to 9.1 mm. By using the same cutter with the same depth control for both grooves, you are sure to obtain a perfectly symmetrical rifling. Don't forget to use enough lubricant.

After the bore is rifled, it should be lapped to remove any chips left from the tools. The description of the operation given in Bill Holmes' book is as follows:

> This may be done by casting a lead slug, some two to four inches long, around a rod inside the bore. Push the slug almost all the way out of the bore and coat it with a mixture of oil and fine emery flour. The unoccupied portion of the bore should also be coated with oil through the opposite end. A stop should be inserted in each end of the barrel to insure against accidentally pushing or pulling out the lapping plug. This plug should never be removed from the bore until its work is finished. The lap should now be pulled (and pushed) back and forth through the bore for about 10 minutes, with additional abrasive and oil being added frequently. After the lap is removed, the barrel should be cleaned thoroughly with gasoline and patches and then examined. If more lapping is needed, the old lap should be melted off the rod and a new one made. Do not try to put the old lap back in the barrel.

The Métral gun will accept a silencer without your having to do major modifications. The only thing you must do is add another front plug to which the silencer can be affixed.

Two different silencer versions are presented here. They are both compromise solutions incorporating known principles, and both were tested and found to be reasonably effective. The bullet remains supersonic, and the mechanical noise of the slamming bolt isn't lessened.

You must not expect your silenced gun to emit only small "plops" as shown in movies. Even the best silenced gun won't do that. However, the suppression you'll achieve with either of these silencers is sufficient to make it extremely difficult to determine the point of origin. In a noisy environment, such as a big city, most bystanders wouldn't even be aware that someone had fired.

A silencer is useful for testing the gun without alarming the neighbors, but its main purpose is for commando-style operations or assassinations. Therefore, most countries either forbid their citizens to own silencers or severely restrict their ability to do so. So be warned again: if you build one, it will almost surely be illegal.

VERSION ONE: SILENCER WITH RUBBER BAFFLES (DRAWINGS 066 AND 067)

This model is slightly more efficient than version two, at least for the first five shots. The rubber

(Top) Ingram M10 with MAC silencer. (Below) Métral submachine gun with the prototype of the version one silencer.

baffles soon wear out, and after about 15 shots this silencer begins to be louder than version two.

As with the World War II silenced STEN gun, you should fire semiauto only.

VERSION TWO:
SILENCER WITHOUT BAFFLES
(DRAWINGS 068 THROUGH 070)

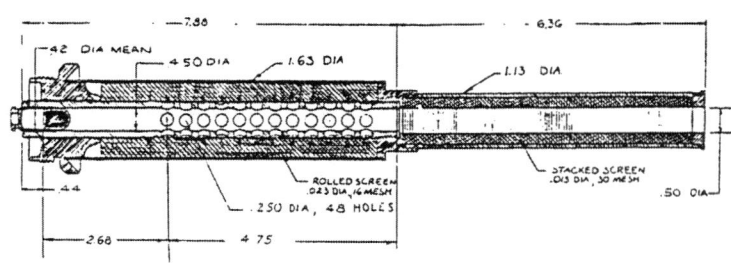

Cross section of .45-caliber Bell Laboratories' silenced M3 submachine gun barrel.

This model is designed to allow a longer use than the former version without loss of performance.

The main working principle is absorption of the propellant gas energy by heating the wire mesh located in the expansion chambers. It was used during World War II with success in the silencer for the U.S. M3 submachine gun ("grease gun"), and since that time has been used in many other silenced weapons.

The middle pressure chamber is my own invention. Its function is to slow down the escaping gasses. It works like an inverted smoke extractor such as those used on tank guns. I didn't do any testing to find out if this system is very effective. It is just a suggestion to carry on further research.

To remain effective the silencer must be thoroughly cleaned periodically, especially the wire mesh. Spray carburetor cleaner works well.

As with version one, avoid full-automatic fire.

FURTHER ADVICE

You may obtain a better silenced submachine gun by using subsonic ammunition and a lightened bolt carrier. The lightened bolt carrier is made by drilling large holes through its left side. Something else to explore is the use of helical channels, as found in the British L34A1 Patchett/Sterling gun or in the Sionics silencer for the Ingram M10 gun. Such silencers are a little more complicated to build, but they are more effective and easier to maintain.

CLANDESTINE LARGE-SCALE PRODUCTION

BASIC PRINCIPLES

These basic principles can be explained by the following joke, believed to have been originated by Jews in Palestine during the last months of the British mandate.

A poor man was working in a plant named Sewing Machines, Inc. He wanted to give to his wife a sewing machine but had no money to buy one, so every evening he'd smuggle home a different piece that his factory was making.

After many days his home stock was complete, and he tried to assemble the machine for his wife. He tried many times, but he always ended up with a machine gun.

A clandestine resistance organization needs considerable quantities of weapons. The importation of complete guns may be difficult and costly, and a single police operation may undo months of effort. Such an event happened to the Irish Republican Army, when on 30 October 1987 the *Eskund II*, a ship loaded with tons of Libyan weapons was intercepted by the French authorities.

The method suggested here consists of a decentralized mass production of harmless metallic pieces that may be used for various purposes. All machining operations requiring heavy machine tools are completed at this stage. The parts are then dispersed in several small workshops where they can be completed without special tools or skilled labor.

COVER

The clandestine organization needs efficient cover to buy large quantities of metallic components without alarming the authorities. The only way to do this is to control at least three small or middle-sized industrial plants used for subcontracting work and with a regular output of some kind of mechanical devices.

You must have a net of interconnecting enterprises devoted to the decentralized production of mechanical devices. The idea is that the orders and movements of the gun components will be completely hidden in a stream of civilian goods.

It is also assumed that you observe all the basic rules of security for a clandestine organization.

PRODUCTION SCHEME

Many components of the submachine gun could belong to any civilian mechanical device, and no one would likely suspect their final destination, at least in their half-finished state. I call these elements "general-purpose pieces." The clandestine organization may order them from ordinary factories. The springs used in the gun are good examples of such pieces, as are the plugs and support rings.

Other components are to be made in two steps. First a bar is machined to the correct profile in an industrial factory. The longer the bar, the better the camouflage. These bars are then dispersed to the smaller workshops, where they are cut like an Italian salami. Most of the resulting rough cuts require only a few drillings to finish the piece. I call these parts "salami-principle pieces." The sear, the bolt, and even bolt carrier are such pieces.

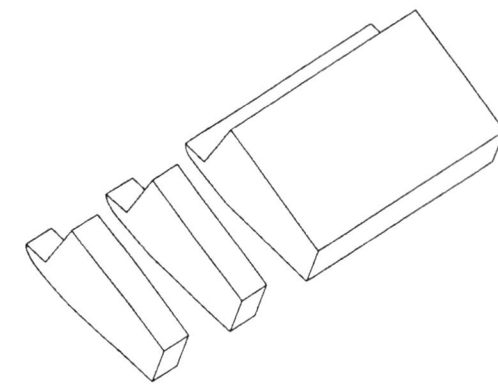

An example of a "salami-principle" part, the sear.

The receivers and trigger mechanism housings are taken from commercial steel tubes and U iron, which appear innocuous. Once the work has begun, it will be difficult to conceal the parts' ultimate function. Fortunately, this phase is done quickly, even in small workshops. For your security, you must remove the pieces from the workshop as soon as they are machined.

The pistol grip, either in its metallic-and-wood or plastic version, is a compromising piece. You have to build it in a secure place. Because it doesn't require special machine tools, it is possible to manufacture it in private homes.

The barrel is the most critical part of the process. For accuracy, a gun must be rifled. As indicated above, it is possible to rifle a barrel with primitive tools, but this is inadequate for a large-scale production. You must therefore find a way to smuggle industrial barrels. I recommend importing finished barrels whose cartridge chambers have already been machined. To smuggle these components, it is wise to use the ant strategy; i.e., import a small number of pieces over and over. It will minimize the loss in case of interception and deflect suspicion of a large-scale operation. Barrels can be easily concealed in metallic pipes, imported as bars, or hidden in a truck chassis.

Magazines should also be purchased from industrial sources.

Final assembly should also be done in a secure place. Since the quality of manufacture is very difficult to control under clandestine conditions, only after the final assembly will it be possible to test whether the guns work or not. Therefore, you must have a place to fire the guns, without alarming the neighborhood, with an adjacent workshop to make the final corrections.

An important element in this production scheme is the distribution of jigs and tools to the various manufacturers, especially for the small pieces.

HOW TO MAKE PARTS WITH RESIN AND GLASS FABRIC

The following text describes how to make parts with epoxy resin reinforced with glass fabric, using a silicone rubber mold.

Make a master form. You may use wood, wax, clay, or any other easy-to-form material. The pistol grip is to be made in two parts.

Make a mold in two parts and use it to reproduce as many copies of the master as you want. Use a suitable silicone rubber elastomer.

1. *Preparation*
    —Prepare a box or simple frame for the mold.
    —Put a layer of modeling clay in the base of the box.
2. *Bedding*
    —Place the object in modeling clay.
3. *Positioning*
    —Make a few 3- or 4-mm holes in the modeling clay to enable you to put the halves of the mold together. Put in a tube about the width of a pencil for the feeder channel. Another tube is necessary to evacuate the air.
    —Coat with a thin layer of petroleum jelly.
4. *Pouring the first half*
    —Catalyze the silicone rubber and pour it into the mold. Wait for the elastomer to cure.
5–6. *Turn over*
    —After curing, invert the mold, and remove the modeling clay completely.
    —Put a thin layer of petroleum jelly on the first half of the mold and the model.
7–8. *Pouring the second half*
    —Catalyze the silicone rubber and pour it into the mold. Wait for the elastomer to cure.
    —Separate the halves, remove the tube to form the feeder channel, and remove the master form.
    —Clean the parts. The mold is now ready.

TO REPRODUCE

*   Cut the glass or Kevlar fabric to the correct dimensions.
*   Impregnate the layers one after the other with catalyzed epoxy resin and put them into the mold.
*   Carefully put the halves of the mold together.
*   Pour the epoxy through the feeder channel to complete the filling.
*   Wait until polymerization occurs and the resin hardens.
*   Open the mold: the molding will be a faithful reproduction of the original, and the mold is ready for further reproductions.

How to make a mold in Two Parts

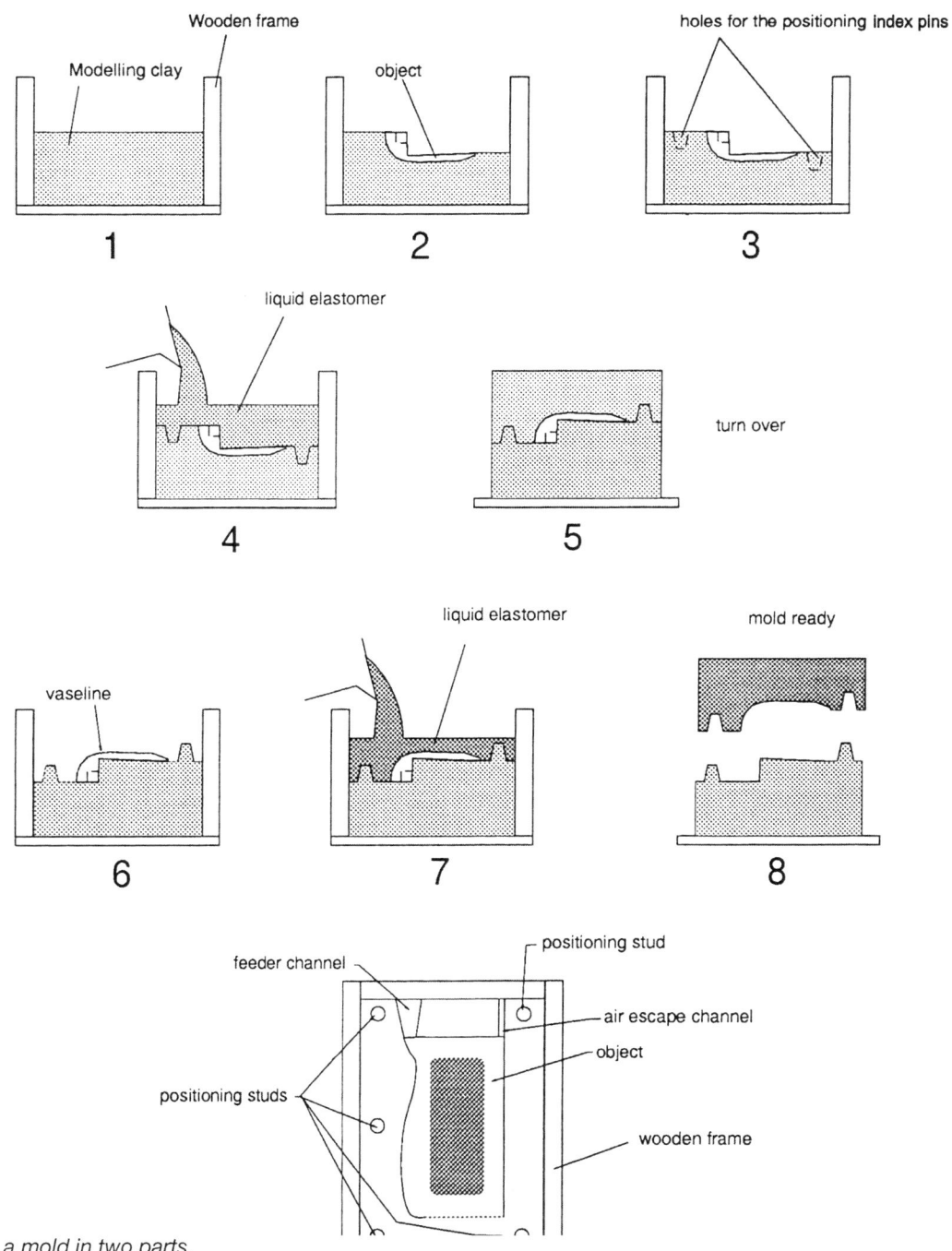

How to make a mold in two parts.

SURFACE TREATMENT: CONVERSION COATINGS

Bluing is the most common treatment for civilian weapons and, outside America, for military arms. In this country the phosphatizing process (Parkerization) has been more widely used for steel military weapons.

For all three methods given below, use iron or steel tanks that are long and wide enough to accept the gun's body. These tanks must not be galvanized, and the seams should be welded, not brazed or soldered. For a heat source, use gas burners.

Because grease is the worst enemy of the iron surface conversion process, be sure not to touch the pieces with your fingers. Use boiled cotton gloves or surgical rubber gloves. Make small wire-screen baskets to handle the small pieces. Also prepare iron wire holders to suspend the large pieces, such as the barrel, receiver, trigger housing, and magazine housing.

Always work in a well-ventilated working place or in the open.

BLUING

There are various methods of bluing, but I will give only two: hot salt bath and hot water.

Hot-Salt-Bath Bluing

This is a quick, professional process recommended for bluing a large number of pieces. However, because it uses highly caustic chemicals, it does require strict adherence to safety precautions to avoid accidents. It is highly caustic and hazardous to the skin and the eyes.

Warning: Bluing should never be done if sulfur is present. This bath is very aggressive and will destroy solder, silver solder, copper, brass, aluminum, zinc alloys, and organic materials.

The parts must first be thoroughly polished and degreased (e.g., with trichlorethylene, TCE). [Editor's note: TCE is virtually unobtainable in the United States because of Environmental Protection Agency regulations. Methyl ketone is a fair substitute for TCE.]

It is sometimes recommended that you etch the parts by immersion in a 10-percent solution of nitric acid (HNO_3). After acid etching, the parts should be thoroughly rinsed in distilled water.

The solution is heated to the boiling point and kept at a gentle boil, which means a temperature of 290–295°F (143–146°C). If the temperature rises, add a small amount of water; allow some to boil away if the temperature gets too low.

Bluing is done by immersing the thoroughly degreased parts in the bath for about 30 minutes. After bluing, the parts are rinsed in hot pure water.

Warning: The description above contains only the main steps of the process. Amateurs should not work with these dangerous chemicals without aid of further references or more experienced helpers. Books describing the entire practical process are given in the Bibliography.

FORMULA FOR HOT-SALT BLUING

	Ounces		Grams
Sodium hydroxide (NaOH)	65	=	1,843
Sodium nitrate ($NaNO_3$)	17	=	482
Sodium nitrite ($NaNO_2$)	4	=	113
Trisodium phosphate (Na_3PO_4)	2	=	57
Distilled water	134	=	3,800

Hot-Water Bluing

This is the safest bluing process for amateurs.

Parts are polished, degreased, and eventually acid-etched as in the hot-salt bluing process.

Bluing is done in a sheet-metal tank, large enough to immerse the largest parts of the gun. The tank will be filled three-fourths full of water and placed over a heat source that will keep it at a hard, rolling boil. A wide-mouthed jar should be placed near the tank, provided with a clean cotton swab on the end of a wood dowel. Some of the bluing solution is placed in the jar.

The gun parts are placed in the tank and boiled for perhaps 15 minutes. They aren't hot enough unless they will dry immediately upon removal from the tank. When they are that hot, remove one part at a time, keeping it very close to the top of the tank. Swab it all over with the bluing formula, using long, uniform strokes. As quickly as the solution dries, immerse that part in the tank. Repeat this on all parts. Then remove each part in turn from the tank and use a wad of steel wool to lightly remove any rust that has formed. Repeat the entire process approximately eight times, or until all parts have taken on a uniform dark-blue color. Finally, boil the parts thoroughly in a bath of distilled water and then dry and oil them.

Warning: nitrates and chlorates are oxidizing chemicals that may be used to prepare explosives. Mercury is a heavy metal and a dangerous pollutant. For these reasons, the above chemicals are difficult to obtain without authorization in many countries.

FORMULA FOR HOT-WATER BLUING

	Ounces		Grams
Sodium nitrate ($NaNO_3$)	0.25	=	7
Potassium nitrate (KNO_3)	0.25	=	7
Mercury dichloride ($HgCl_2$)	0.50	=	14
Potassium chlorate ($KClO_3$)	0.50	=	14
Distilled water	10.00	=	283
*Sweet spirits of niter	0.50	=	14

*Sweet spirits of niter is a solution of 3.5 to 4.5 percent of ethyl nitrite (C_2H_5ONO) in ethanol.

PHOSPHATIZING

This process is fast and easy and much less dangerous than the hot-salt bluing process.

The parts are cleaned and eventually sandblasted to provide them with a dull nonreflecting finish.

Once this is done, the parts should be thoroughly degreased.

The phosphatizing solution is heated to the boiling point and kept at a gentle boil. The parts are immersed for about 30 minutes (or more) to obtain the desired color. Place the parts in boiling water to clean them.

Remove, dry, and coat the parts with a good gun oil or rust-inhibiting oil.

Use a commercially available solution (and work according to the directions, which may be slightly different than the description given above). In the United States the phosphatizing process was developed and sold by the Parker Rust-Proof Company of Cleveland, Ohio, hence the name Parkerizing.

If you can't purchase a ready-to-use solution, you can make a very usable substitute with the following recipe, based on French patent # 698878:

Recipe for Phosphatizing

1. Pour 200 milliliters of 85-percent phosphoric acid (H_3PO_4) in 300 milliliters distilled water.
2. Heat the solution and add as much manganese carbonate ($MnCO_3$) as it will dissolve.
3. Mix 30 milliliters of this solution with 1 liter of distilled water to obtain the final phosphatizing solution.
4. Phosphatizing is done by boiling the parts in this solution until the desired color is obtained (usually 30 to 60 minutes). Maintain the proper concentration by adding water to compensate for evaporation.

CONVERSION FROM METRIC TO U.S. MEASUREMENT SYSTEM

GENERAL DIMENSIONS

Use a spreadsheet home computer program or a pocket calculator to do the following:

- Convert millimeters to inches by multiplying by 0.03937
- Convert grams to ounces by dividing by 28.35

TUBING

For the receiver, the nearest U.S. dimension is a 1 1/2-inch exterior diameter, with 1/12-inch wall thickness; in this case you must adapt the drawings slightly for the following parts:

- Bolt carrier
- Bolt front ring
- Front and back support rings
- Rear barrel support
- Front and back plugs

THREADING

The following table of conversion may be used:

Metric	U.S.
M38x1.5	UNEF 1 1/2–18
M3	UNC 5–40
M4	UNC 8–32
M5	UNC 10–24

DRAWINGS

ADVICE

These drawings were made to be used as separate full-scale units in several workshops. Before using them pay attention to the following points:

1. Protection of the original:
- Don't use the original plans in the workshop because they can be easily damaged by oil or dirt. Use photocopies instead.

2. Scaling:
- The drawings presented vertically (for example #003) are already full scale and don't need any adaptation.
- The drawings presented horizontally (those denoted by an * above the scale box, for example #001) *should be photocopied at 150 percent to obtain a full-scale plan*.
- Measure some element of the first copy and compare it with the dimensions given on the drawing to check that the copier is correctly set. If necessary modify the enlargement factor.

3. Warning:
- Any other use of the copies would be in violation of the copyright regulations.

LIST OF DRAWINGS

Gun's assembly groups:
1. Receiver with barrel and main spring   Total: 22 pieces
2. Bolt   Total: 17 pieces
3. Trigger mechanism housing   Total: 16 pieces
4. Trigger mechanism   Total: 21 pieces
5. Pistol grip   Total: 8 pieces
6. Sights   Total: 18 pieces
7. Folding stock   Total: 21 pieces
8. Handguard and front grip

Tools
Expedient Solutions
Silencers

GROUP 1: RECEIVER WITH BARREL AND MAIN SPRING

Code	Designation	Quantity	Drawing #
R1	Receiver		001, 002
R2	Rear plug		003
R3	Front plug		003
R4	Support ring	2 pieces	004, 005
R5	Support ring positioning stud	2 pieces	006
R6	Positioning stud spring	2 pieces	006
R7	Positioning stud retaining pin	2 pieces	006
R8	Ejector base		007
R9	Ejector		007
R10	Ejector base blocking screw		007
R11	Main spring guide		008
R12	Main spring guide end pieces	2 pieces	008
R13	Main spring		008
R14	Barrel		009
R15	Rear barrel support with feeding ramp		010
R16	Rear barrel support screws	2 pieces	

GROUP 2: BOLT

Code	Designation	Quantity	Drawing #
B1	Bolt carrier		011–014
B2	Bolt carrier front ring		015
B3	Bolt carrier front ring screws	3 pieces	
B4	Bolt pins	2 pieces	016
B5	Bolt		017
B6	Extractor pin		018
B7	Extractor		018
B8	Extractor spring		018
B9	Firing pin		018
B10	Firing pin blocking screw		018
B11	Cocking handle		019
B12	Cocking handle positioning stud		019
B13	Positioning stud spring		019
B14	Positioning stud retaining screw		019

GROUP 3: TRIGGER MECHANISM HOUSING

Code	Designation	Quantity	Drawing #
H1	Housing		020, 021
H2	End plates	2 pieces	022
H3	Rear hook		023
H4	Rear screws	2 pieces	
H5	Front hook		023
H6	Front screws	2 pieces	
H7	Pistol grip support block		024

Code	Designation	Quantity	Drawing #
H8	Pistol grip retaining screw		
H9	Support block retaining screws	2 pieces	
H10	Trigger guard		025
H11	Bottom screw	2 pieces	

GROUP 4: TRIGGER MECHANISM

Code	Designation	Quantity	Drawing #
T1	Trigger		026
T2	Trigger arms	2 pieces	027
T3	Rivets	2 pieces	027
T4	Trigger spring		028
T5	Disconnector		028
T6	Disconnector and spring axis pin	2 pieces	027
T7	Trigger and sear axis pin	2 pieces	029
T8	Trigger and sear spacers	2 pieces	029
T9	Sear		030
T10	Plunger		028
T11	Sear spring		028
T12	Selector guide		031
T13	Selector		032
T14	Axis retaining spring		029
T15	Sear positioning screw		029
T16	M3 self-locking nut		

GROUP 5: PISTOL GRIP

Code	Designation	Quantity	Drawing #
G1	Magazine housing		033, 034
G2	Magazine latch support		034
G3	Magazine latch		035
G4	Spring guide		035
G5	Magazine latch spring		035
G6	Magazine latch axis (also grip screw)		
G7	M3 self-locking nut		
G8	Pistol grip shell		036

GROUP 6: SIGHTS

Code	Designation	Quantity	Drawing #
S1	Collars	2 pieces	037
S2	Bases	2 pieces	037
S3	Blind rivets	8 pieces	
S4	Rear sight		038
S5	Sights screws	2 pieces	038
S6	M3 self-locking nut		
S7	Front sight support		039
S8	Front sight		039

GROUP 7: FOLDING STOCK

Code	Designation	Quantity	Drawing #
F1	Butt stock		040
F2	Butt stock front plug		041
F3	Butt stock front plug screw		
F4	Butt stock locking spring		041
F5	Spring rest		041
F6	Sliding guide		042
F7	Hinge		042
F8	Hinge screw		
F9	Butt stock retaining screw		
F10	M4 self-locking nut	4 pieces	
F11	Locking tube		043
F12	Folding stock support		043
F13	Axis pin		
F14	Folding stock assembly retaining screws	2 pieces	
F15	Washer		
F16	Front locking stud		041
F17	M3 self-locking nut		

GROUP 8: HANDGUARD AND FRONT GRIP

Code	Designation	Quantity	Drawing #
W1	Handguard		044
W2	Handguard screw		
W3	Front grip		045
W4	Front grip screw		

Tools

Code	Designation	Drawing #
Tool 1	Template to drill the holes in parts R4, B1, B2	046
Tool 2	Guiding tool to drill the main pin holes	047
Tool 3	Device to chuck the bolt carrier on a lathe	048
Tool 4	Device to form the sight collars	049
Dummy round 9mm Parabellum		050
Tool 5	Magazine housing forming die	051
Trigger mechanism test fixture		052

EXPEDIENT SOLUTIONS

Group 1 Receiver and plugs without threading

Code	Designation	Quantity	Drawing #
	List of parts		053
R1E	Receiver		054, 055
R2E	Rear plug		056
R3E	Front plug		056
R4E	Support ring	2 pieces	057

Code	Designation	Quantity	Drawing #
R4E-S	Support ring screws	5 pieces	057
R5E	Retaining stud	4 pieces	057
R6E	Retaining stud spring	4 pieces	057
R7E	Inner ring	2 pieces	057
R8E	Ejector base		058
R9E	Ejector		058

Group 2 Bolt carrier, 3 part-version, ensemble view — 059

B1E-1	Bolt carrier module 1		059, 062
B1E-2	Bolt carrier module 2		059, 060, 061, 062
B1E-3	Bolt carrier module 3		059, 061, 062

Bolt, solution without use of a milling machine

| B5E | Bolt | | 063 |

Welded bracket solution to assemble the trigger housing to the receiver, ensemble view — 064

H5E-1	Bracket		064
H5E-2	Retaining pin		064
H5E-3	Retaining pin spring		064

Rifling head — 065

SILENCER

Silencer version 1, with rubber baffles, ensemble view	066
Silencer version 1, parts, including fixation	067
Silencer version 2, ensemble view	068
Silencer version 2, parts, including fixation	069
Silencer version 2, inner tubes and deflector	070

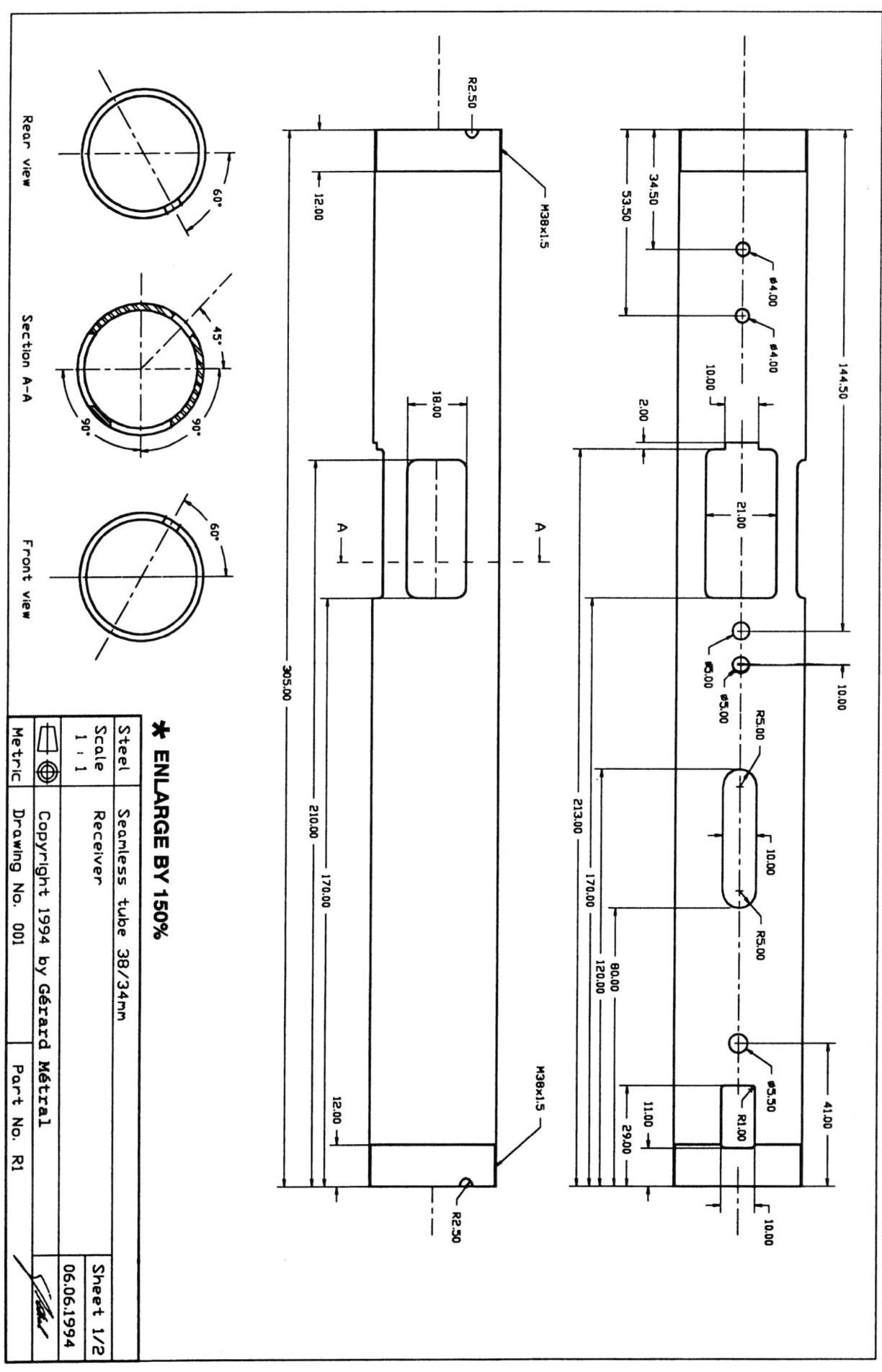

Rear view

Section A-A

Front view

60°

45°

90°

90°

60°

R2.50

12.00

34.50

53.50

144.50

Ø4.00

Ø4.00

10.00

2.00

21.00

M38x1.5

A

18.00

A

Ø5.00

Ø5.00

R5.00

10.00

R5.00

305.00

210.00

170.00

213.00

170.00

80.00

120.00

Ø5.50

R1.00

11.00

29.00

41.00

10.00

12.00

M38x1.5

R2.50

* ENLARGE BY 150%

Steel	Seamless tube 38/34mm
Scale	Receiver
1 : 1	

Copyright 1994 by Gérard Métral

Metric | Drawing No. 001 | Part No. R1

Sheet 1/2

06.06.1994

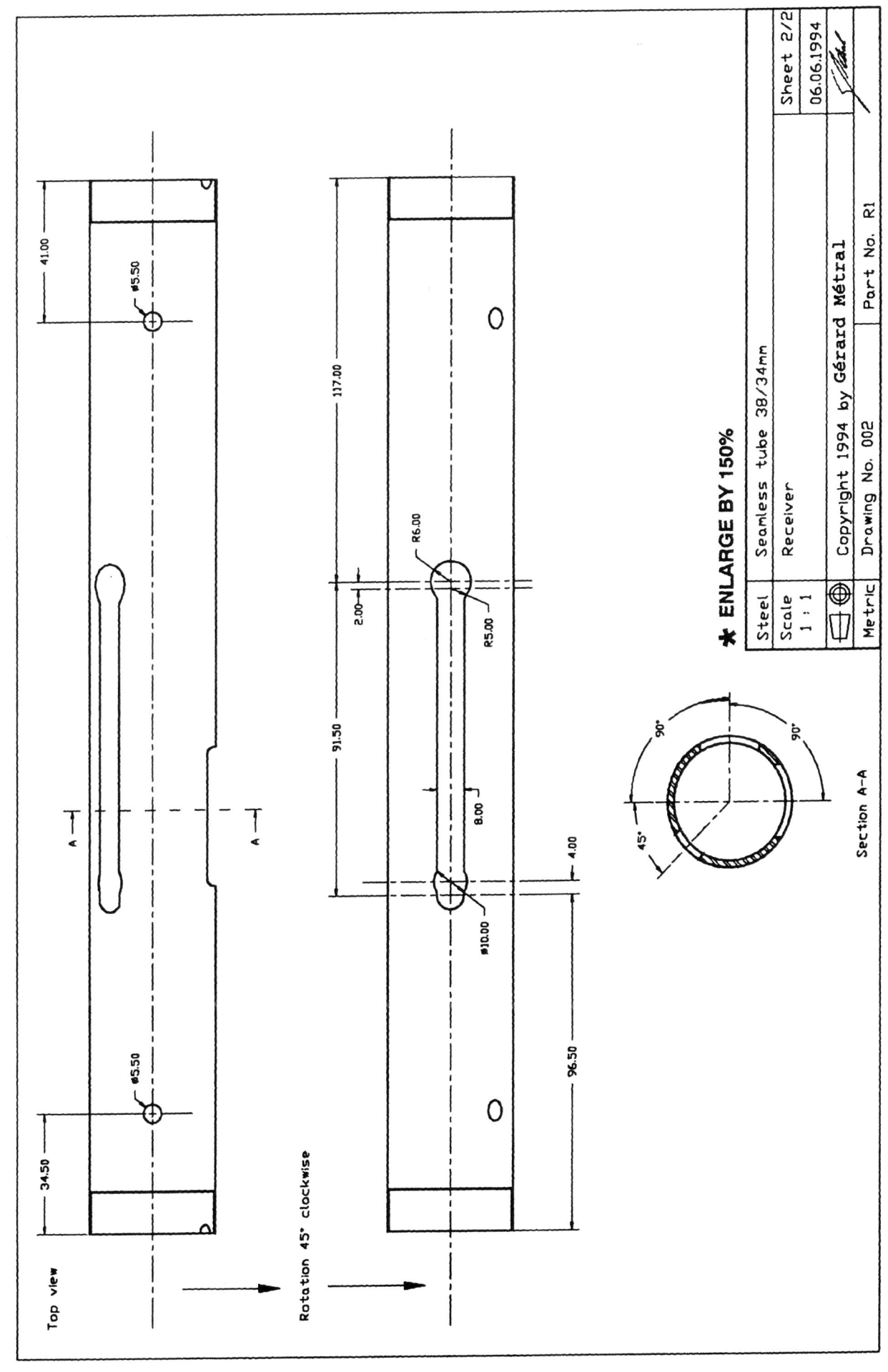

Top view

Rotation 45° clockwise

41.00
117.00
⌀5.50
R6.00
2.00
R5.00
91.50
8.00
4.00
⌀10.00
96.50
34.50
⌀5.50

90°
90°
45°

Section A-A

✶ ENLARGE BY 150%

Steel	Seamless tube 38/34mm		Sheet 2/2
Scale 1 : 1	Receiver		06.06.1994
⊕	Copyright 1994 by Gérard Métral		
Metric	Drawing No. 002	Part No. R1	

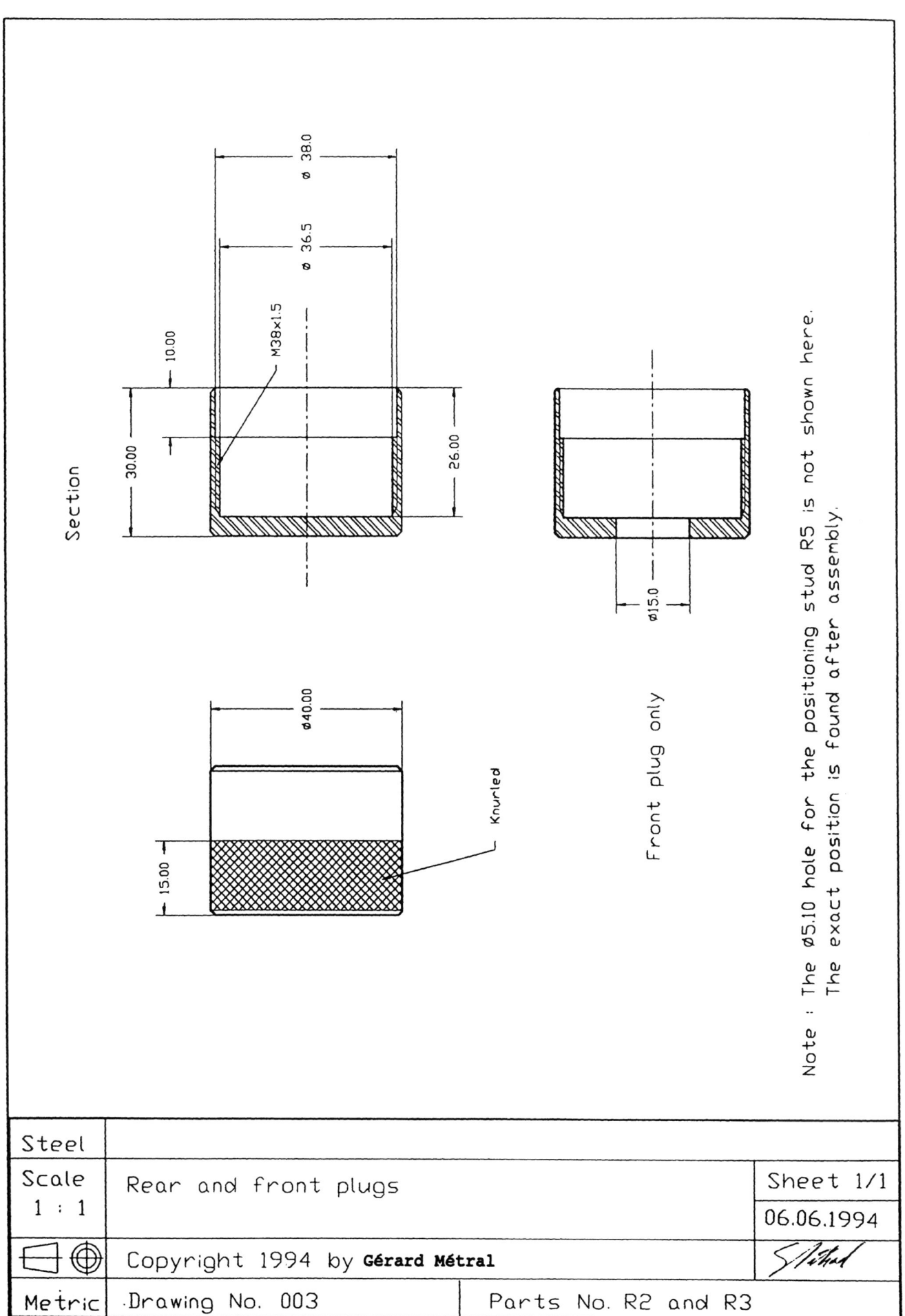

Section

Ø 38.0

Ø 36.5

M38×1.5

10.00

30.00

26.00

Ø40.00

15.00

Knurled

Ø15.0

Front plug only

Note : The Ø5.10 hole for the positioning stud R5 is not shown here.
The exact position is found after assembly.

Steel			
Scale 1 : 1	Rear and front plugs		Sheet 1/1
			06.06.1994
⌳ ⊕	Copyright 1994 by **Gérard Métral**		
Metric	Drawing No. 003	Parts No. R2 and R3	

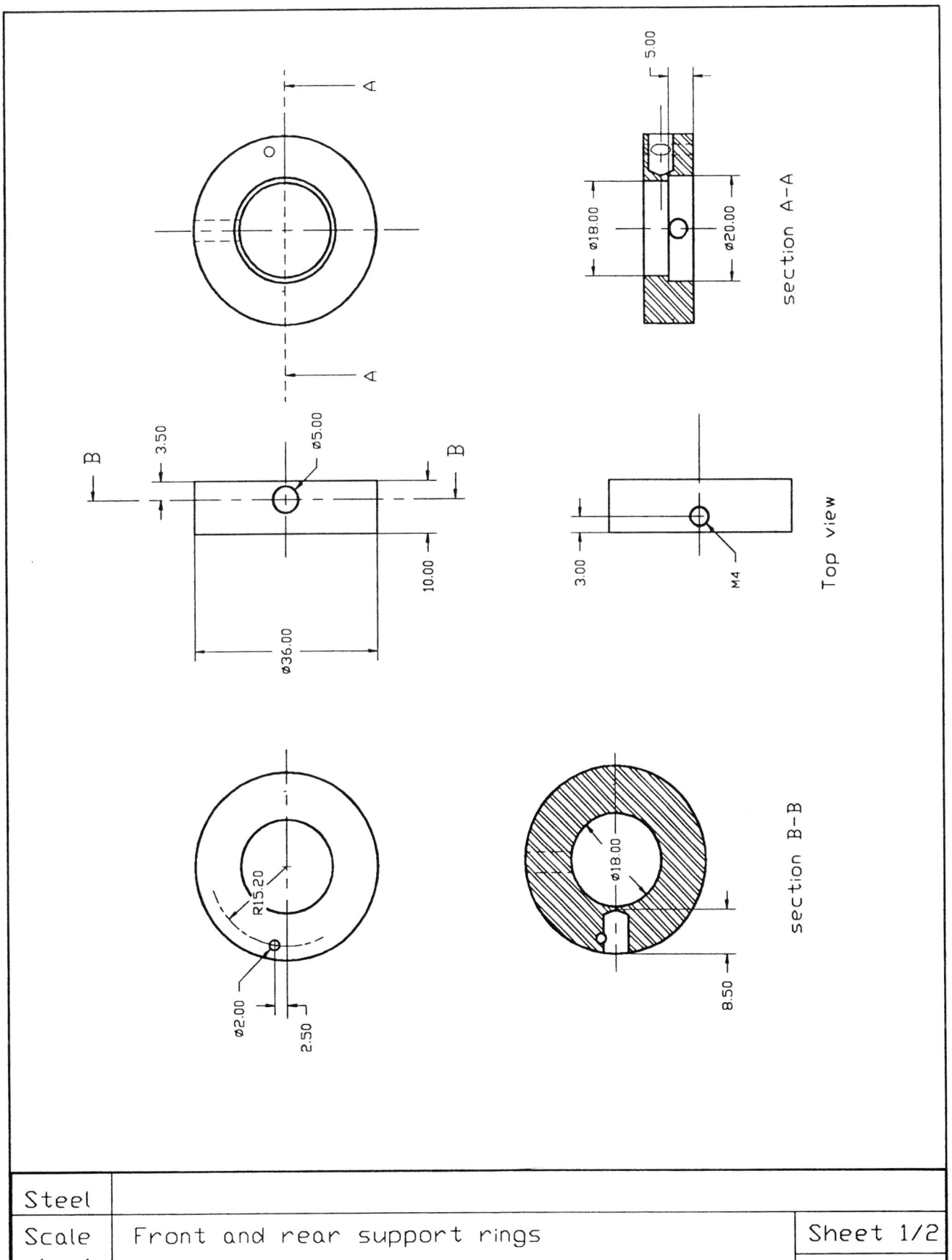

section A-A

5.00

⌀18.00   ⌀20.00

Top view

3.00

M4

A — A

⌀5.00

3.50

B — B

10.00

⌀36.00

section B-B

⌀18.00

8.50

R15.20

⌀2.00

2.50

Steel			
Scale 1 : 1	Front and rear support rings		Sheet 1/2
	Construction step 1		06.06.1994
	Copyright 1994 by **Gérard Métral**		
Metric	Drawing No. 004	Part No. R4	

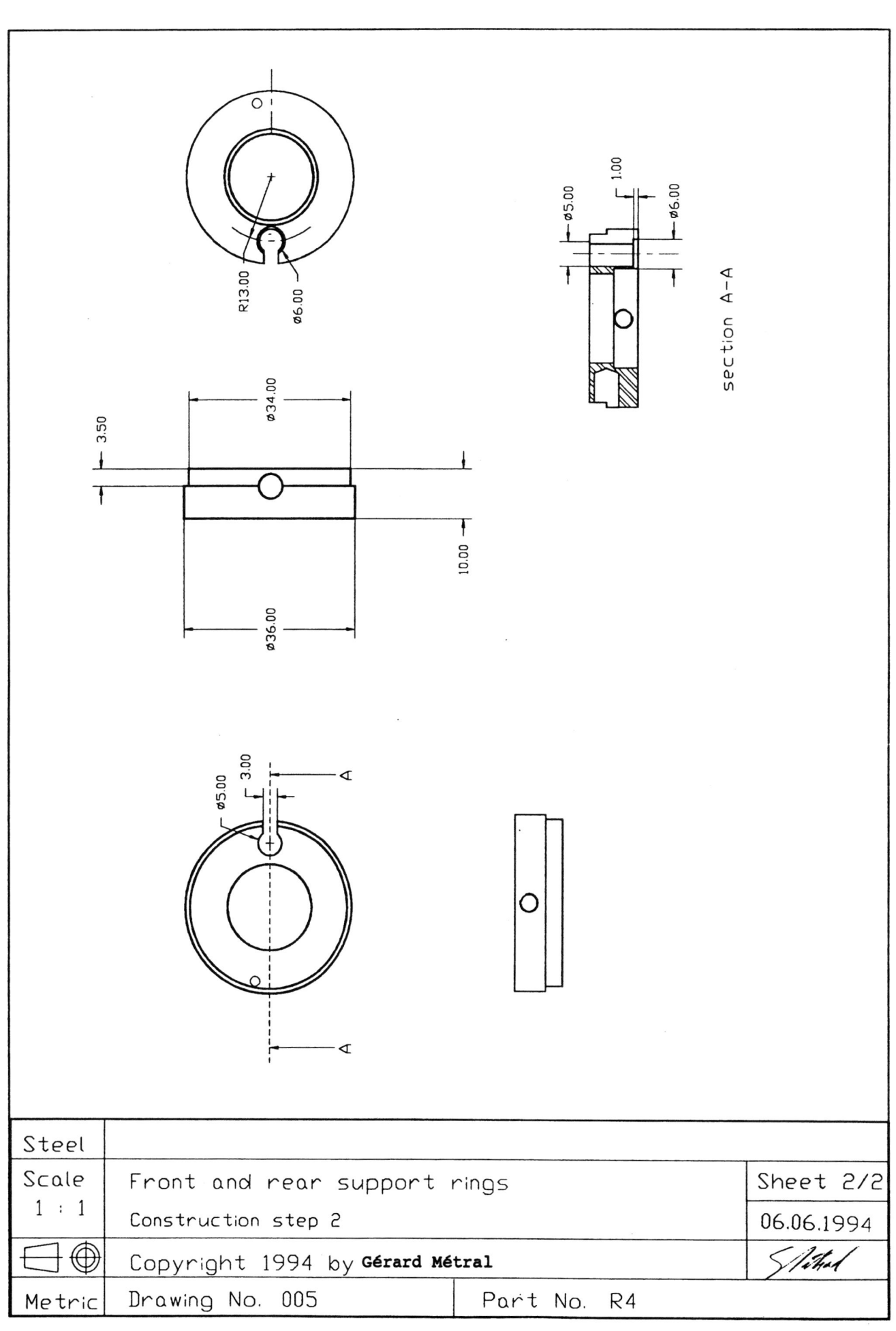

section A-A

Ø5.00
1.00
Ø6.00

R13.00
Ø6.00

3.50
Ø34.00
10.00
Ø36.00

Ø5.00
3.00
A
A

Steel		
Scale 1 : 1	Front and rear support rings	Sheet 2/2
	Construction step 2	06.06.1994
	Copyright 1994 by **Gérard Métral**	
Metric	Drawing No. 005	Part No. R4

spring

⌀3.00

10.00

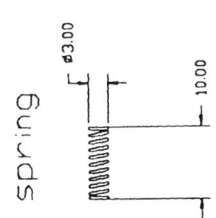

stud

1.00

4.50

⌀5.00

6.50

6.00

⌀3.50

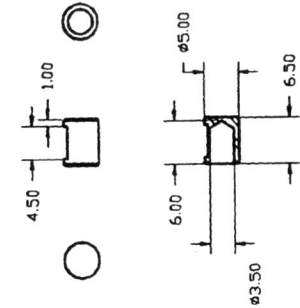

retaining pin

10.00

⌀2.00

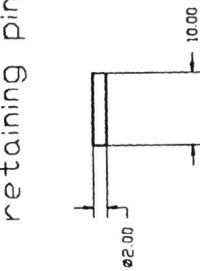

Steel			
Scale 1 : 1	Front and rear ring positioning stud with retaining pin and spring		Sheet 1/1
			06.06.1994
⊟ ⊕	Copyright 1994 by **Gérard Métral**		
Metric	Drawing No. 006	Parts No. R5, R6 and R7	

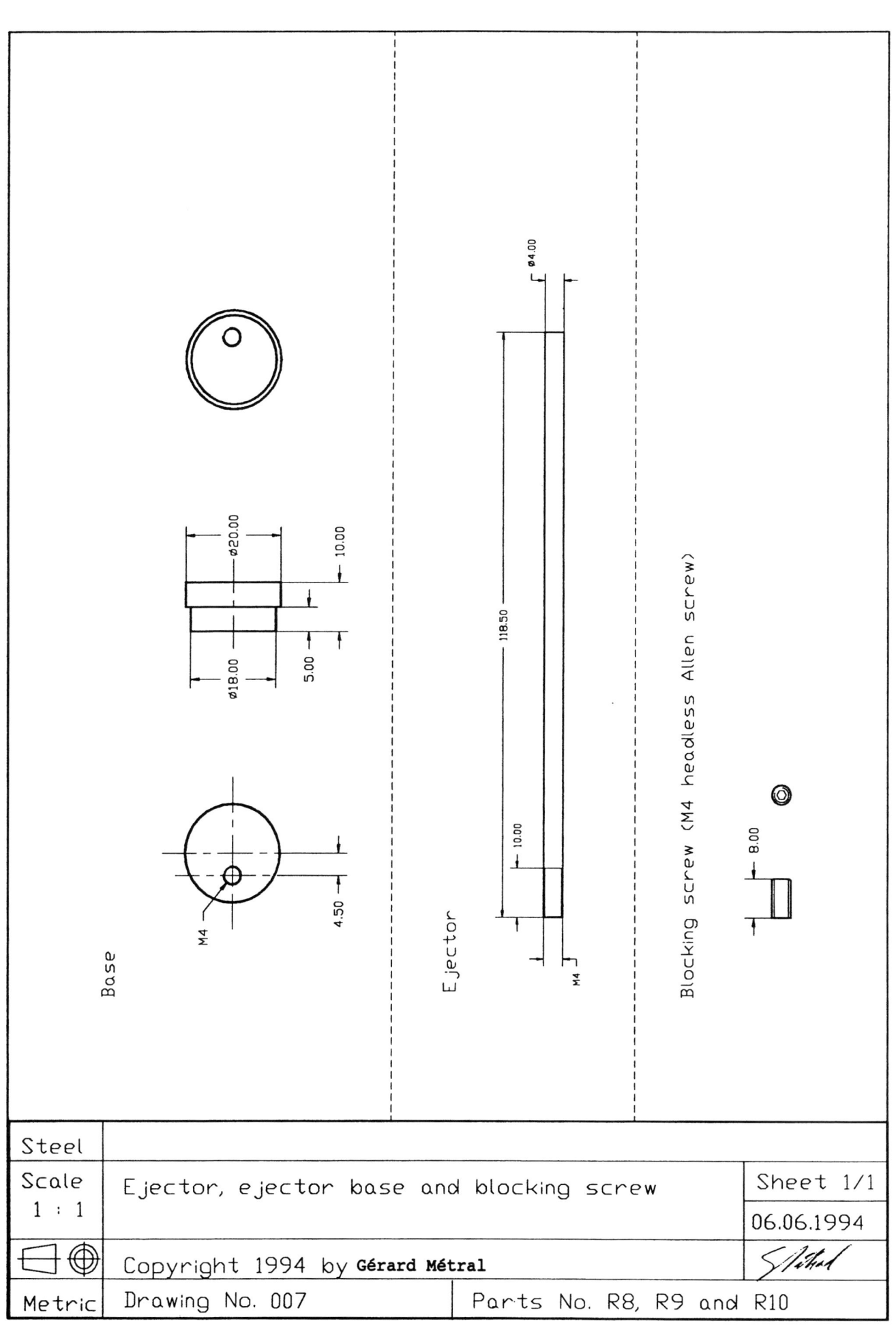

Base

Ejector

Blocking screw (M4 headless Allen screw)

Ø20.00
10.00
Ø18.00
5.00
4.50
M4

118.50
10.00
Ø4.00
M4
8.00

Steel		
Scale 1 : 1	Ejector, ejector base and blocking screw	Sheet 1/1
		06.06.1994
	Copyright 1994 by **Gérard Métral**	
Metric	Drawing No. 007	Parts No. R8, R9 and R10

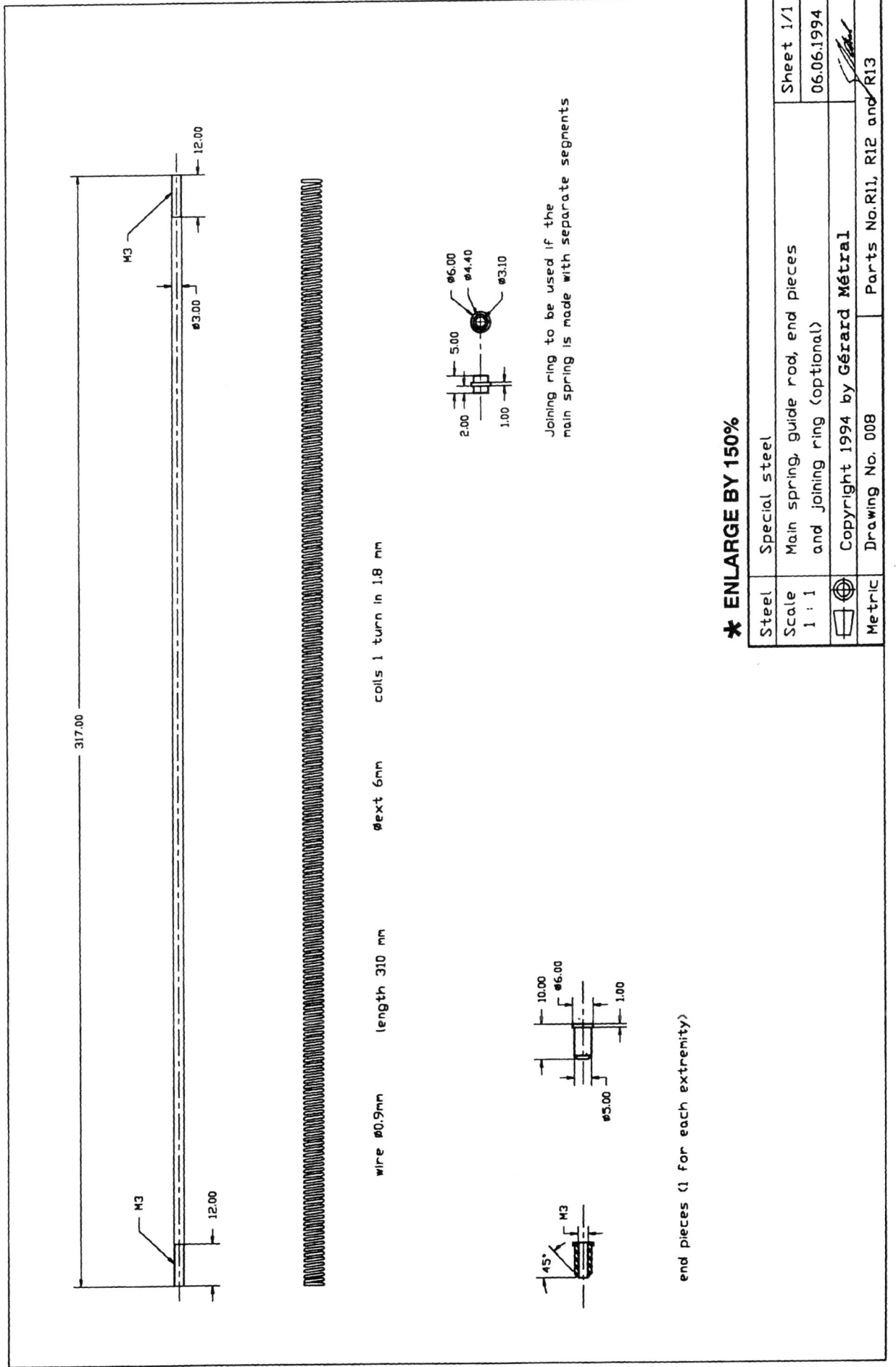

317.00

M3

Ø3.00

12.00

M3

12.00

wire Ø0.9mm   length 310 mm   Øext 6mm   coils 1 turn in 1.8 mm

Ø6.00
Ø4.40
Ø3.10

5.00

2.00

1.00

Joining ring to be used if the
main spring is made with separate segments

10.00
Ø6.00

1.00

Ø5.00

M3

45°

end pieces (1 for each extremity)

✱ ENLARGE BY 150%

Steel	Special steel		Sheet 1/1
Scale 1 : 1	Main spring, guide rod, end pieces and joining ring (optional)		
	Copyright 1994 by Gérard Métral		06.06.1994
Metric	Drawing No. 008	Parts No.R11, R12 and R13	

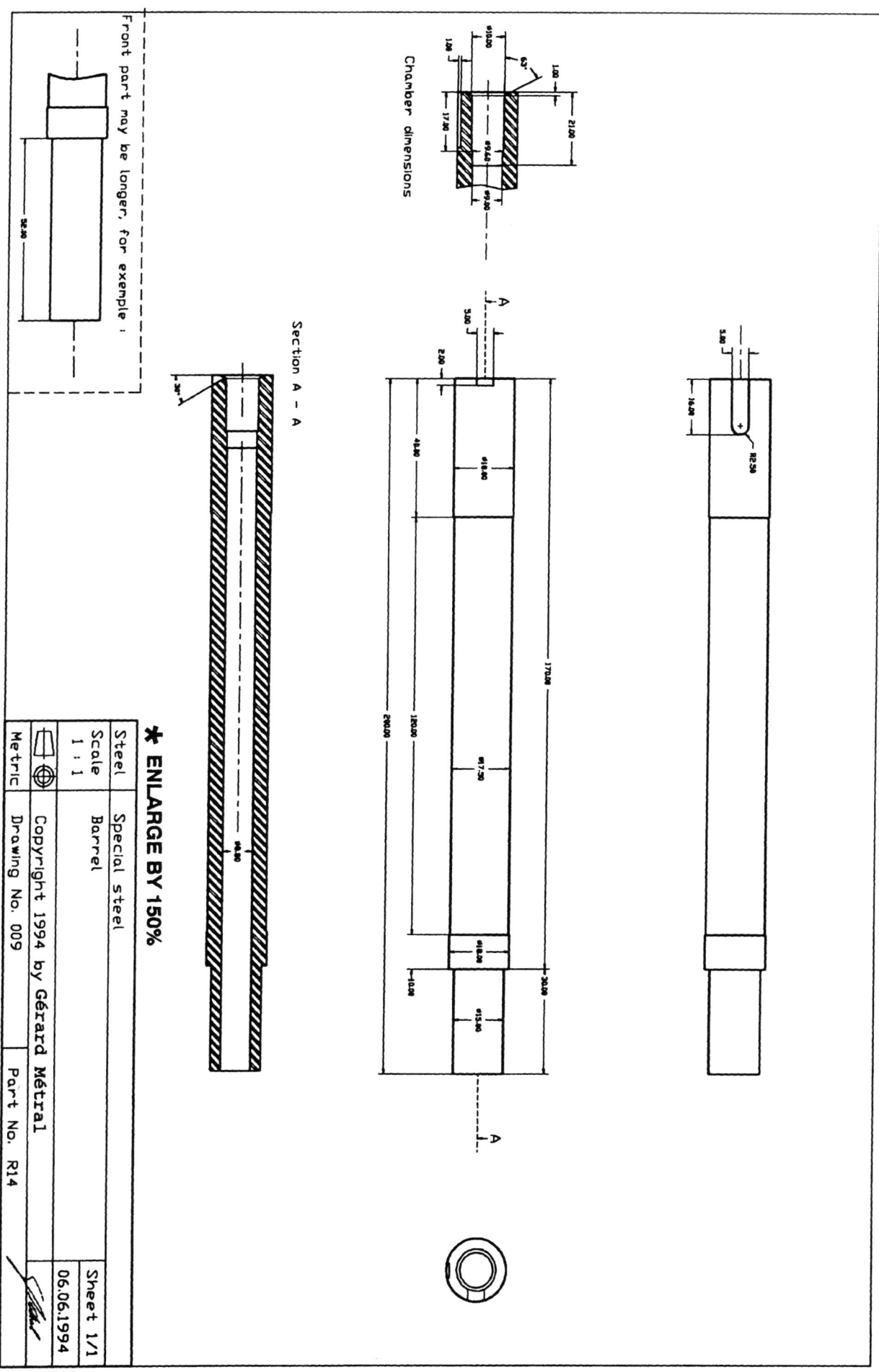

Front part may be longer, for exemple :

Chamber dimensions

Section A – A

✳ ENLARGE BY 150%

Steel	Special steel	
Scale	Barrel	
1 : 1		
	Copyright 1994 by Gérard Métral	
Metric	Drawing No. 009	Part No. R14

	Sheet 1/1
	06.06.1994

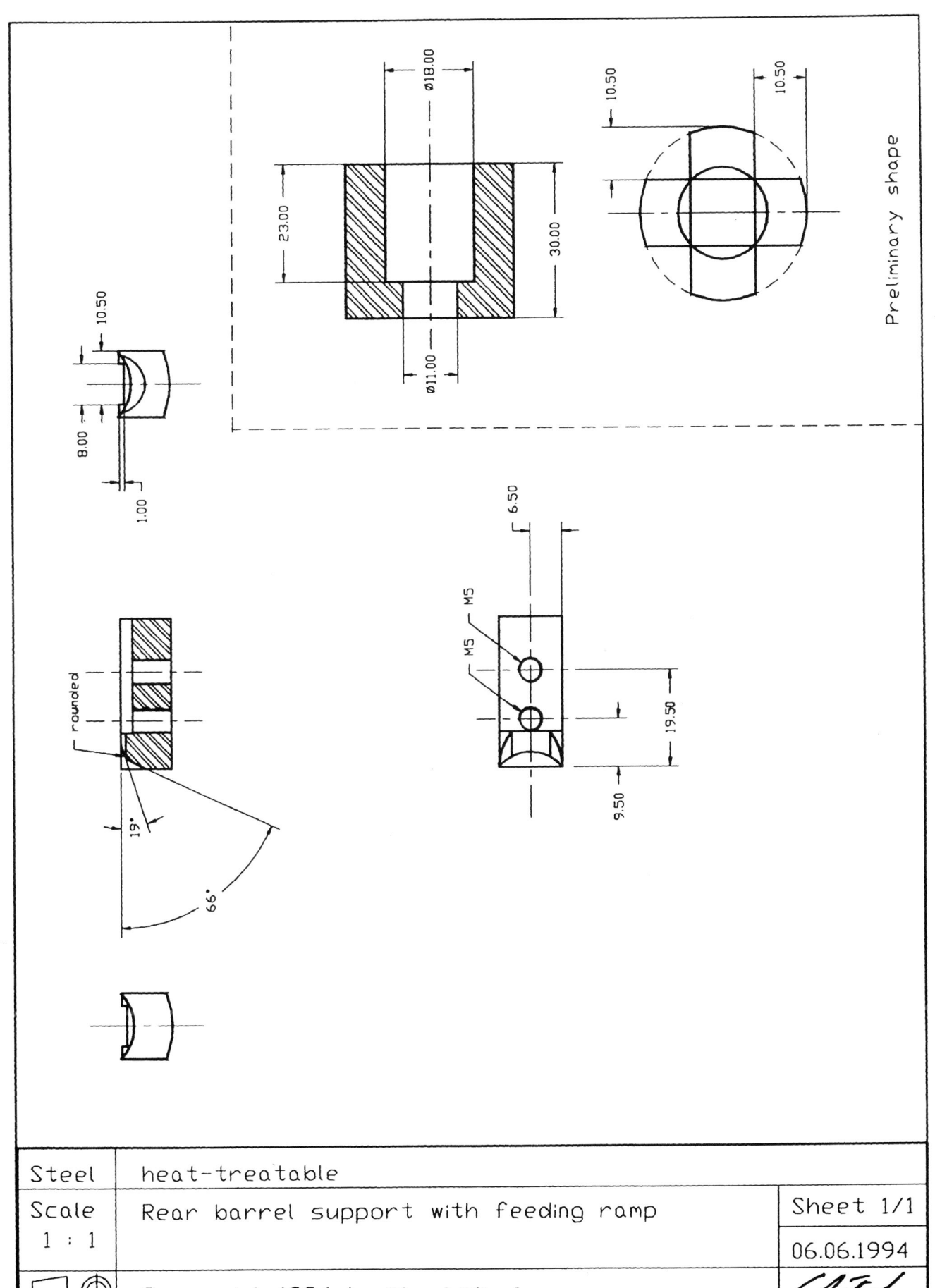

Preliminary shape

ø18.00

23.00

30.00

ø11.00

10.50

10.50

10.50

8.00

1.00

rounded

19°

66°

6.50

M5

M5

M5

19.50

9.50

Steel	heat-treatable	
Scale 1 : 1	Rear barrel support with feeding ramp	Sheet 1/1
		06.06.1994
⊟ ⊕	Copyright 1994 by **Gérard Métral**	
Metric	Drawing No. 010	Part No. R15

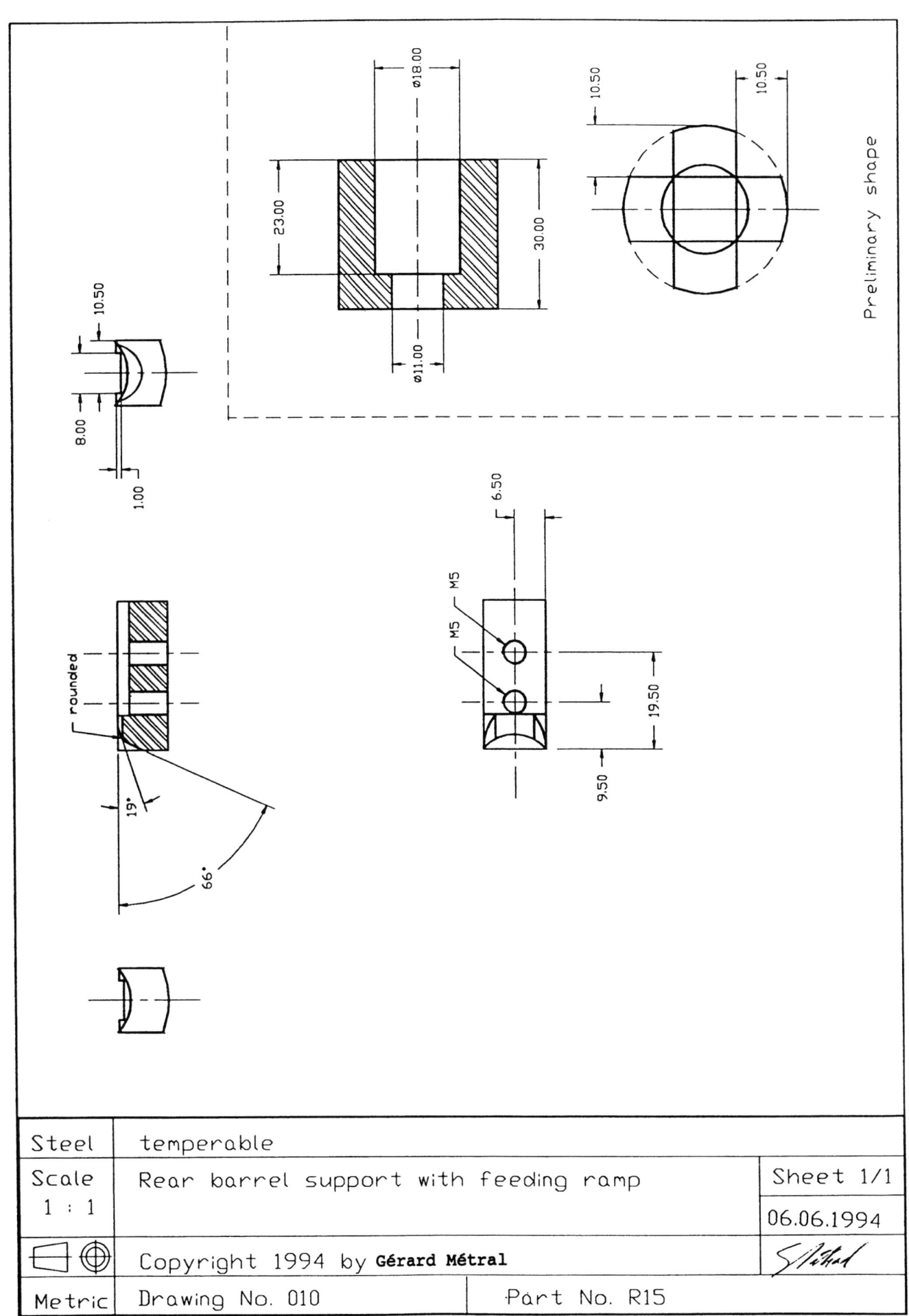

Preliminary shape

Ø18.00

10.50

10.50

23.00

30.00

Ø11.00

10.50

8.00

1.00

6.50

M5   M5

M5

19.50

9.50

rounded

19°

66°

Steel	temperable	
Scale 1 : 1	Rear barrel support with feeding ramp	Sheet 1/1
		06.06.1994
⊟ ⊕	Copyright 1994 by **Gérard Métral**	
Metric	Drawing No. 010	Part No. R15

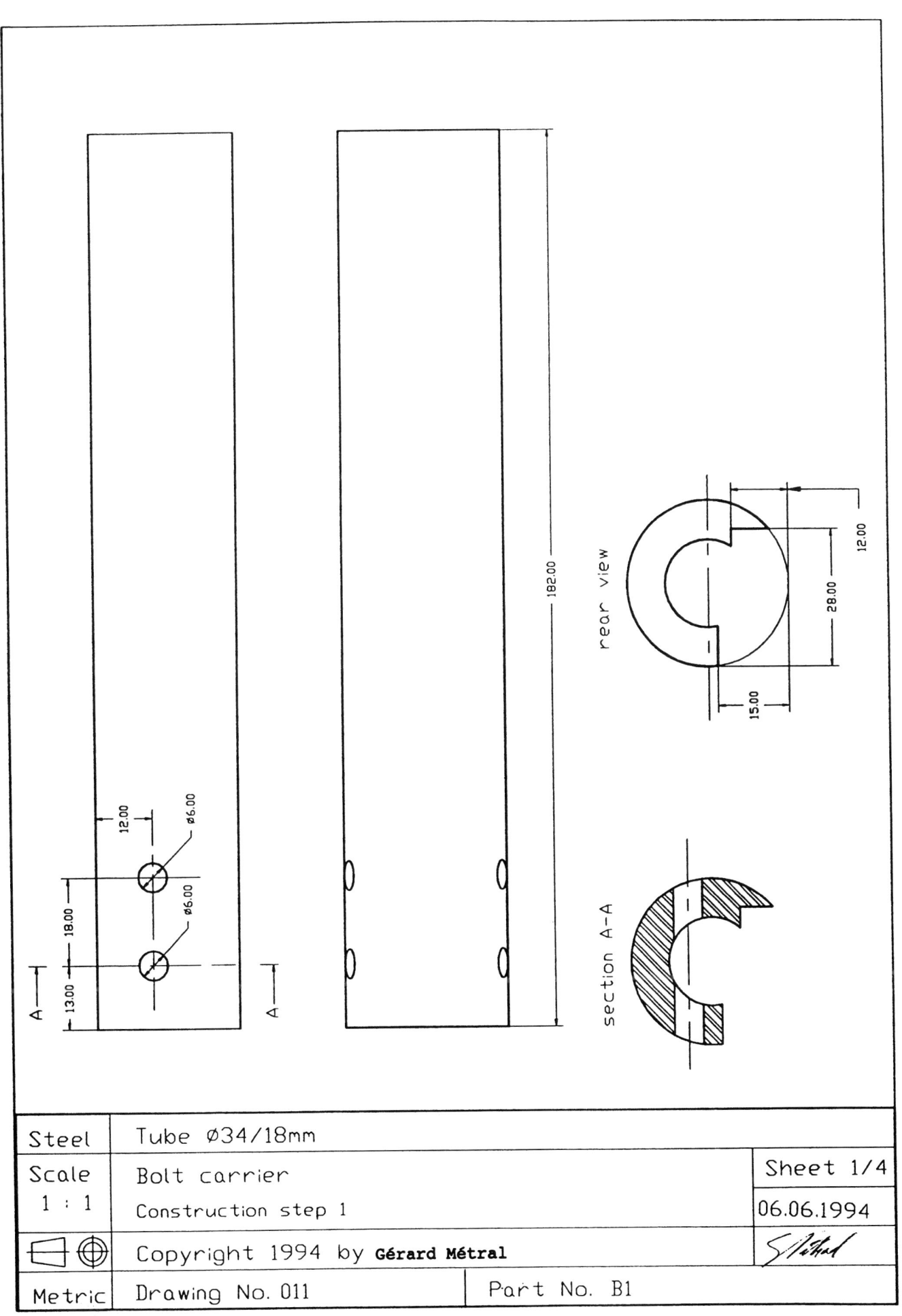

rear view

12.00

28.00

15.00

182.00

section A-A

12.00

Ø6.00

18.00

Ø6.00

13.00

A

A

Steel	Tube Ø34/18mm	
Scale	Bolt carrier	Sheet 1/4
1 : 1	Construction step 1	06.06.1994
⊟ ⊕	Copyright 1994 by **Gérard Métral**	
Metric	Drawing No. 011	Part No. B1

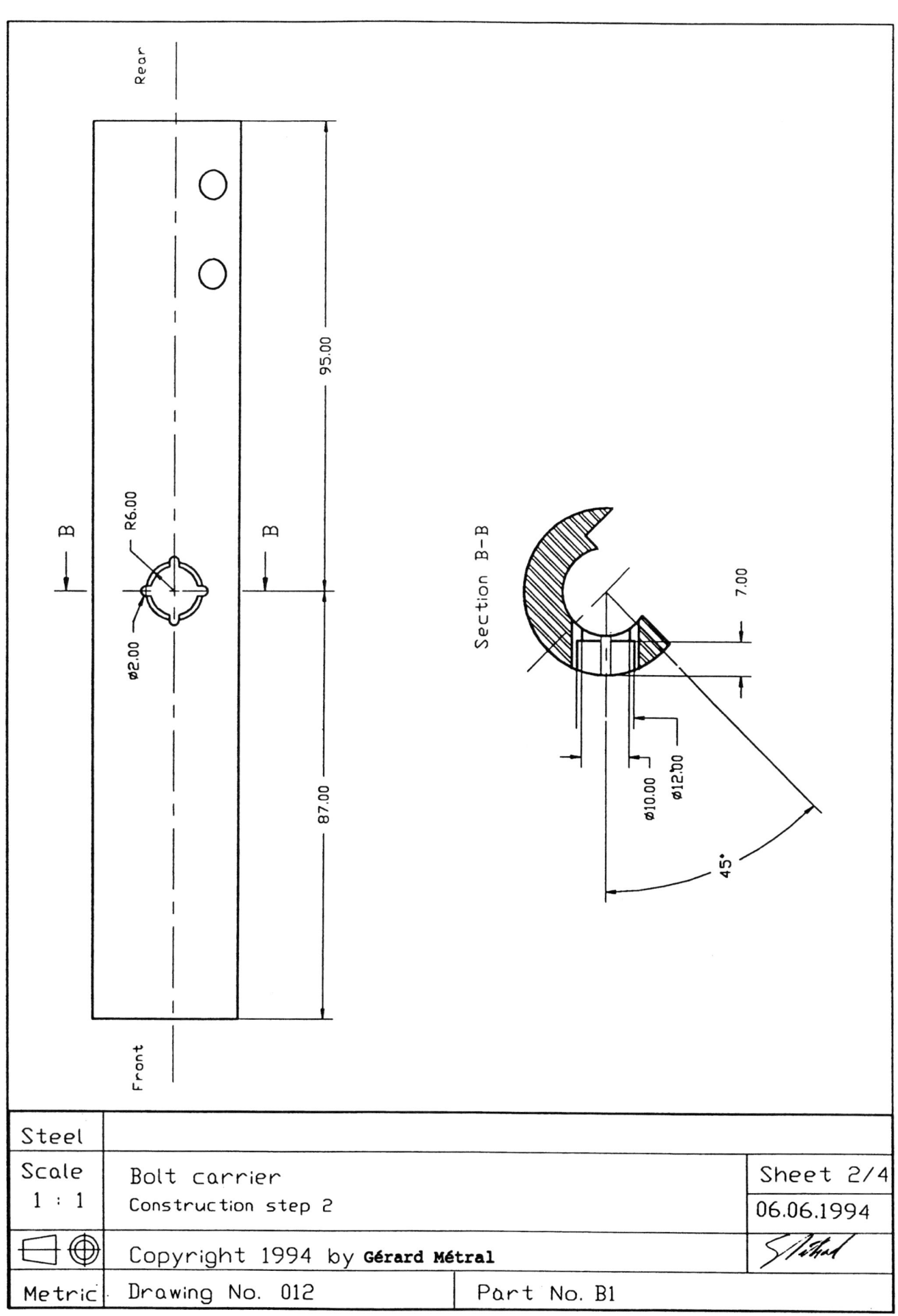

Rear

B

R6.00

Ø2.00

B

95.00

87.00

Front

Section B-B

7.00

Ø10.00

Ø12.00

45°

Steel		
Scale 1 : 1	Bolt carrier Construction step 2	Sheet 2/4
		06.06.1994
⊟ ⊕	Copyright 1994 by **Gérard Métral**	
Metric	Drawing No. 012	Part No. B1

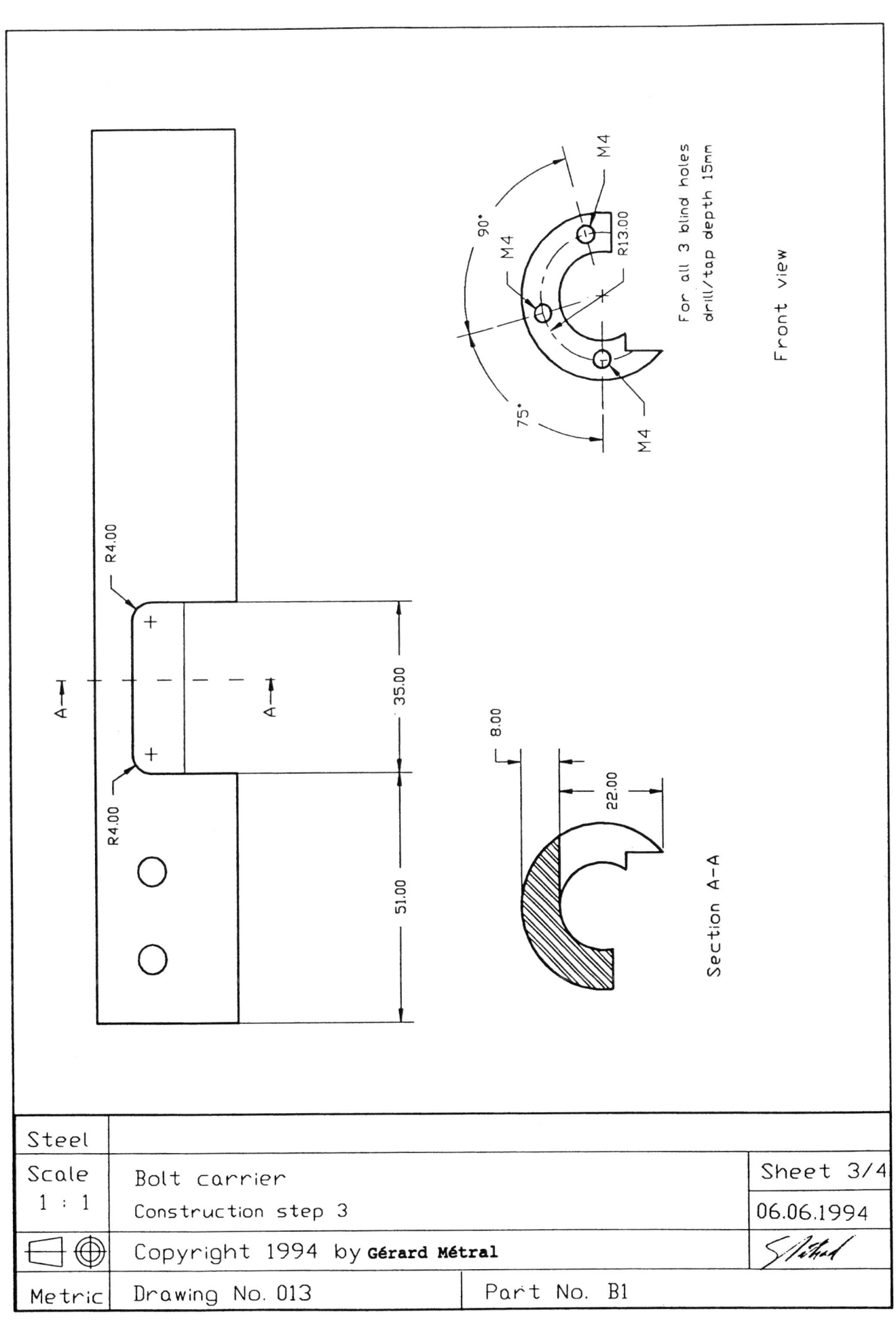

M4

M4

M4

90°

75°

R13.00

For all 3 blind holes
drill/tap depth 15mm

Front view

R4.00

R4.00

A

A

35.00

51.00

8.00

22.00

Section A-A

Steel		
Scale 1 : 1	Bolt carrier	Sheet 3/4
	Construction step 3	06.06.1994
⊟ ⊕	Copyright 1994 by **Gérard Métral**	
Metric	Drawing No. 013	Part No. B1

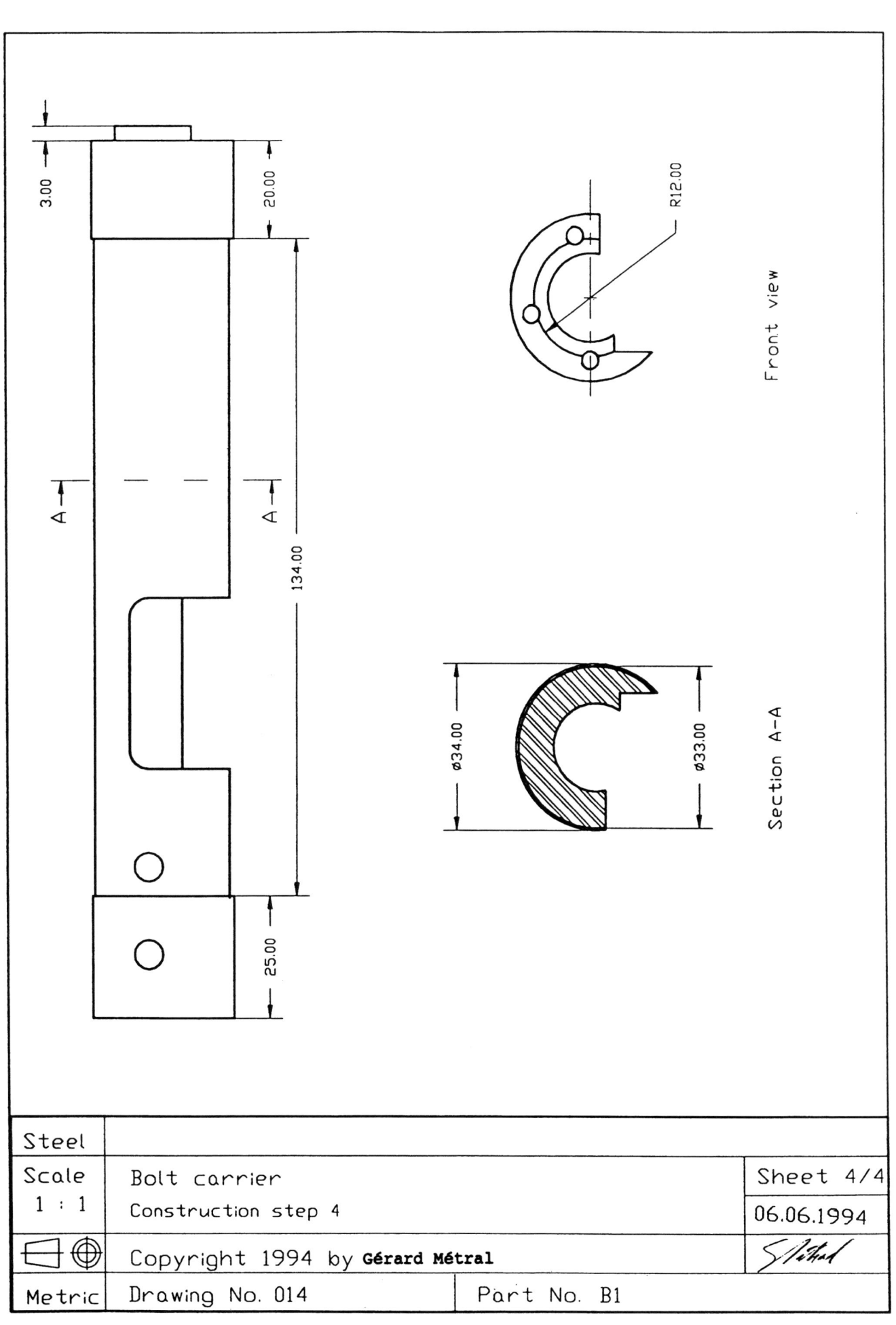

3.00

20.00

A

A

134.00

25.00

R12.00

Front view

ø34.00

ø33.00

Section A-A

Steel		
Scale 1 : 1	Bolt carrier	Sheet 4/4
	Construction step 4	06.06.1994
⊟ ⊕	Copyright 1994 by **Gérard Métral**	
Metric	Drawing No. 014	Part No. B1

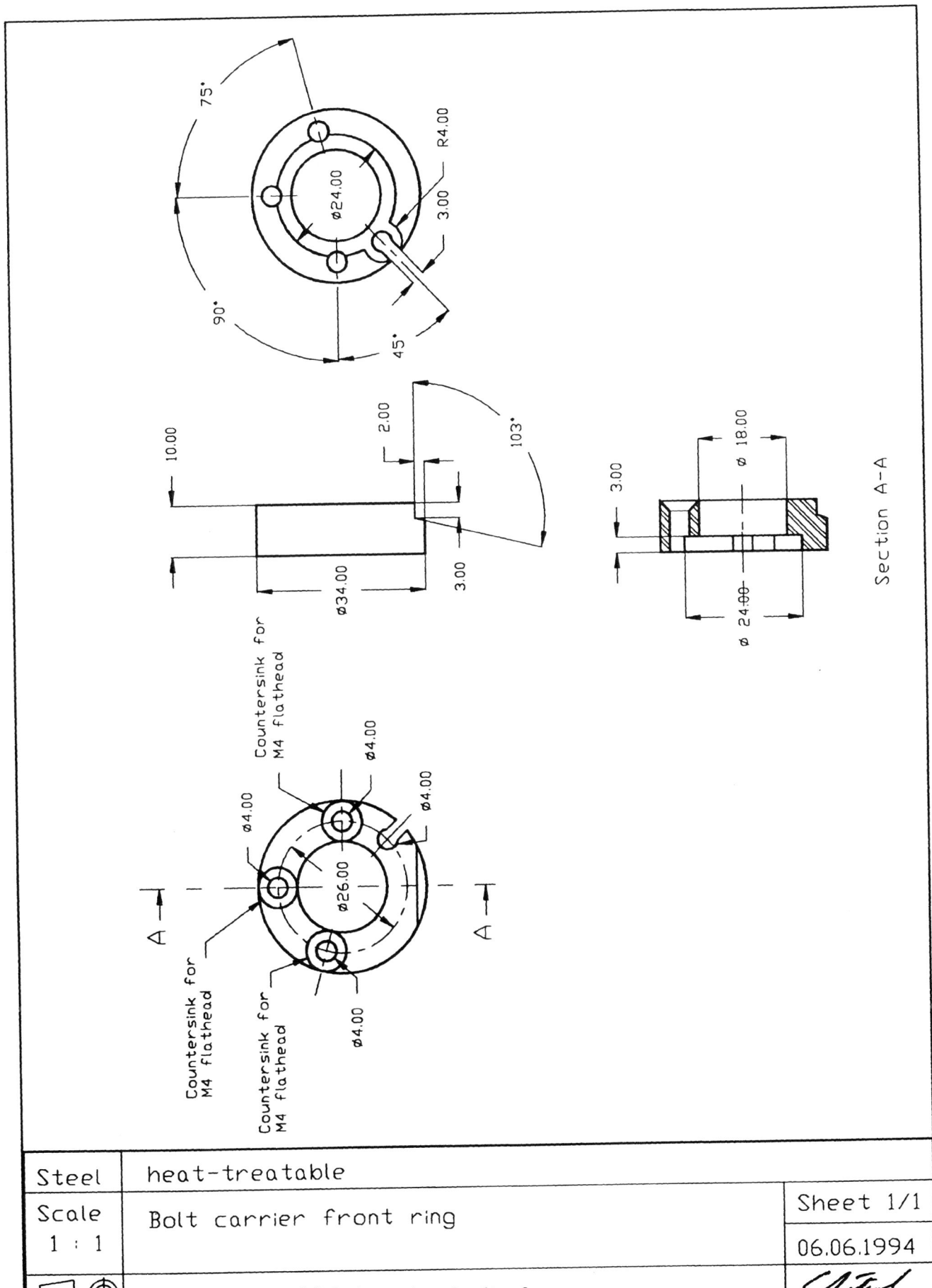

Steel	heat-treatable	
Scale 1 : 1	Bolt carrier front ring	Sheet 1/1
		06.06.1994
⬚ ⊕	Copyright 1994 by **Gérard Métral**	
Metric	Drawing No. 015	Part No. B2

Section A-A

Countersink for M4 flathead

Ø24.00
R4.00
3.00
75°
90°
45°
10.00
2.00
103°
34.00
3.00
3.00
Ø 18.00
Ø 24.00
Ø26.00
Ø4.00

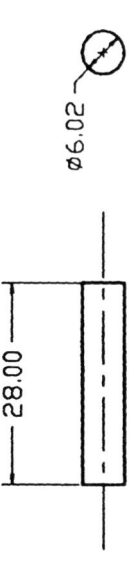

ø6.02

28.00

Steel	980-1180N/mm^2 DIN 34 CrNiMo 6		
Scale 1 : 1	Bolt pins		Sheet 1/1
			06.06.1994
	Copyright 1994 by **Gérard Métral**		
Metric	Drawing No. 016	Part No. B4	

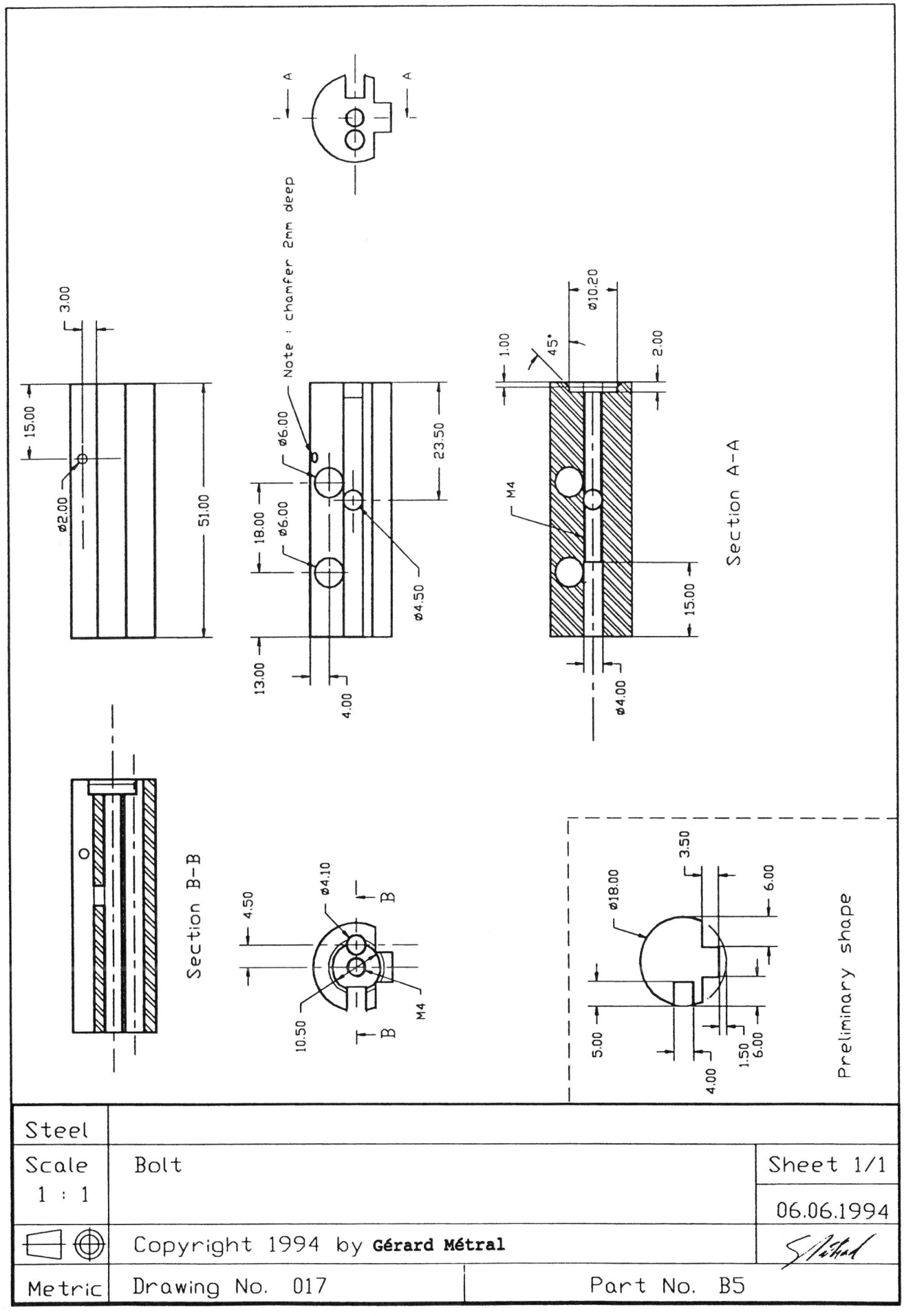

Note : chamfer 2mm deep

Section A-A

Section B-B

Preliminary shape

Steel		
Scale 1 : 1	Bolt	Sheet 1/1
		06.06.1994
⬒ ⊕	Copyright 1994 by **Gérard Métral**	
Metric	Drawing No. 017	Part No. B5

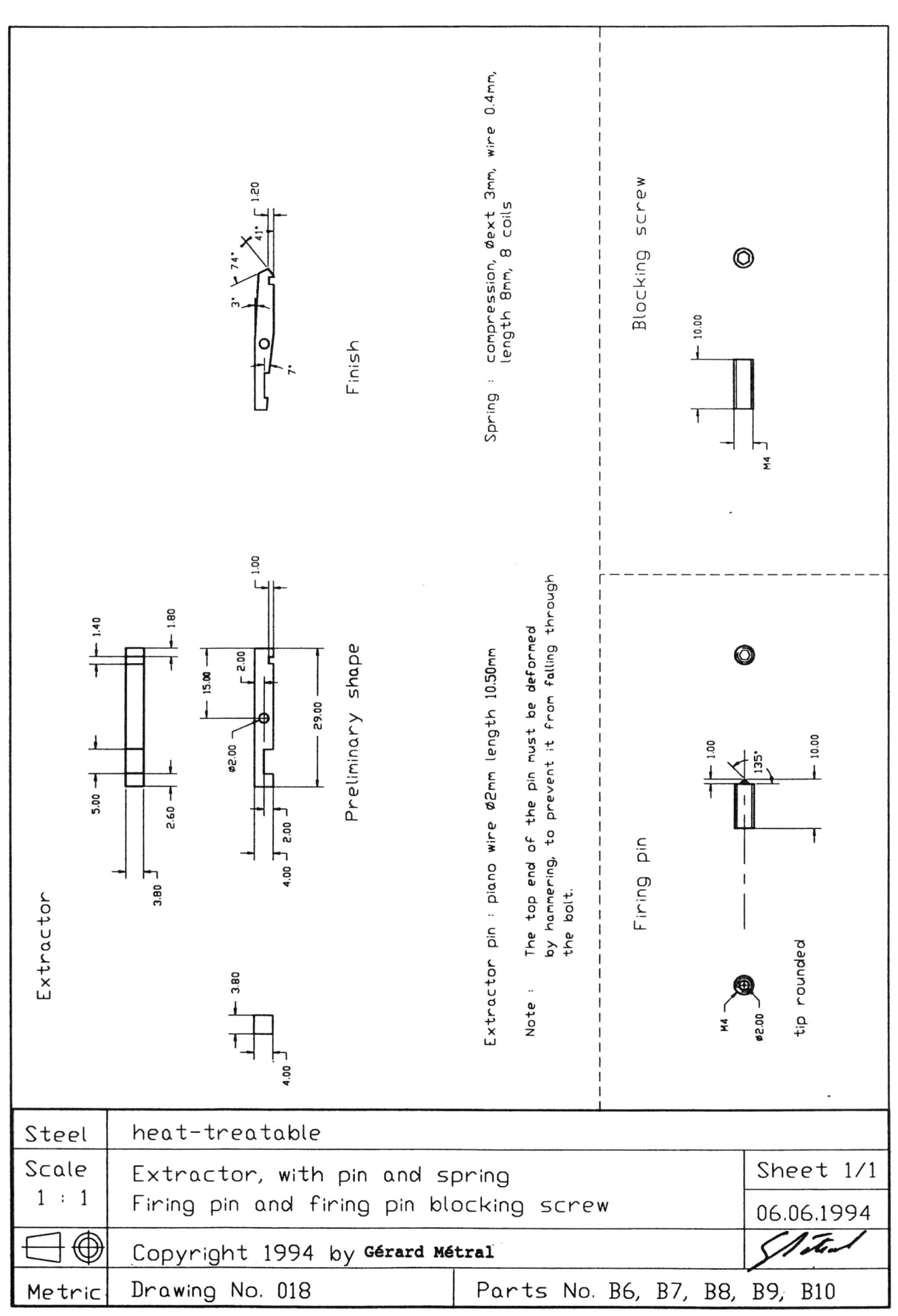

Extractor

Finish

Preliminary shape

Spring : compression, Øext 3mm, wire 0.4mm, length 8mm, 8 coils

Extractor pin : piano wire Ø2mm length 10.50mm

Note : The top end of the pin must be deformed by hammering, to prevent it from falling through the bolt.

Blocking screw

Firing pin

tip rounded

Steel	heat-treatable	
Scale 1 : 1	Extractor, with pin and spring Firing pin and firing pin blocking screw	Sheet 1/1
		06.06.1994
	Copyright 1994 by **Gérard Métral**	
Metric	Drawing No. 018	Parts No. B6, B7, B8, B9, B10

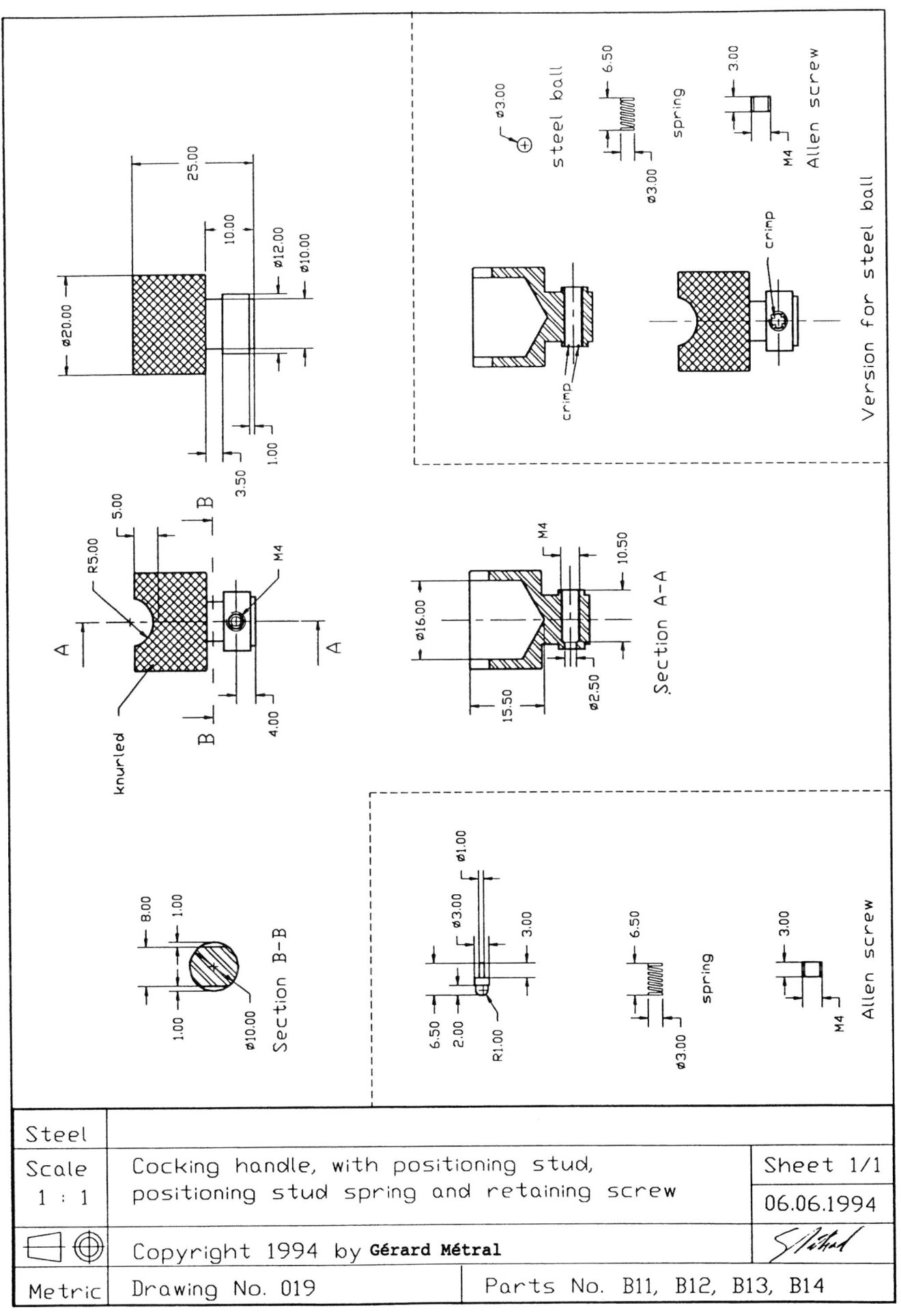

steel ball

Ø3.00

6.50

Ø3.00

spring

3.00

M4

Allen screw

Version for steel ball

crimp

25.00

10.00

Ø20.00

Ø12.00

Ø10.00

1.00

3.50

5.00

R5.00

B

M4

A

A

knurled

B

4.00

Section A-A

Ø16.00

15.50

M4

10.50

Ø2.50

8.00

1.00

1.00

Ø10.00

Section B-B

Ø1.00

Ø3.00

3.00

6.50

2.00

R1.00

6.50

Ø3.00

spring

3.00

M4

Allen screw

Steel		
Scale 1 : 1	Cocking handle, with positioning stud, positioning stud spring and retaining screw	Sheet 1/1
		06.06.1994
⊟ ⊕	Copyright 1994 by **Gérard Métral**	
Metric	Drawing No. 019	Parts No. B11, B12, B13, B14

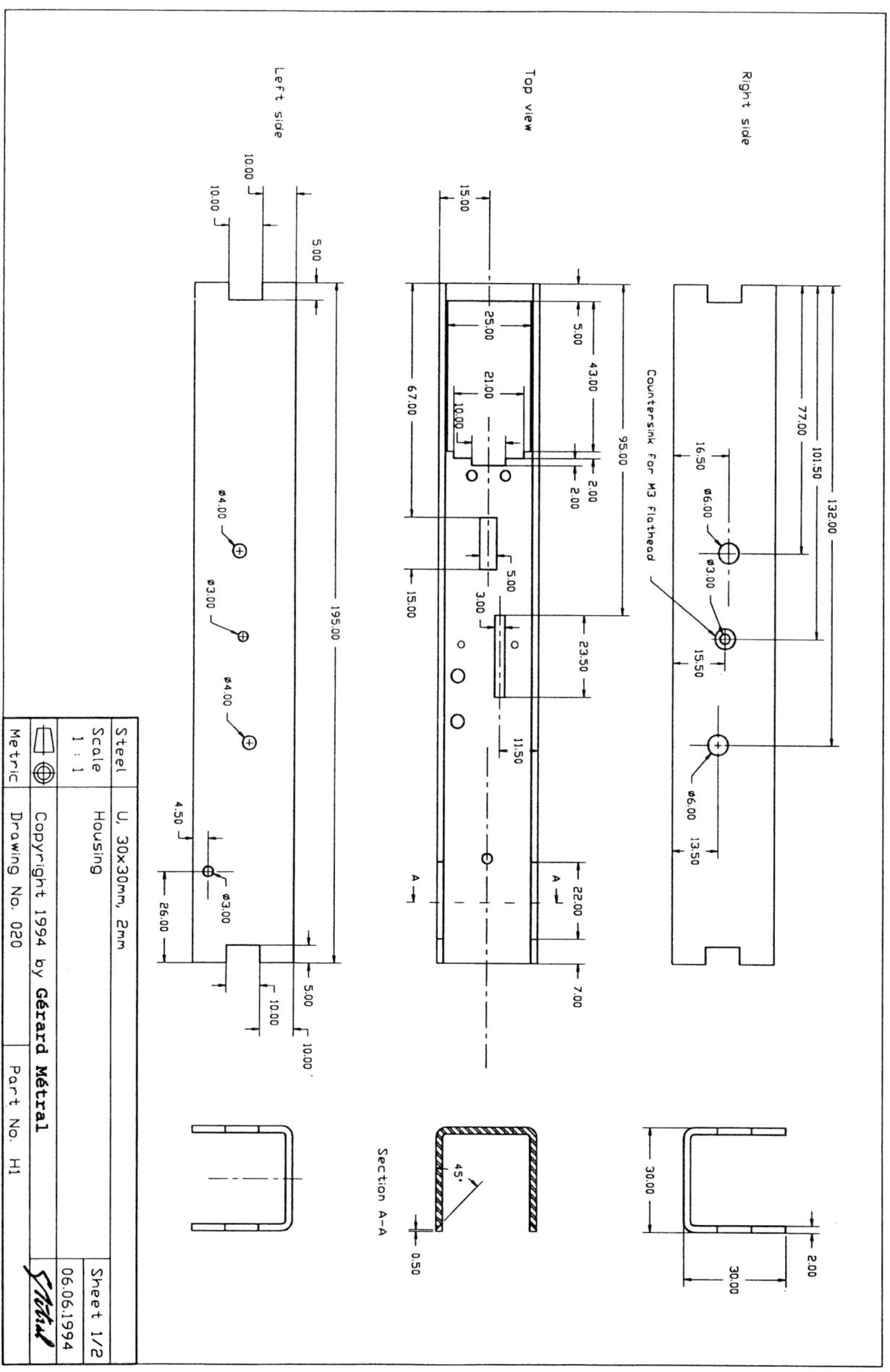

Right side

Top view

Left side

Countersink for M3 flathead

Section A-A

ø4.00

ø3.00

ø4.00

ø3.00

45°

Steel	U, 30x30mm, 2mm
Scale	Housing
1 : 1	
Metric	
	Copyright 1994 by Gérard Métral
	Drawing No. 020	Part No. H1
	06.06.1994	Sheet 1/2

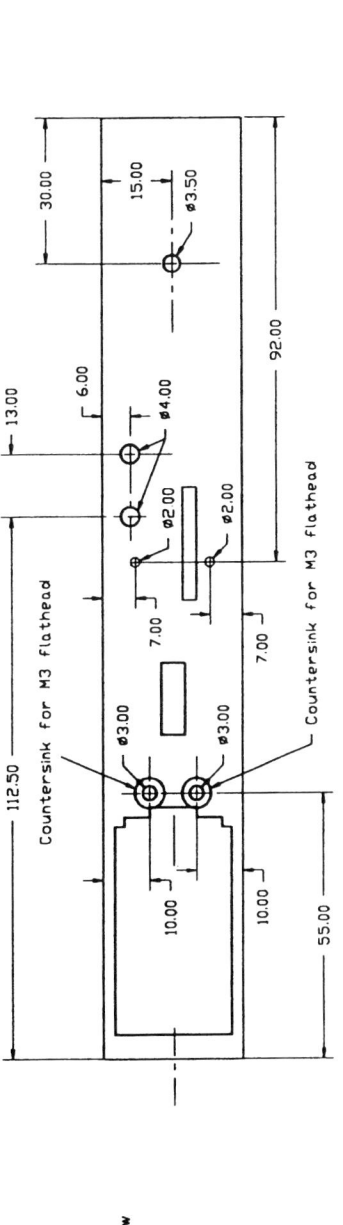

Seen from below

Countersink for M3 Flathead

Countersink for M3 Flathead

112.50

30.00
15.00
ø3.50

13.00
6.00
ø4.00

92.00

ø2.00
ø2.00

7.00
7.00

ø3.00
ø3.00

10.00
10.00

55.00

* ENLARGE BY 150%

Steel	
Scale 1:1	Housing
⊕	Copyright 1994 by **Gérard Métral**
Metric	Drawing No. 021	Part No. H1

Sheet 2/2

06.06.1994

Métral

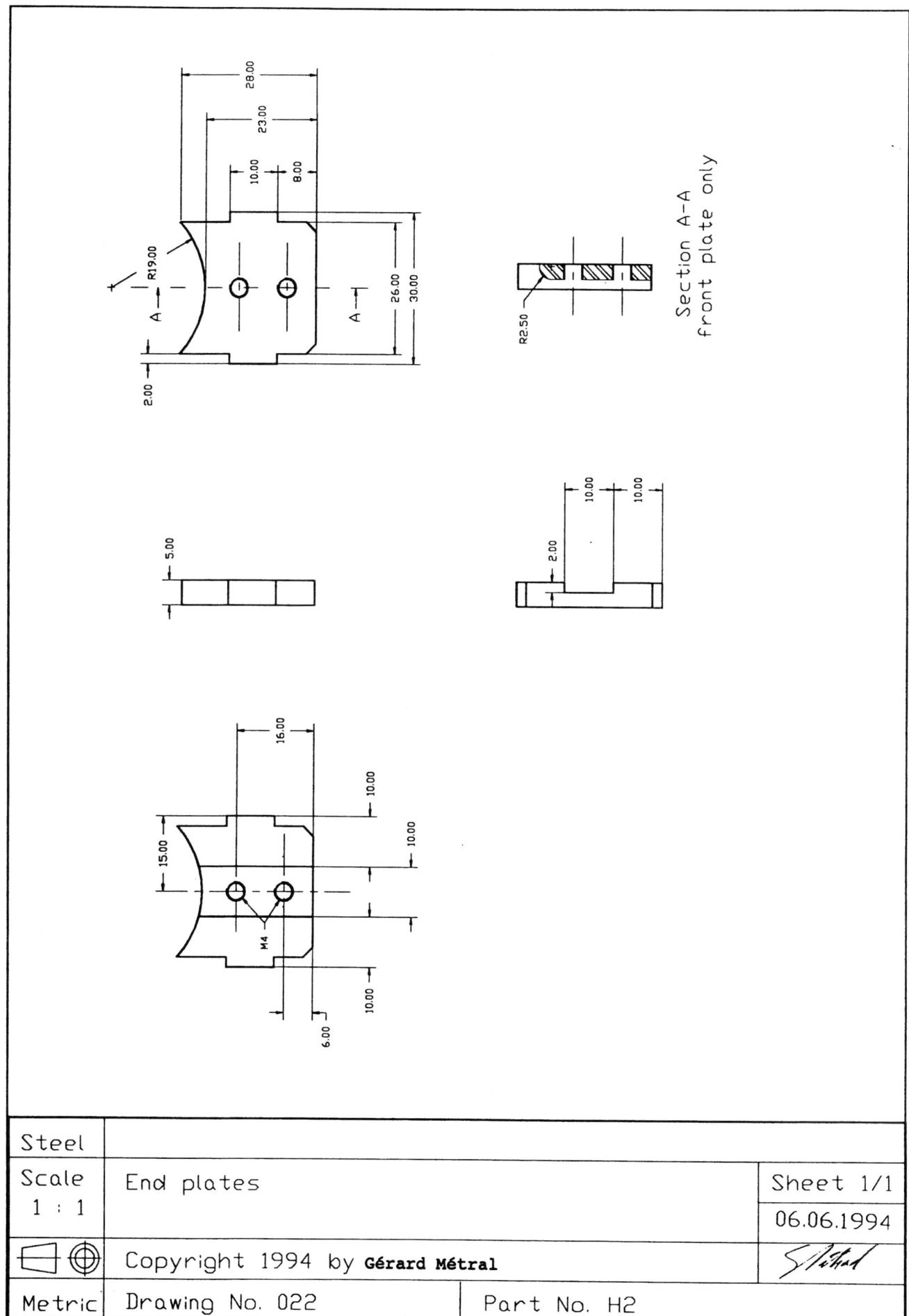

Section A-A
front plate only

Steel		
Scale 1 : 1	End plates	Sheet 1/1
		06.06.1994
⬓ ⊕	Copyright 1994 by **Gérard Métral**	
Metric	Drawing No. 022	Part No. H2

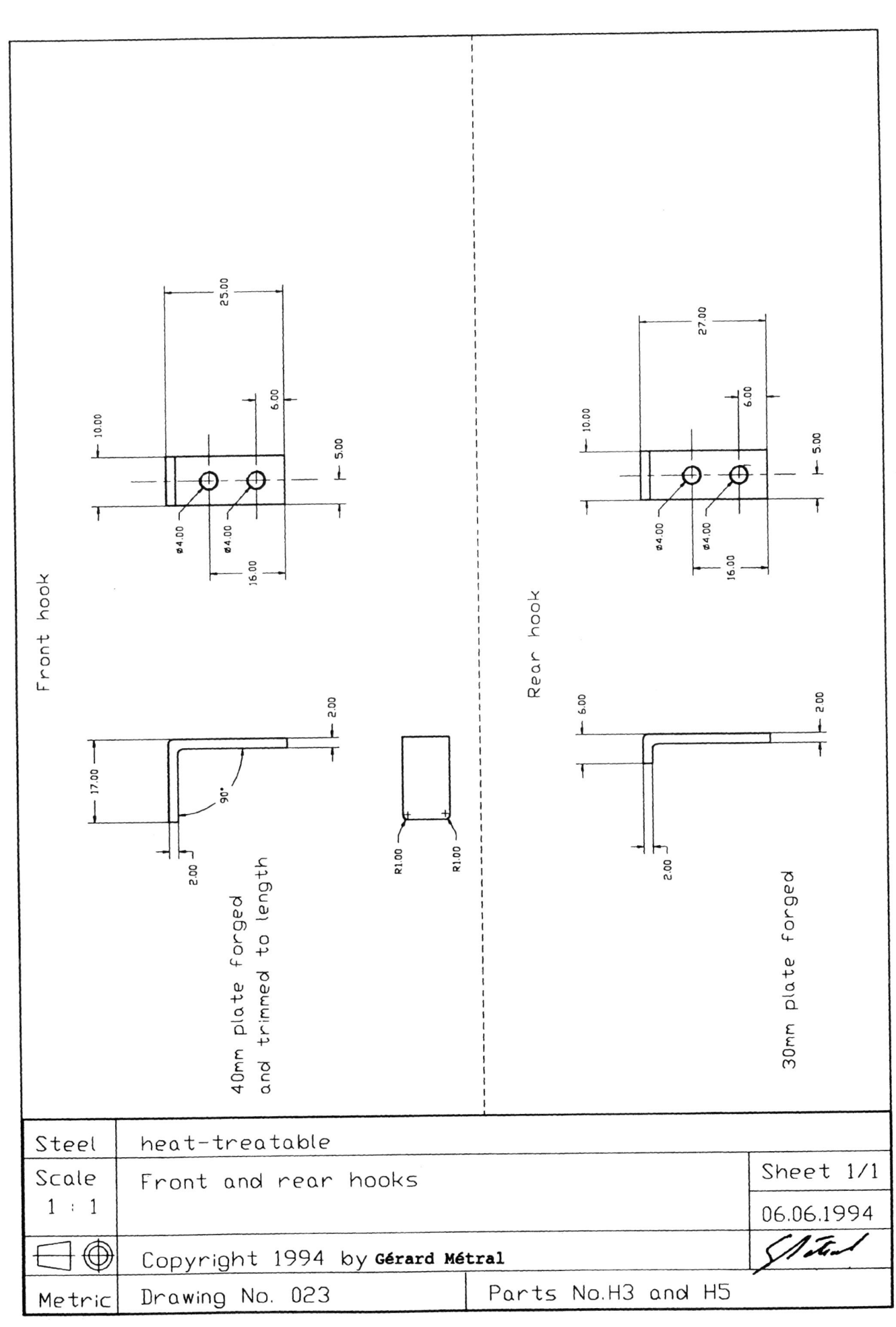

Front hook

25.00
10.00
6.00
5.00
16.00
Ø4.00
Ø4.00

17.00
2.00
2.00
90°
R1.00
R1.00

40mm plate forged
and trimmed to length

Rear hook

27.00
10.00
6.00
5.00
16.00
Ø4.00
Ø4.00

6.00
2.00
2.00

30mm plate forged

Steel	heat-treatable	
Scale	Front and rear hooks	Sheet 1/1
1 : 1		06.06.1994
⊟ ⊕	Copyright 1994 by **Gérard Métral**	
Metric	Drawing No. 023	Parts No.H3 and H5

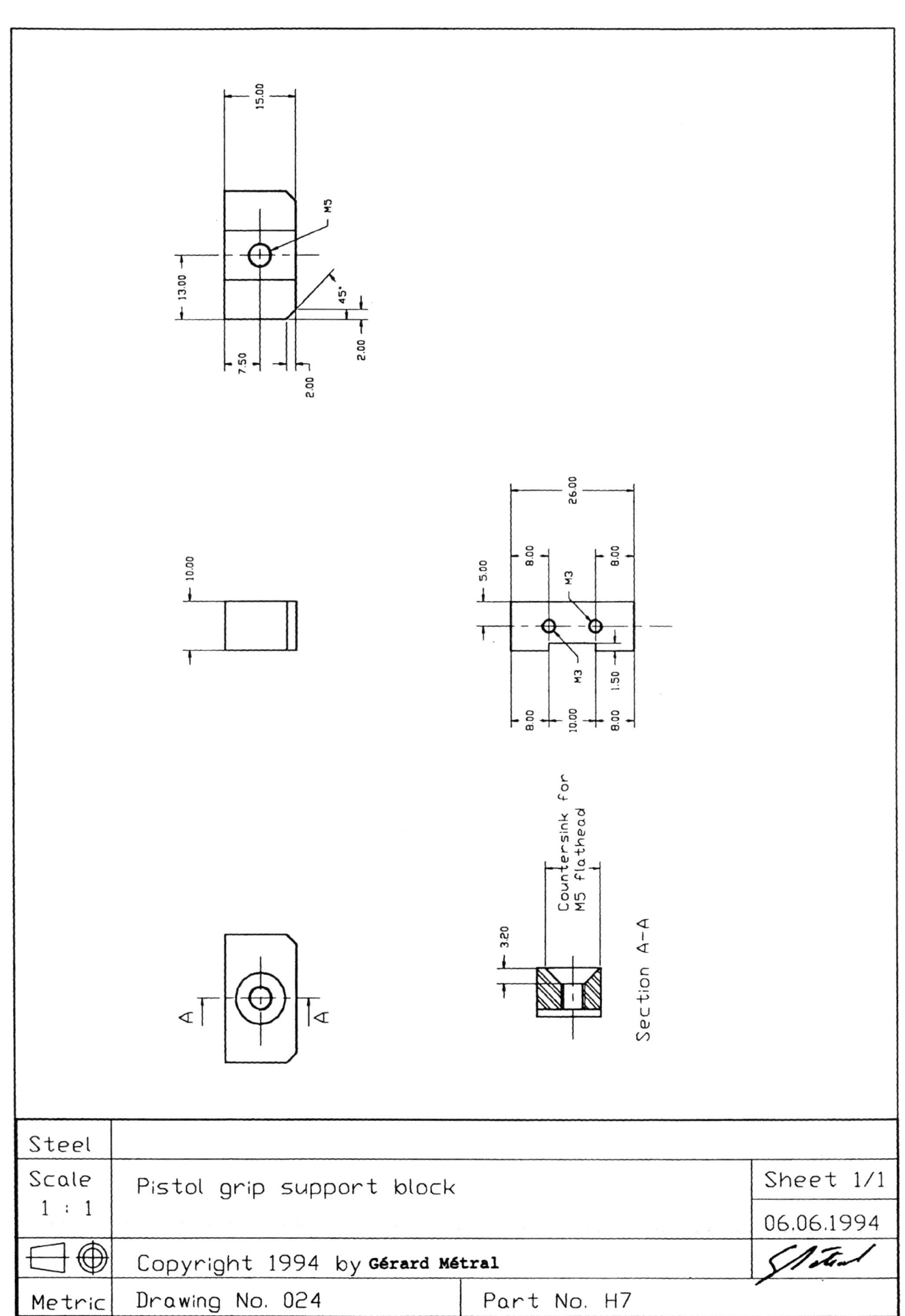

15.00

M5

13.00

45°

7.50

2.00

2.00

10.00

26.00

5.00

8.00

8.00

M3

M3

8.00

10.00

8.00

1.50

Countersink for M5 flathead

3.20

Section A-A

A

A

Steel		
Scale 1 : 1	Pistol grip support block	Sheet 1/1
		06.06.1994
	Copyright 1994 by **Gérard Métral**	
Metric	Drawing No. 024	Part No. H7

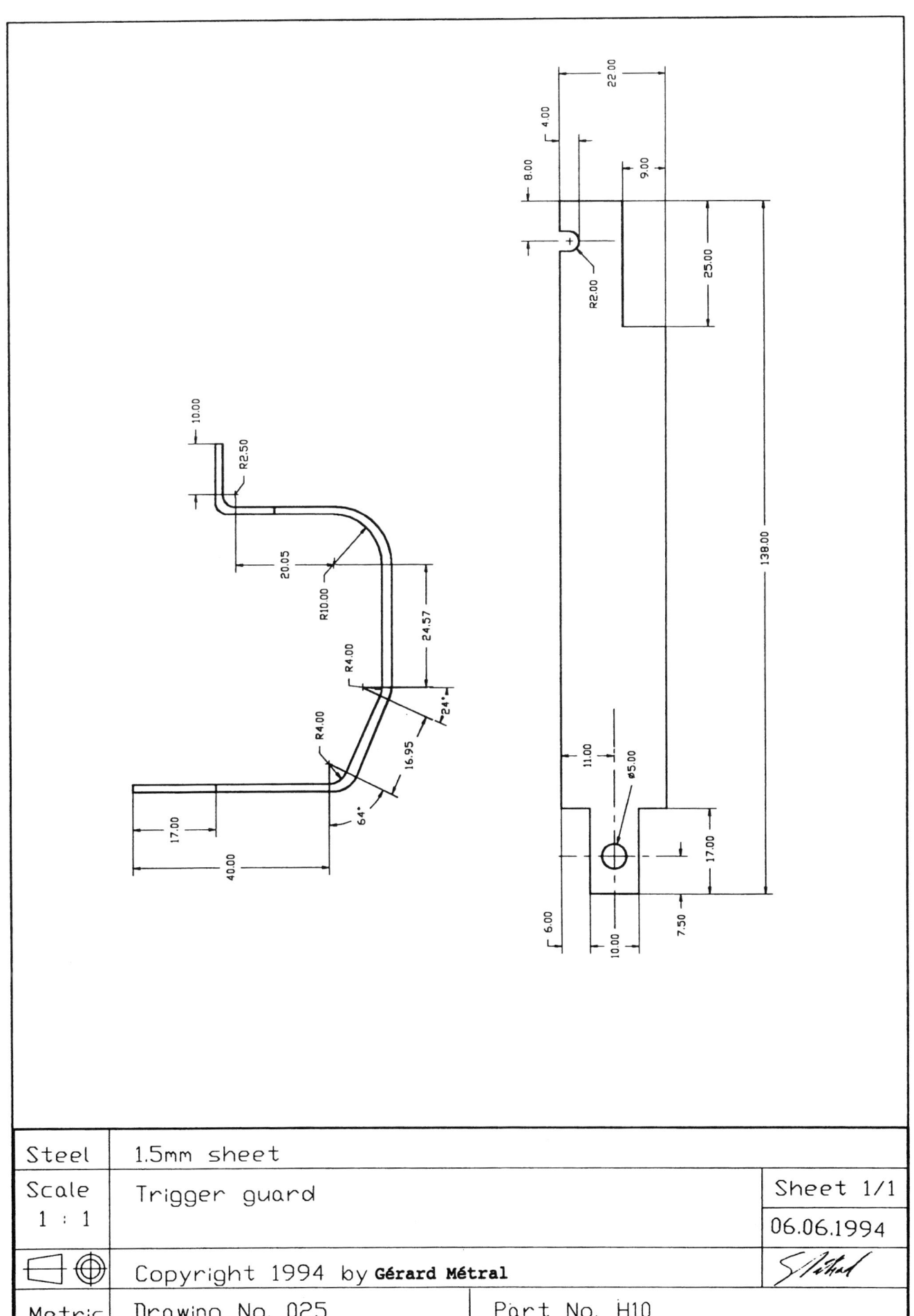

Steel	1.5mm sheet		
Scale 1 : 1	Trigger guard		Sheet 1/1
			06.06.1994
	Copyright 1994 by **Gérard Métral**		
Metric	Drawing No. 025	Part No. H10	

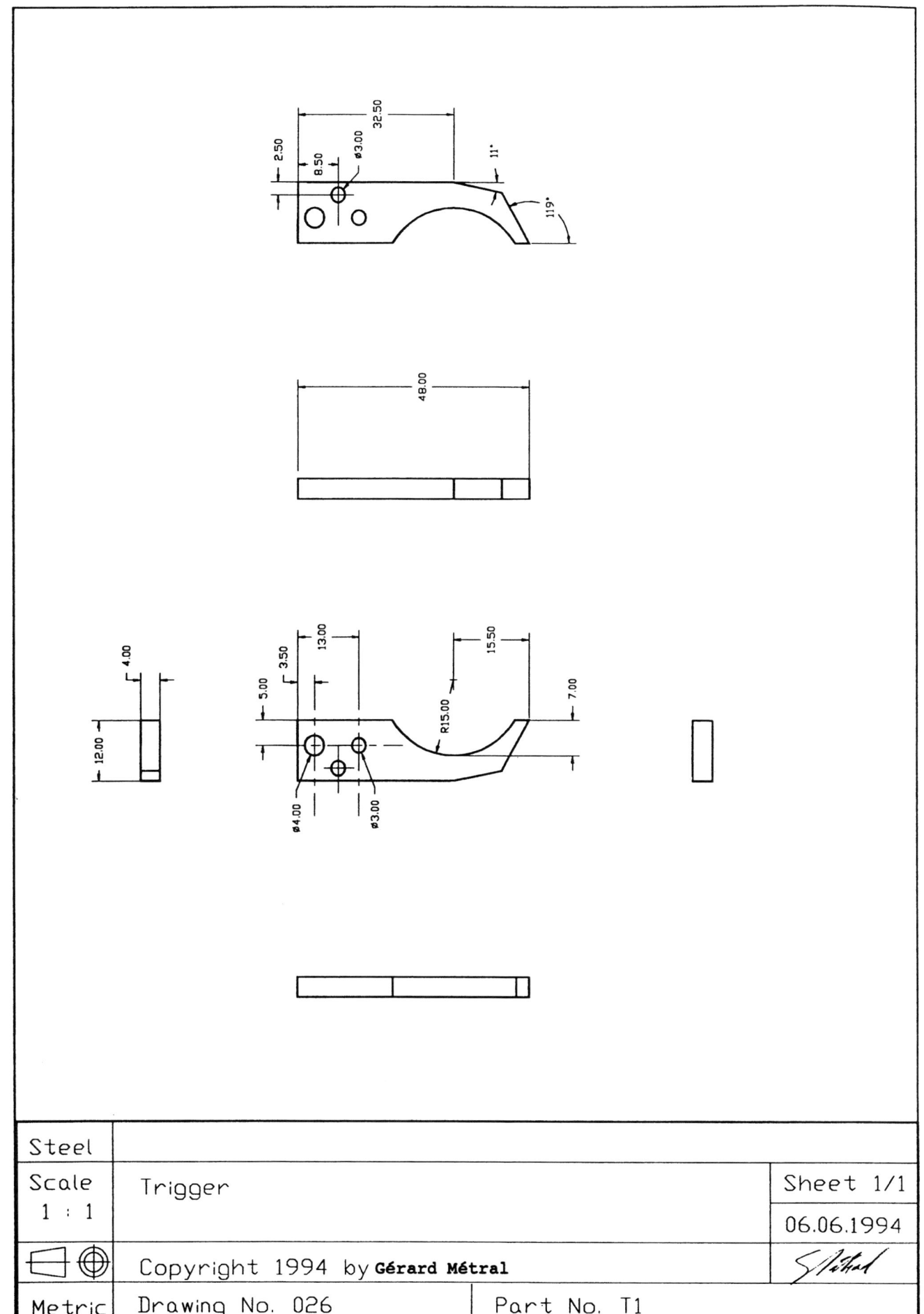

Steel		
Scale 1 : 1	Trigger	Sheet 1/1
		06.06.1994
	Copyright 1994 by **Gérard Métral**	
Metric	Drawing No. 026	Part No. T1

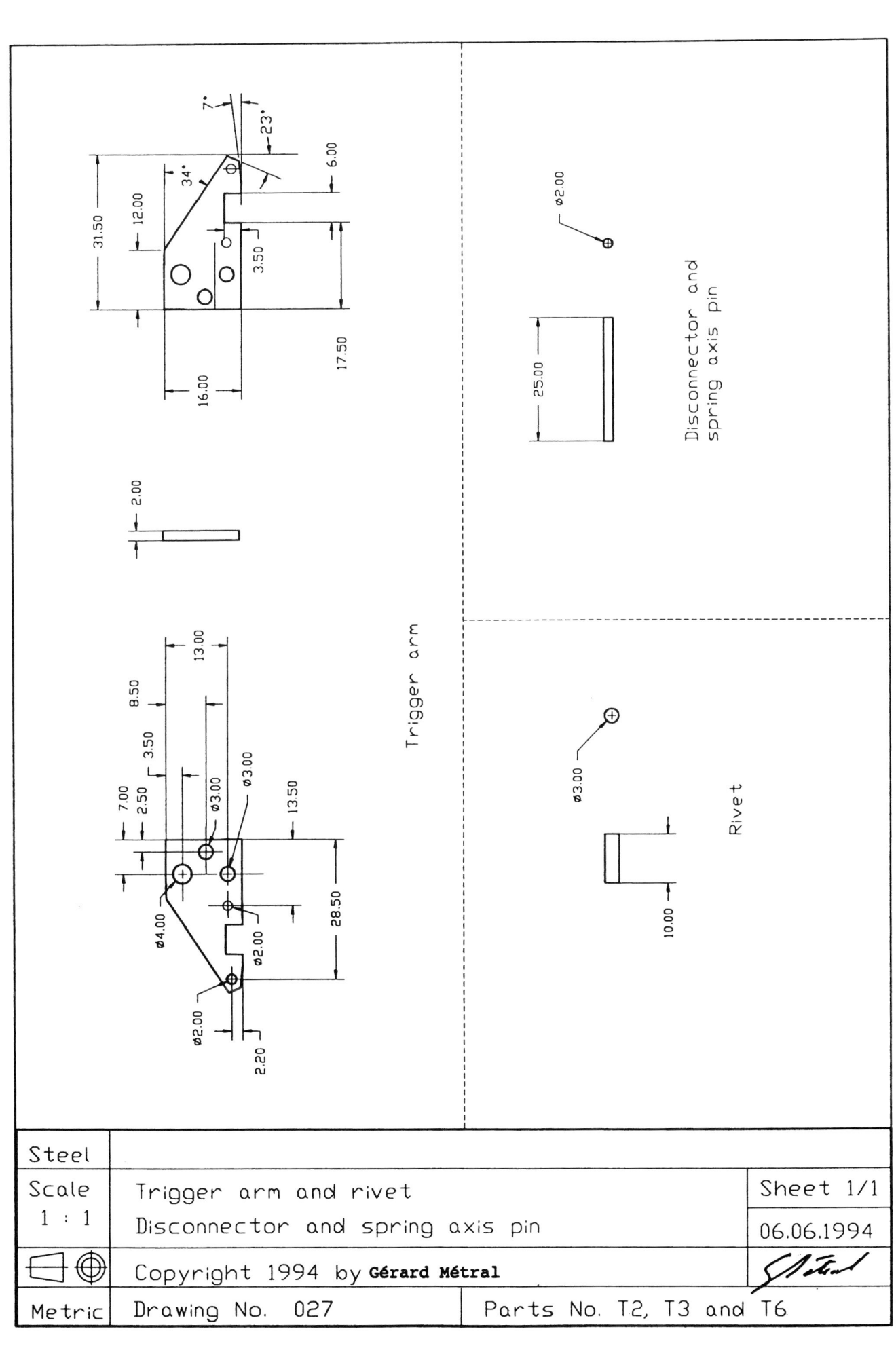

Trigger arm

Disconnector and spring axis pin

Rivet

Steel		
Scale 1 : 1	Trigger arm and rivet	Sheet 1/1
	Disconnector and spring axis pin	06.06.1994
⏛ ⊕	Copyright 1994 by **Gérard Métral**	
Metric	Drawing No. 027	Parts No. T2, T3 and T6

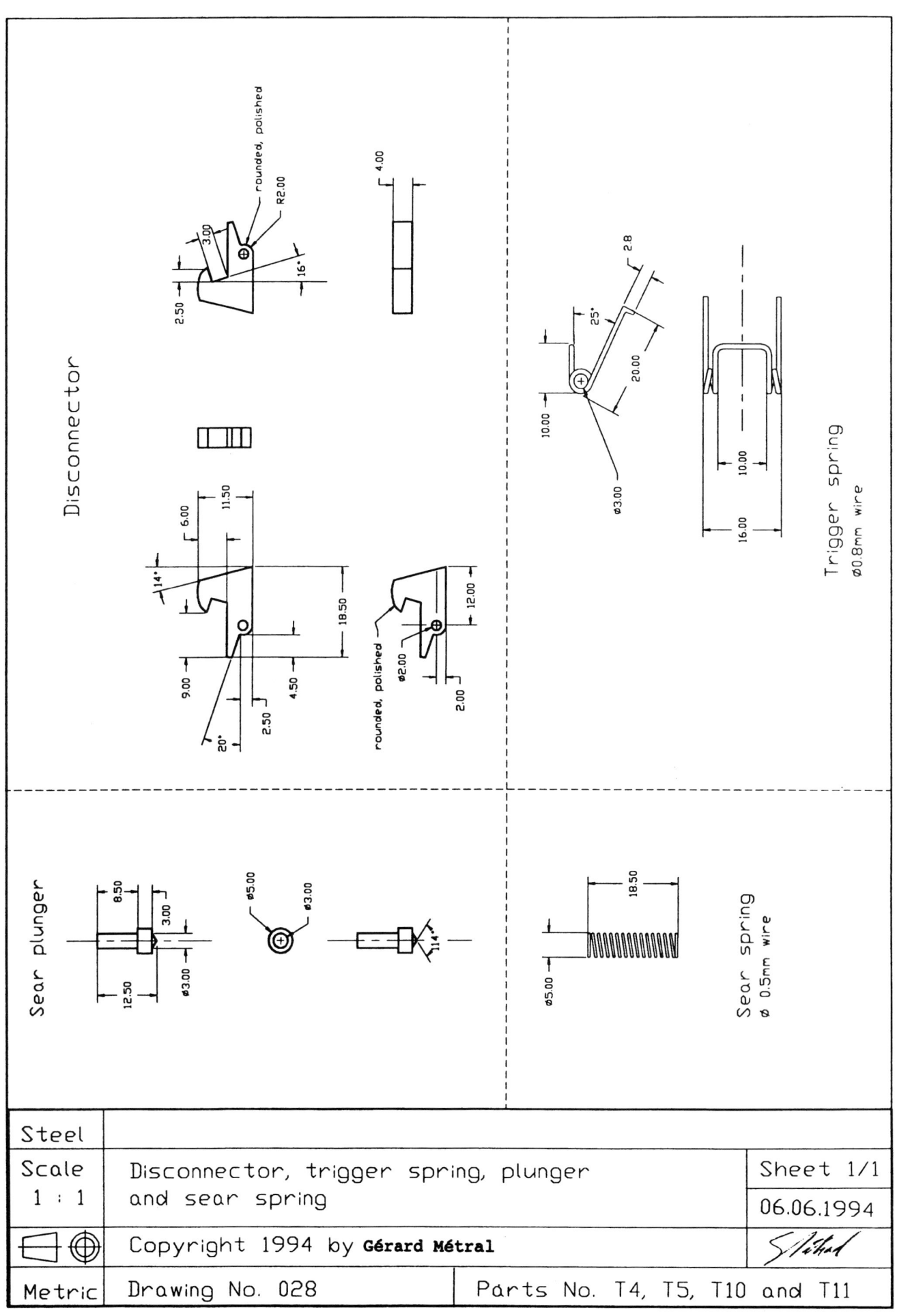

Disconnector

rounded, polished
R2.00
3.00
16°
2.50
4.00

Trigger spring
Ø0.8mm wire
28
25°
20.00
10.00
Ø3.00
10.00
16.00

11.50
6.00
14°
18.50
9.00
2.50
4.50
20°

rounded, polished
Ø2.00
12.00
2.00

Sear plunger
8.50
3.00
12.50
Ø3.00
Ø5.00
Ø3.00
14°

18.50
Ø5.00

Sear spring
Ø 0.5mm wire

Steel		
Scale 1 : 1	Disconnector, trigger spring, plunger and sear spring	Sheet 1/1
		06.06.1994
⊟ ⊕	Copyright 1994 by **Gérard Métral**	
Metric	Drawing No. 028	Parts No. T4, T5, T10 and T11

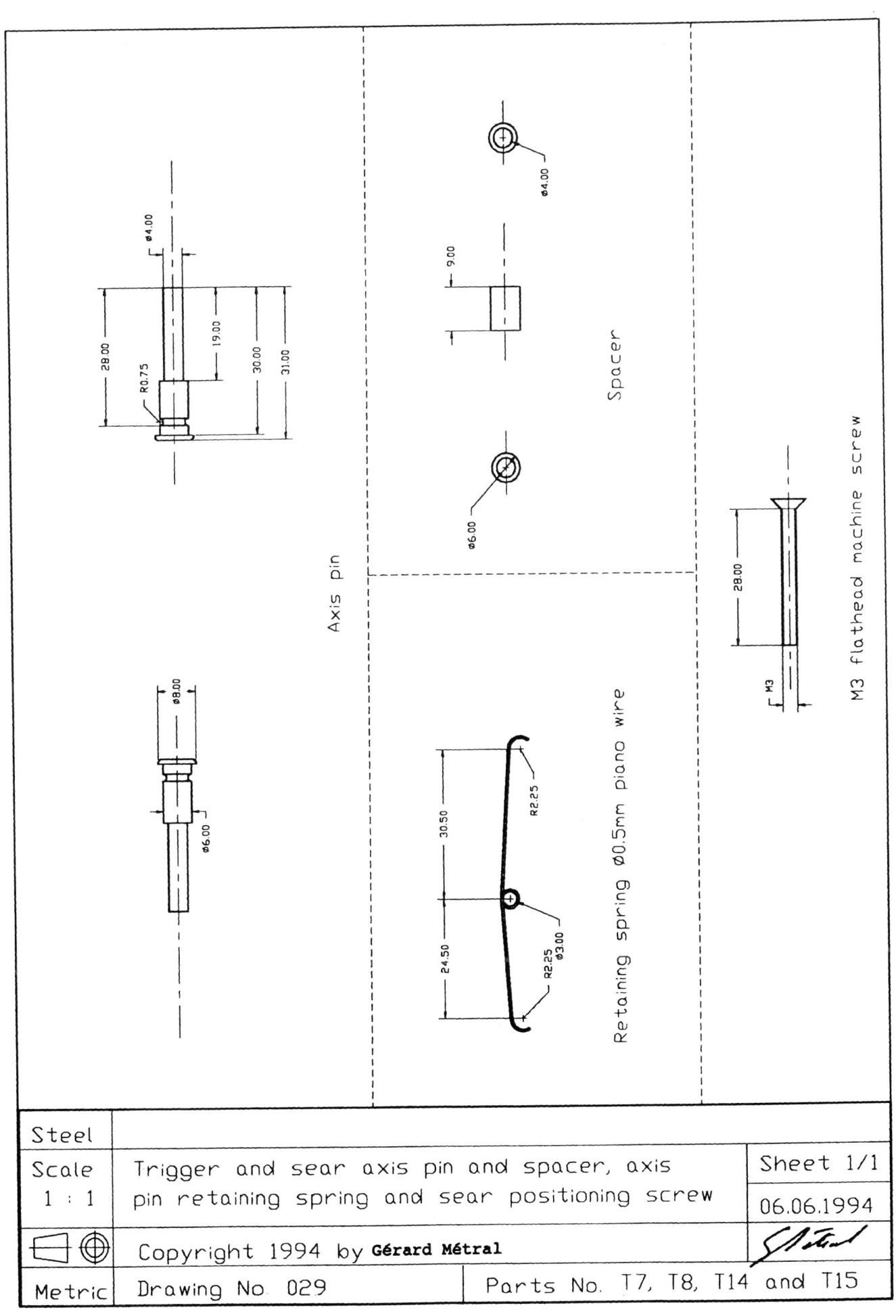

Axis pin

Spacer

Ø4.00

9.00

Ø6.00

Ø4.00

Ø8.00

Ø6.00

R0.75
28.00
19.00
30.00
31.00

Retaining spring Ø0.5mm piano wire

30.50
24.50
R2.25
R2.25
Ø3.00

M3 flathead machine screw

28.00
M3

Steel		
Scale 1 : 1	Trigger and sear axis pin and spacer, axis pin retaining spring and sear positioning screw	Sheet 1/1
		06.06.1994
⬡ ⊕	Copyright 1994 by **Gérard Métral**	
Metric	Drawing No. 029	Parts No. T7, T8, T14 and T15

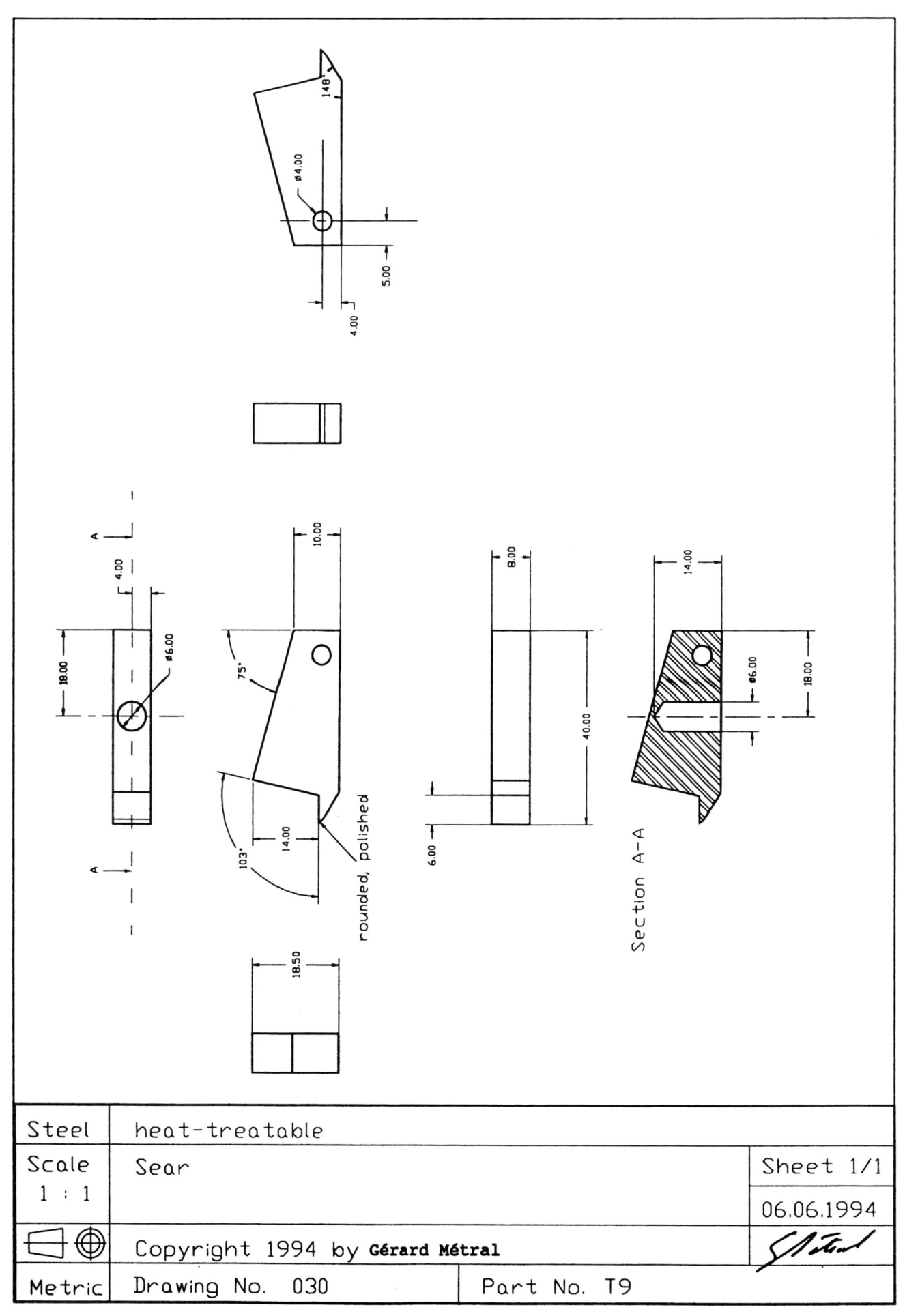

Steel	heat-treatable	
Scale 1 : 1	Sear	Sheet 1/1
		06.06.1994
⊟⊕	Copyright 1994 by **Gérard Métral**	
Metric	Drawing No. 030	Part No. T9

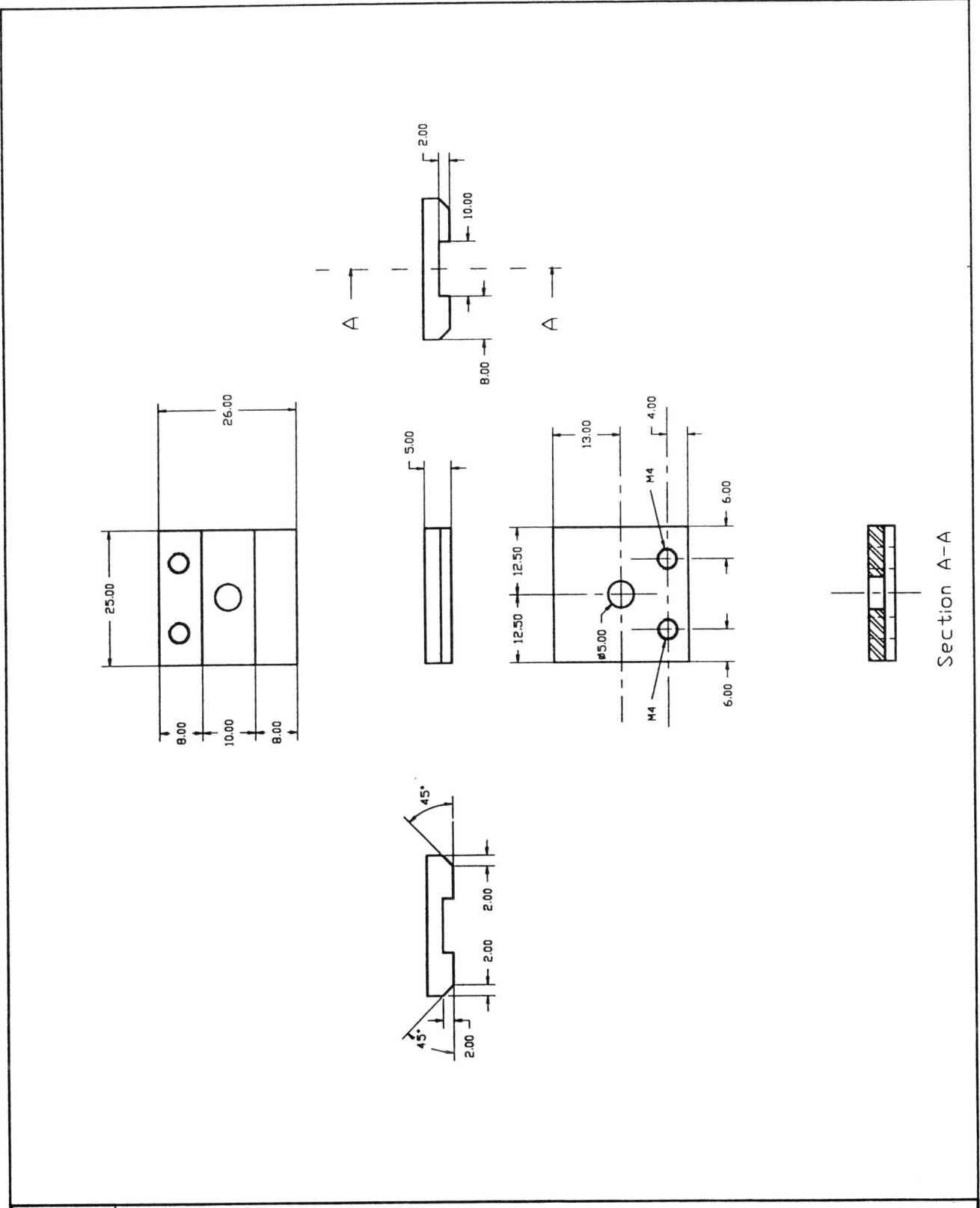

Steel		
Scale 1 : 1	Selector guide	Sheet 1/1
		06.06.1994
⊟ ⊕	Copyright 1994 by **Gérard Métral**	
Metric	Drawing No. 031	Part No. T12

Section A-A

M4

Ø5.00

45°

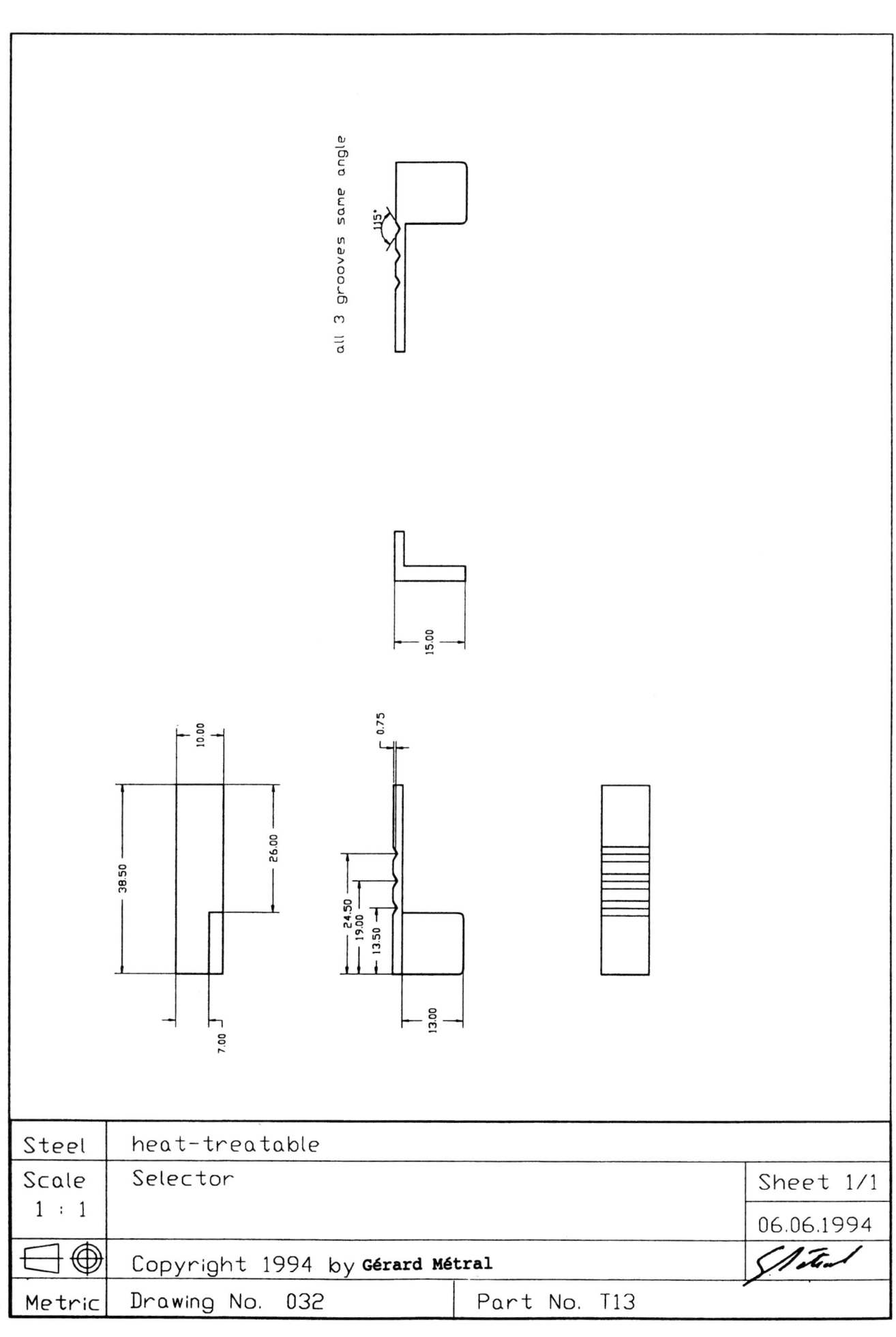

all 3 grooves same angle

115°

15.00

10.00

0.75

38.50

26.00

24.50

19.00

13.50

7.00

13.00

Steel	heat-treatable	
Scale 1 : 1	Selector	Sheet 1/1
		06.06.1994
⬭ ⊕	Copyright 1994 by **Gérard Métral**	
Metric	Drawing No. 032	Part No. T13

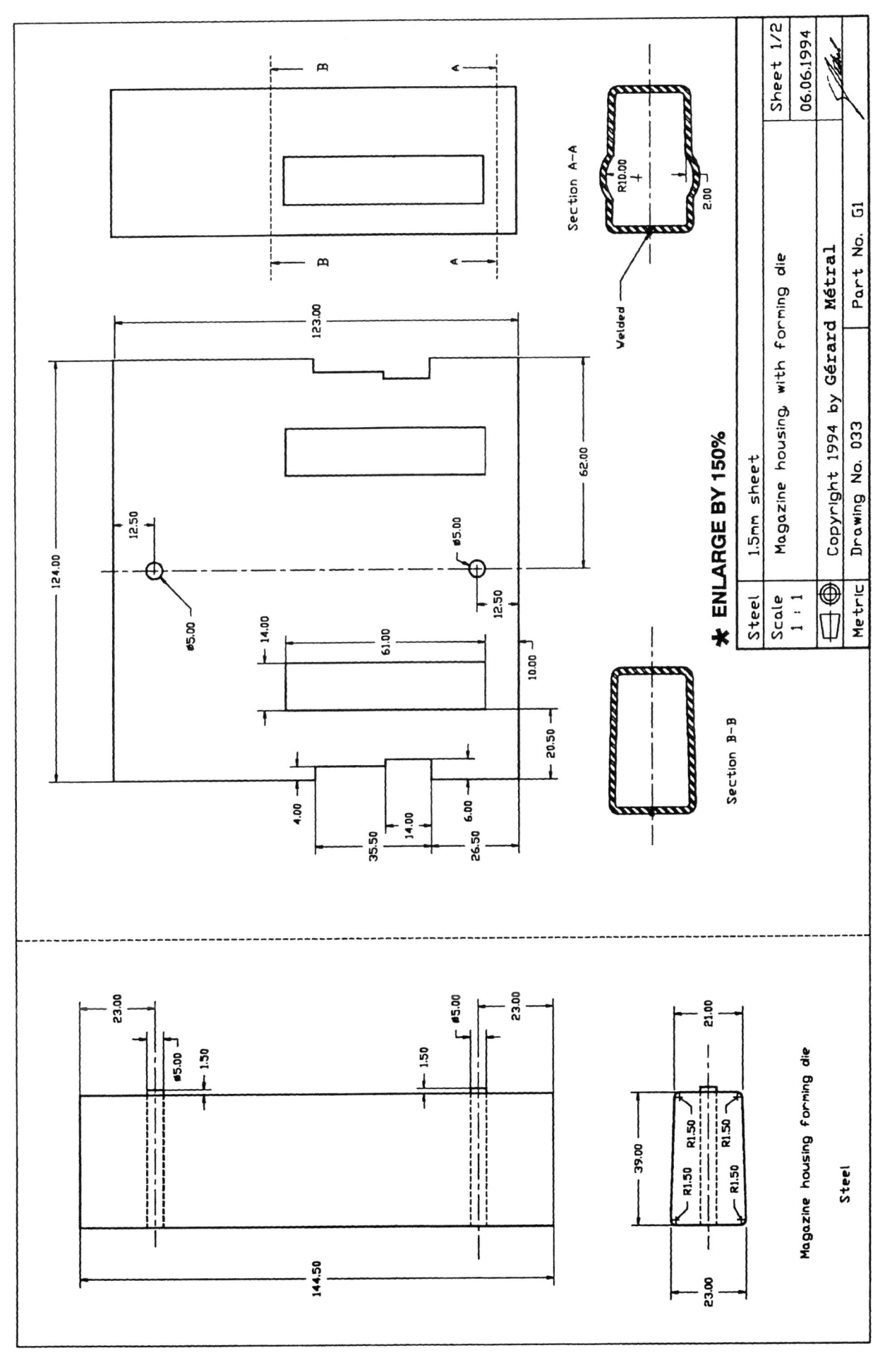

Section A-A

Welded

R10.00

2.00

Section B-B

123.00

62.00

124.00

12.50

ø5.00

ø5.00

12.50

14.00

61.00

10.00

20.50

4.00

35.50

14.00

26.50

B   A

B   A

* ENLARGE BY 150%

Steel	1.5mm sheet
Scale 1:1	Magazine housing with forming die
⊕	Copyright 1994 by Gérard Métral
Metric	Drawing No. 033	Part No. G1

Sheet 1/2

06.06.1994

23.00

ø5.00

1.50

ø5.00

1.50

23.00

144.50

21.00

39.00

R1.50 R1.50 R1.50

R1.50 R1.50

23.00

Magazine housing forming die

Steel

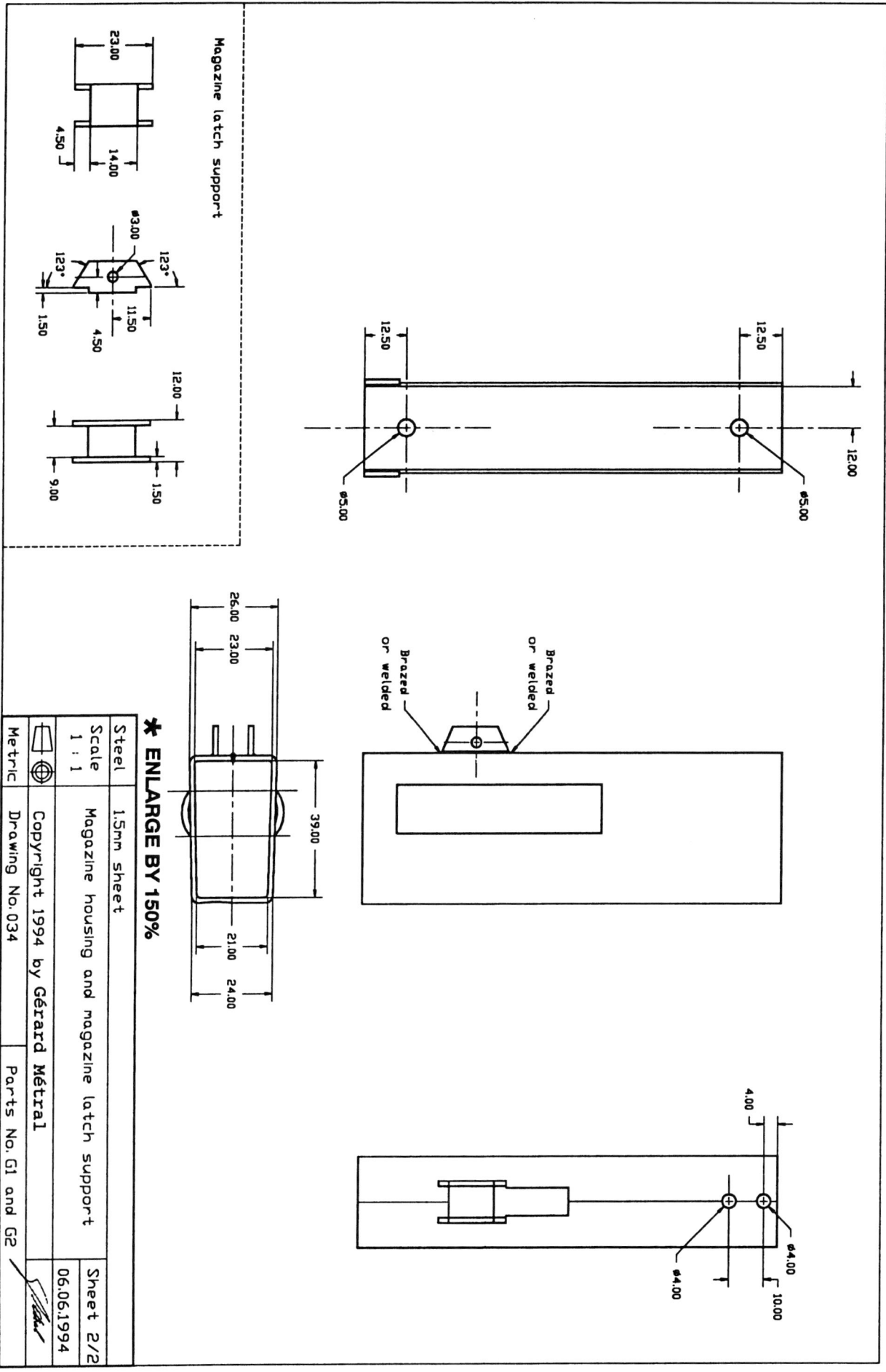

Magazine latch support

23.00
4.50
14.00

∅3.00
123°   123°
11.50
1.50   4.50
11.50

12.00
9.00   1.50

12.50
12.00
∅5.00
12.50
∅5.00

Brazed or welded
Brazed or welded

26.00
23.00
39.00
21.00
24.00

4.00
∅4.00
∅4.00
10.00

★ ENLARGE BY 150%

Steel	1.5mm sheet	
Scale	1 : 1	Magazine housing and magazine latch support
Metric		
Copyright 1994 by Gérard Métral		
Drawing No.034	Parts No. G1 and G2	Sheet 2/2
		06.06.1994

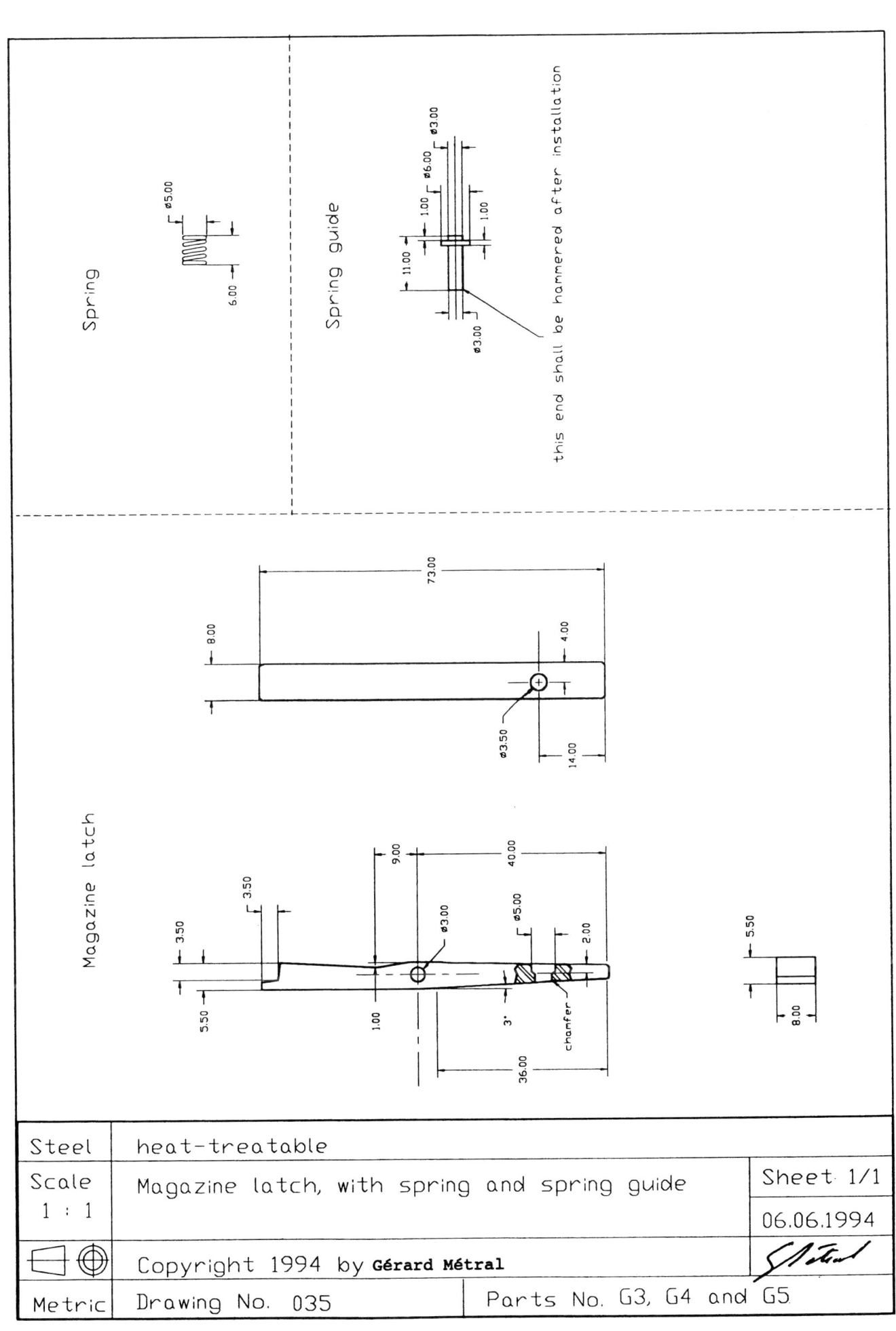

Spring

∅5.00

6.00

Spring guide

∅6.00

∅3.00

11.00

1.00

1.00

∅3.00

this end shall be hammered after installation

Magazine latch

73.00

8.00

∅3.50

4.00

14.00

3.50

3.50

9.00

40.00

∅3.00

∅5.00

2.00

5.50

1.00

3°

chamfer

36.00

5.50

8.00

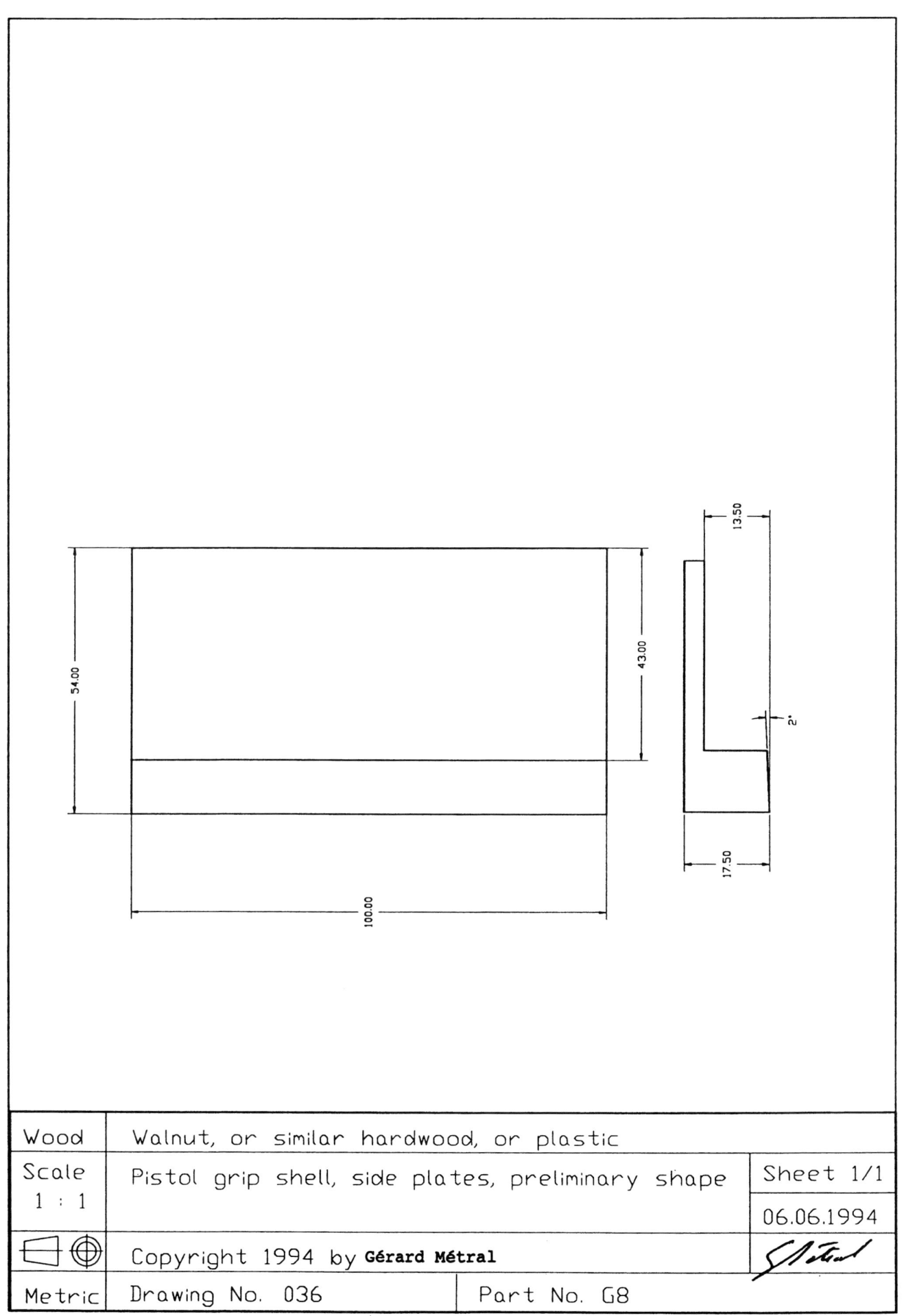

Wood	Walnut, or similar hardwood, or plastic	
Scale 1 : 1	Pistol grip shell, side plates, preliminary shape	Sheet 1/1
		06.06.1994
⊟ ⊕	Copyright 1994 by **Gérard Métral**	
Metric	Drawing No. 036	Part No. G8

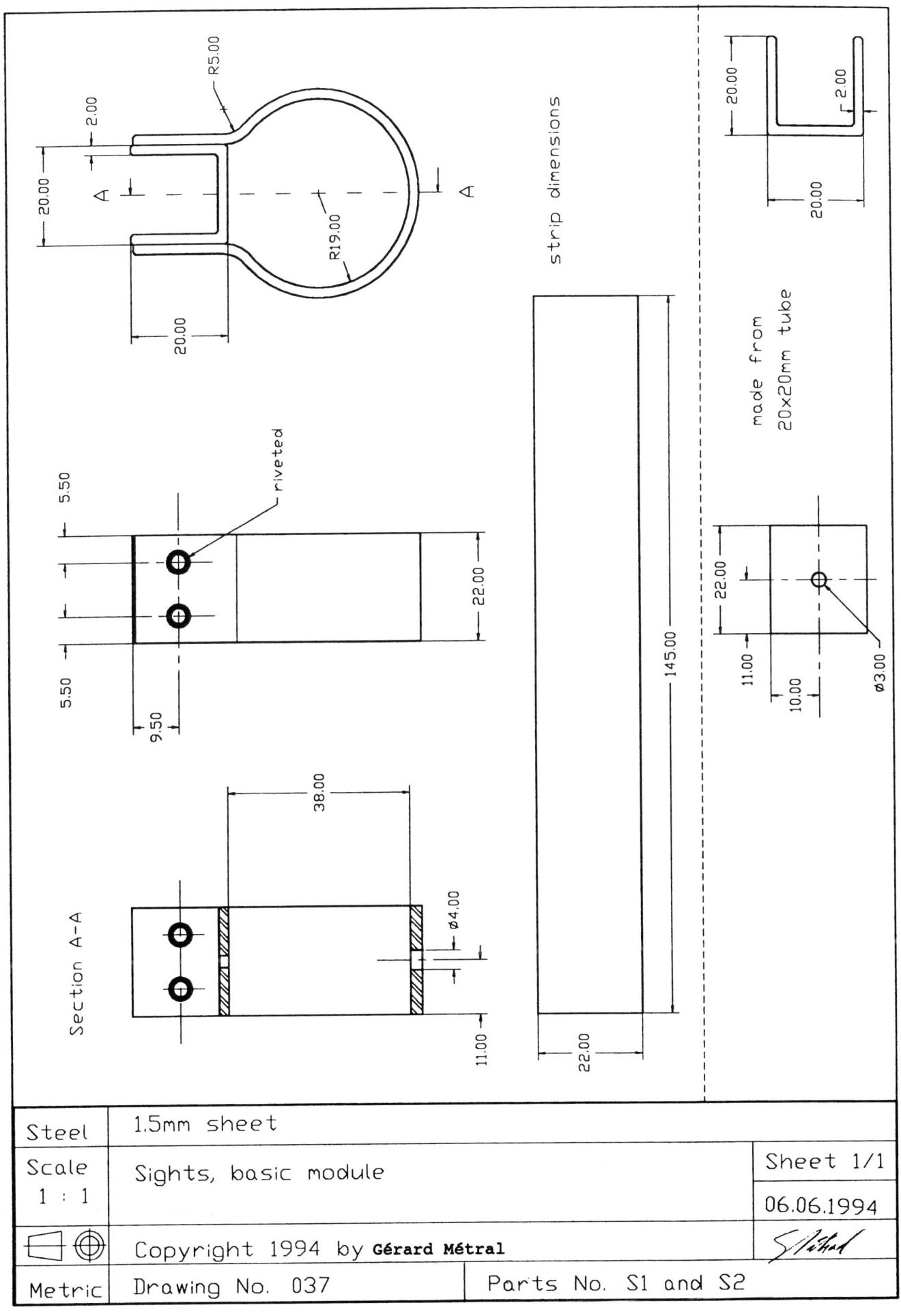

R5.00

2.00

20.00

A — — A

R19.00

20.00

strip dimensions

20.00

2.00

20.00

made from
20x20mm tube

5.50

riveted

22.00

5.50

9.50

22.00

11.00

10.00

Ø3.00

38.00

Section A-A

Ø4.00

145.00

11.00

22.00

Steel	1.5mm sheet	
Scale 1 : 1	Sights, basic module	Sheet 1/1
		06.06.1994
	Copyright 1994 by **Gérard Métral**	
Metric	Drawing No. 037	Parts No. S1 and S2

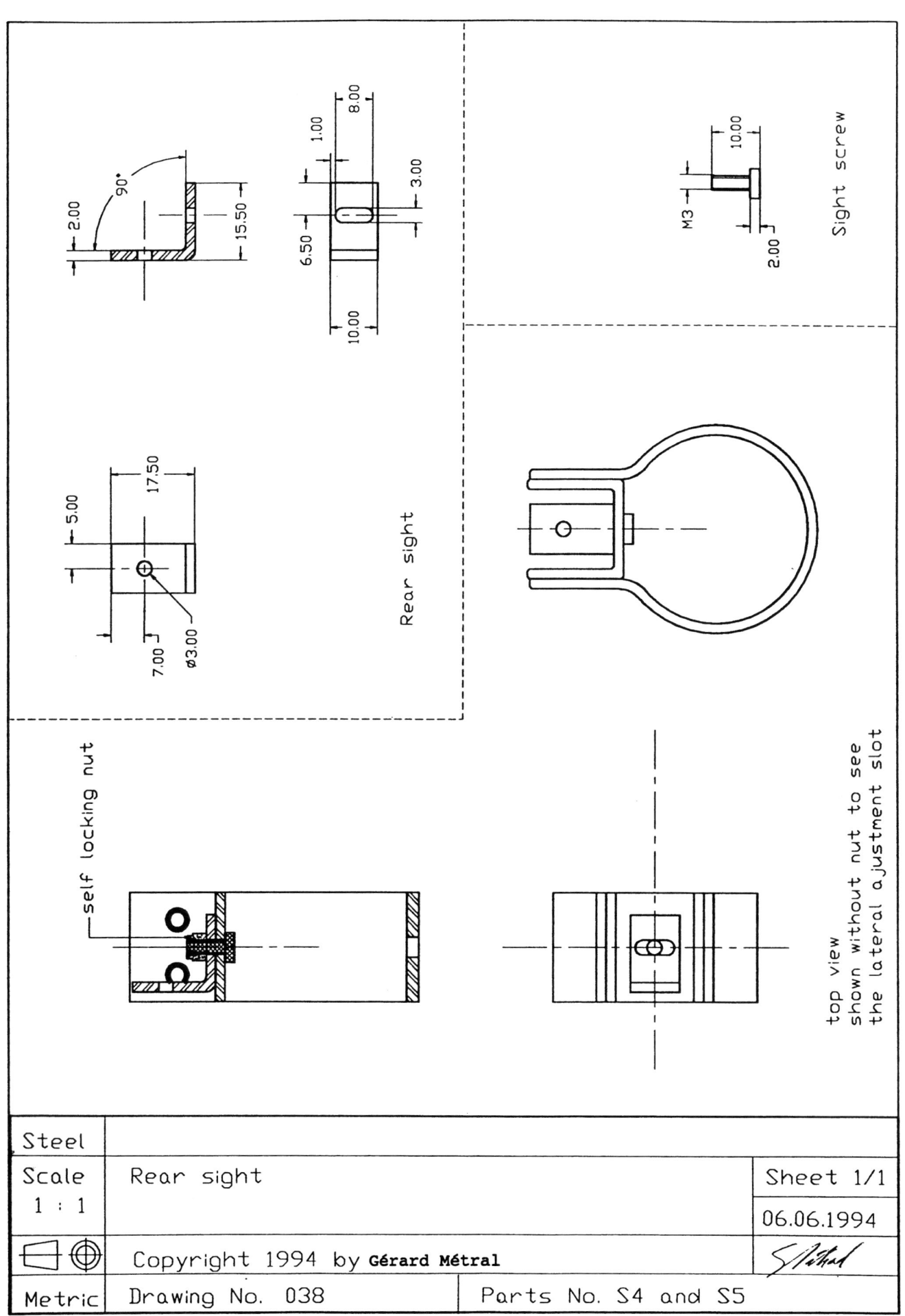

90°

2.00

15.50

1.00

8.00

3.00

6.50

10.00

Sight screw

M3

10.00

2.00

5.00

17.50

7.00

ø3.00

Rear sight

self locking nut

top view
shown without nut to see
the lateral ajustment slot

Steel		
Scale 1 : 1	Rear sight	Sheet 1/1
		06.06.1994
	Copyright 1994 by **Gérard Métral**	
Metric	Drawing No. 038	Parts No. S4 and S5

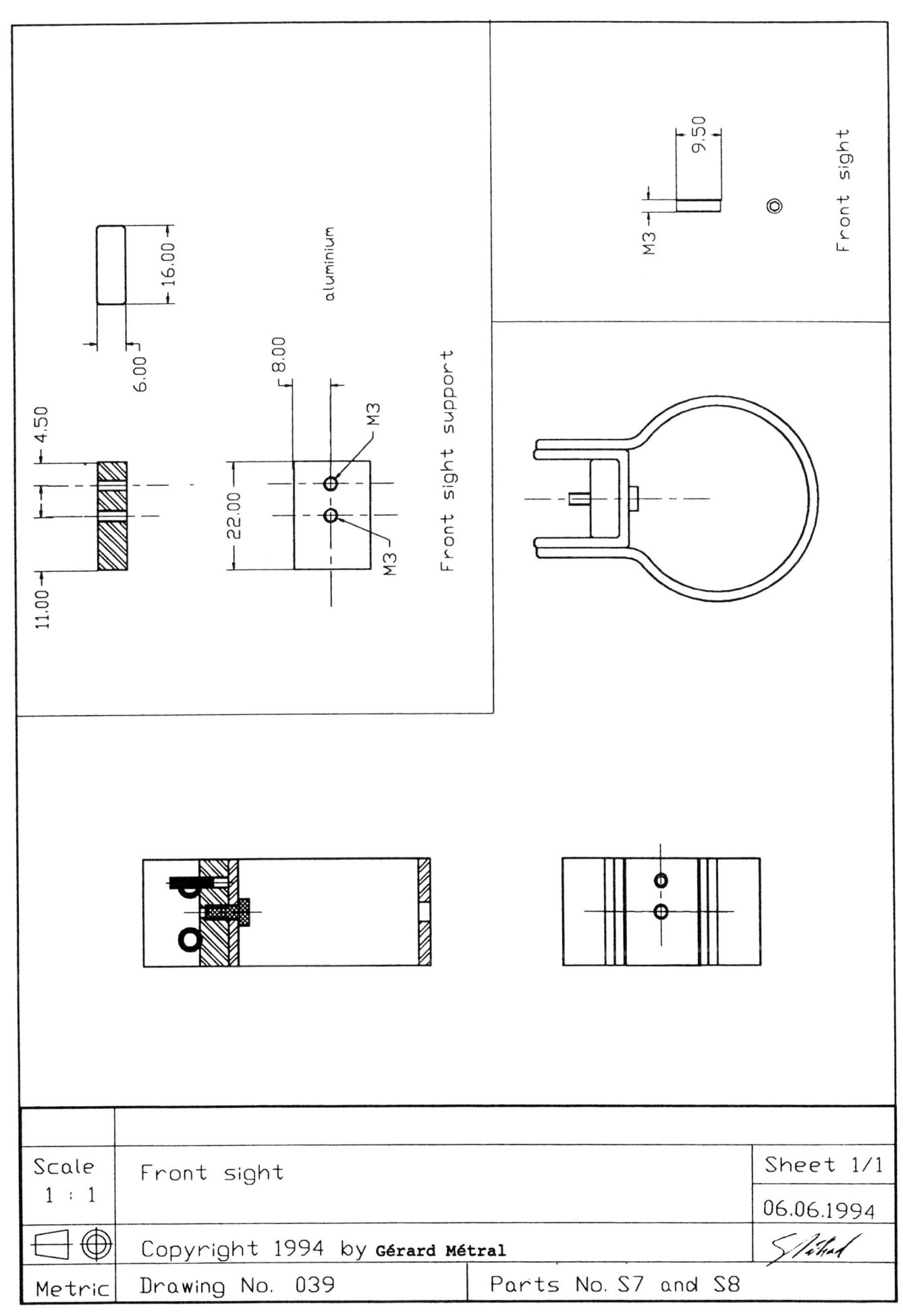

16.00

6.00

4.50

11.00

8.00

22.00

M3

M3

aluminium

Front sight support

9.50

M3

Front sight

Scale 1 : 1	Front sight	Sheet 1/1
		06.06.1994
	Copyright 1994 by **Gérard Métral**	
Metric	Drawing No. 039	Parts No. S7 and S8

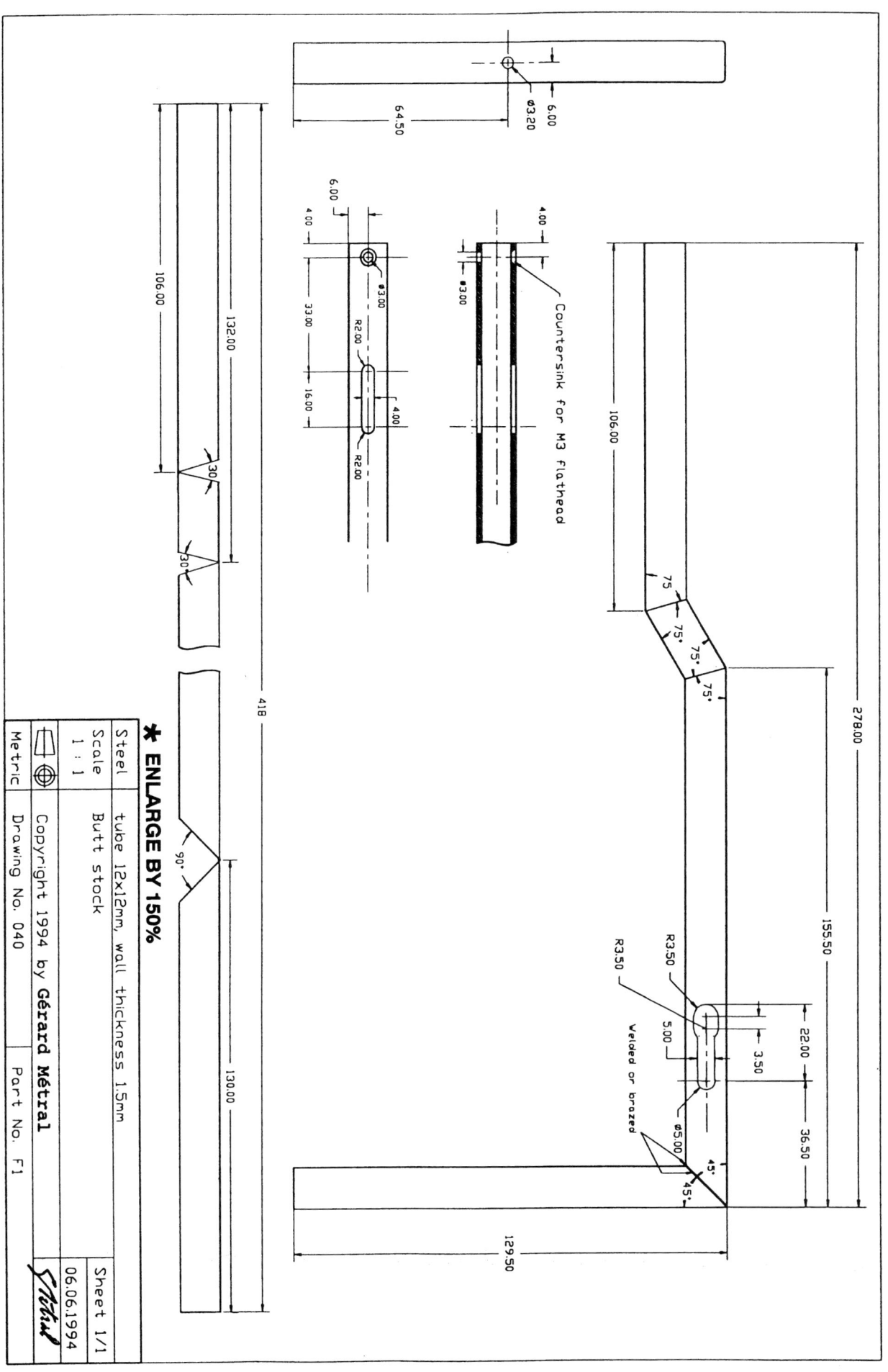

Countersink for M3 flathead

Welded or brazed

★ ENLARGE BY 150%

Steel	tube 12x12mm, wall thickness 1.5mm		
Scale	Butt stock		
1:1			
	Copyright 1994 by **Gérard Métral**	Sheet 1/1	
Metric	Drawing No. 040	Part No. F1	06.06.1994

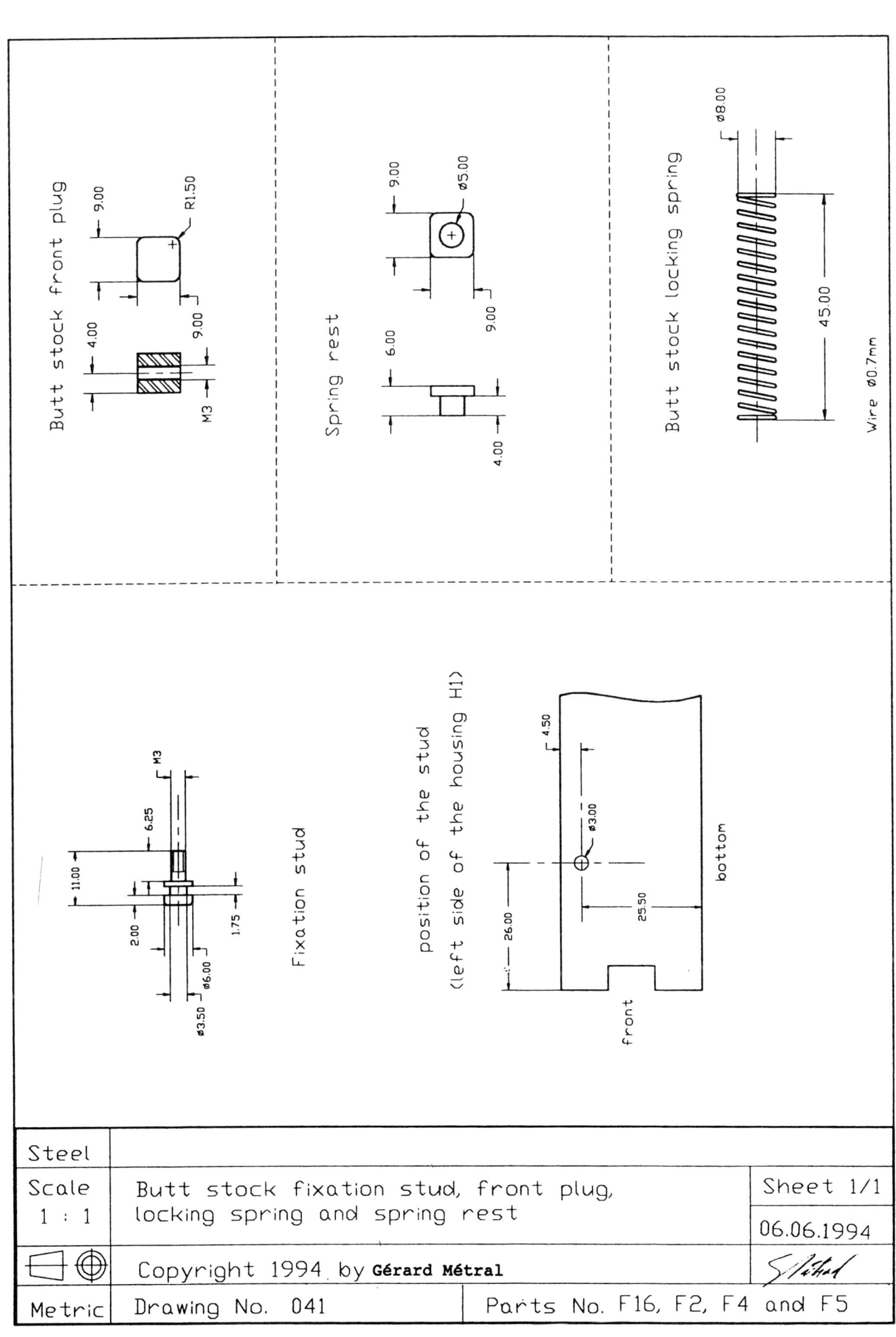

Butt stock front plug

9.00

R1.50

4.00

9.00

M3

Spring rest

9.00

ø5.00

6.00

9.00

4.00

Butt stock locking spring

ø8.00

45.00

Wire ø0.7mm

M3

6.25

11.00

2.00

1.75

ø6.00

ø3.50

Fixation stud

position of the stud
(left side of the housing H1)

4.50

ø3.00

26.00

25.50

front

bottom

Steel		
Scale 1 : 1	Butt stock fixation stud, front plug, locking spring and spring rest	Sheet 1/1
		06.06.1994
⊟ ⊕	Copyright 1994 by **Gérard Métral**	
Metric	Drawing No. 041	Parts No. F16, F2, F4 and F5

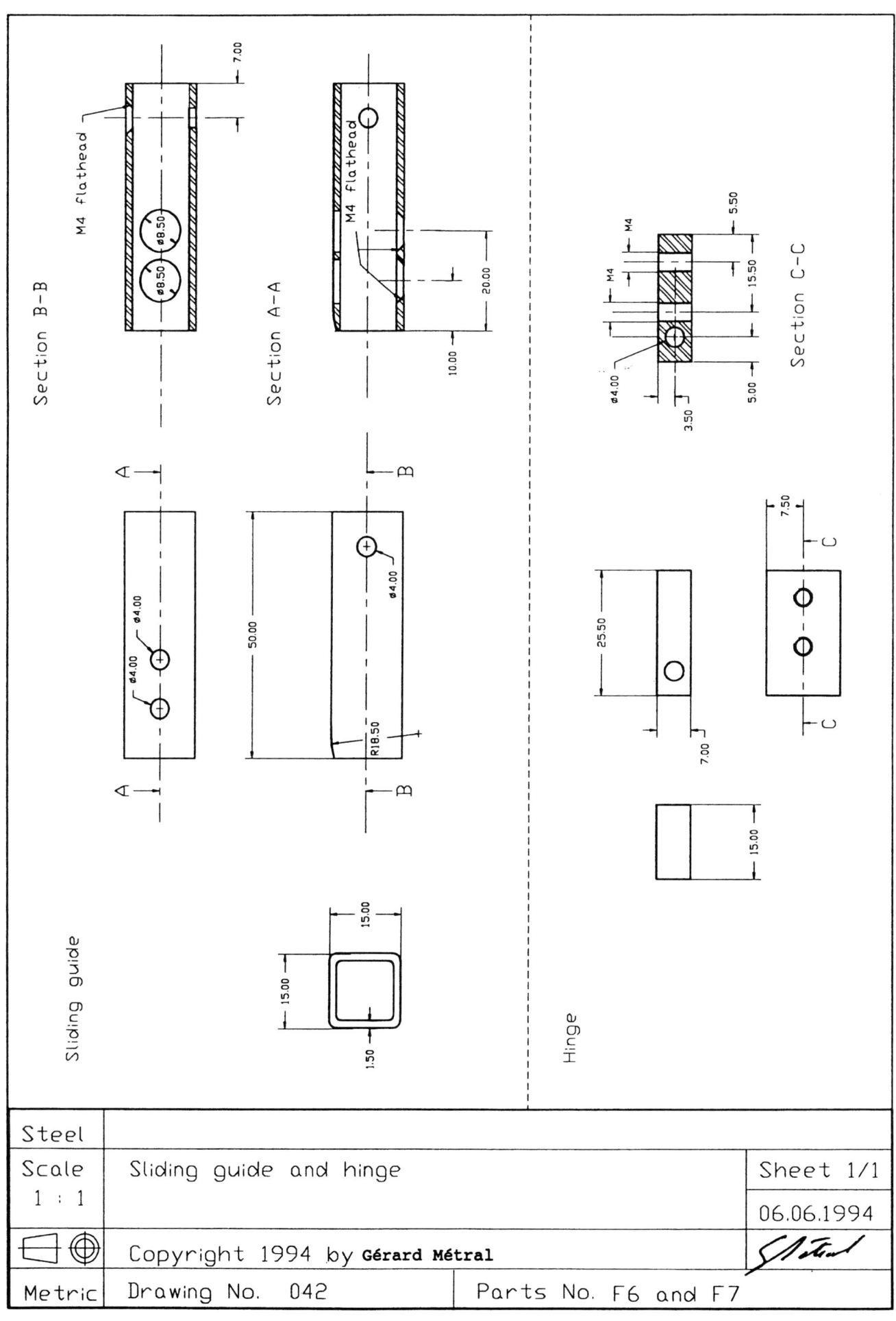

Section B-B

M4 flathead

ø8.50

ø8.50

7.00

Section A-A

M4 flathead

ø4.00

20.00

10.00

A

B

Sliding guide

ø4.00

ø4.00

50.00

R18.50

15.00

15.00

1.50

Section C-C

M4

M4

ø4.00

3.50

5.50

15.50

5.00

7.50

25.50

7.00

C

C

15.00

Hinge

Steel		
Scale 1 : 1	Sliding guide and hinge	Sheet 1/1
		06.06.1994
⬡ ⊕	Copyright 1994 by **Gérard Métral**	
Metric	Drawing No.　042	Parts No.　F6 and F7

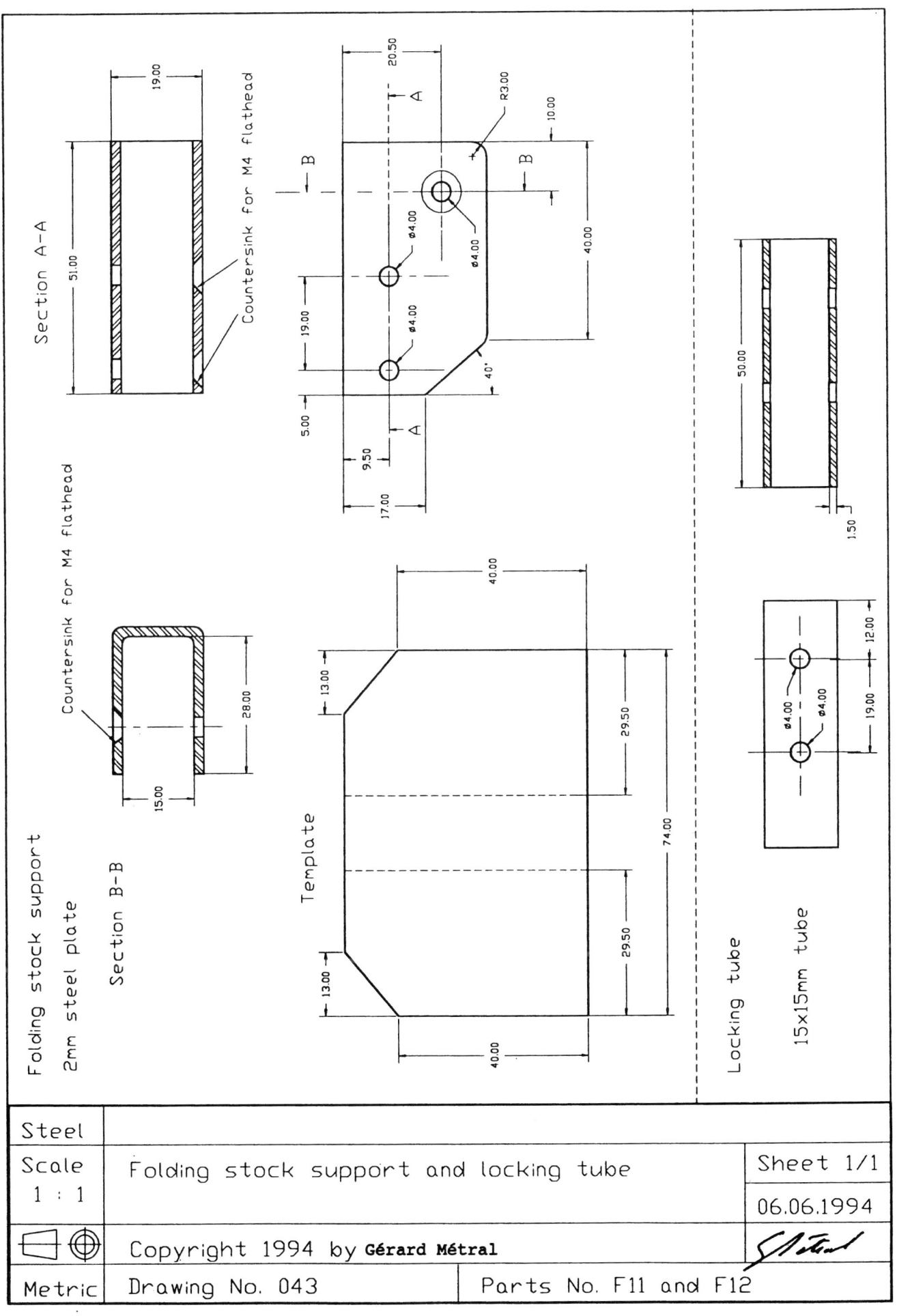

Section A-A

Countersink for M4 flathead

Countersink for M4 flathead

Section B-B

Folding stock support
2mm steel plate

Template

Locking tube

15x15mm tube

Countersink for M4 flathead

R3.00

Ø4.00
Ø4.00
Ø4.00

40°

Steel		
Scale 1 : 1	Folding stock support and locking tube	Sheet 1/1
		06.06.1994
	Copyright 1994 by **Gérard Métral**	
Metric	Drawing No. 043	Parts No. F11 and F12

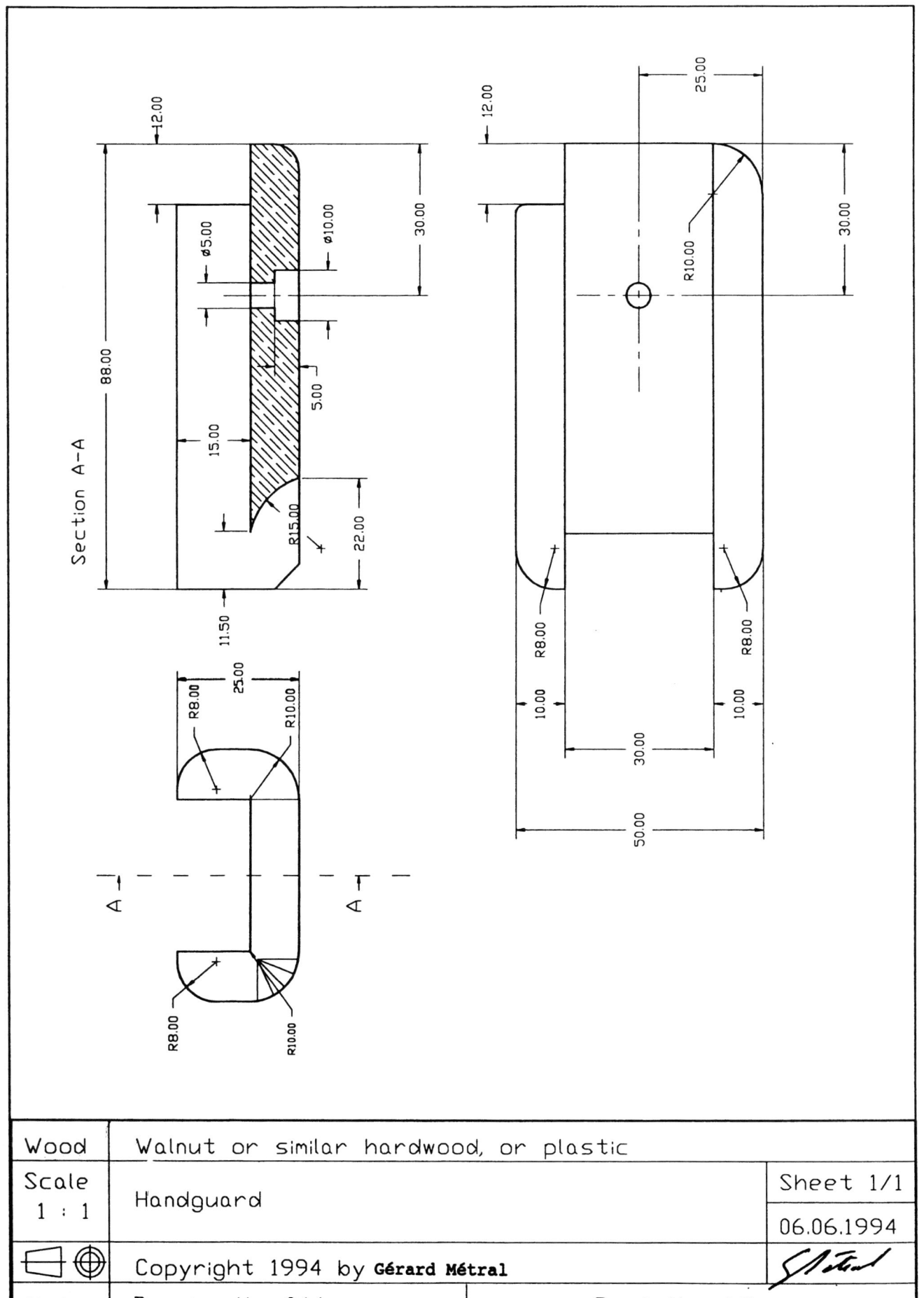

Section A-A

12.00

88.00

ø5.00

ø10.00

30.00

15.00

5.00

R15.00

22.00

11.50

25.00

R8.00

R10.00

A

A

R8.00

R10.00

12.00

25.00

R10.00

30.00

R8.00

R8.00

10.00

10.00

30.00

50.00

Wood	Walnut or similar hardwood, or plastic	
Scale 1 : 1	Handguard	Sheet 1/1
		06.06.1994
⊟⊕	Copyright 1994 by **Gérard Métral**	
Metric	Drawing No. 044	Part No. W1

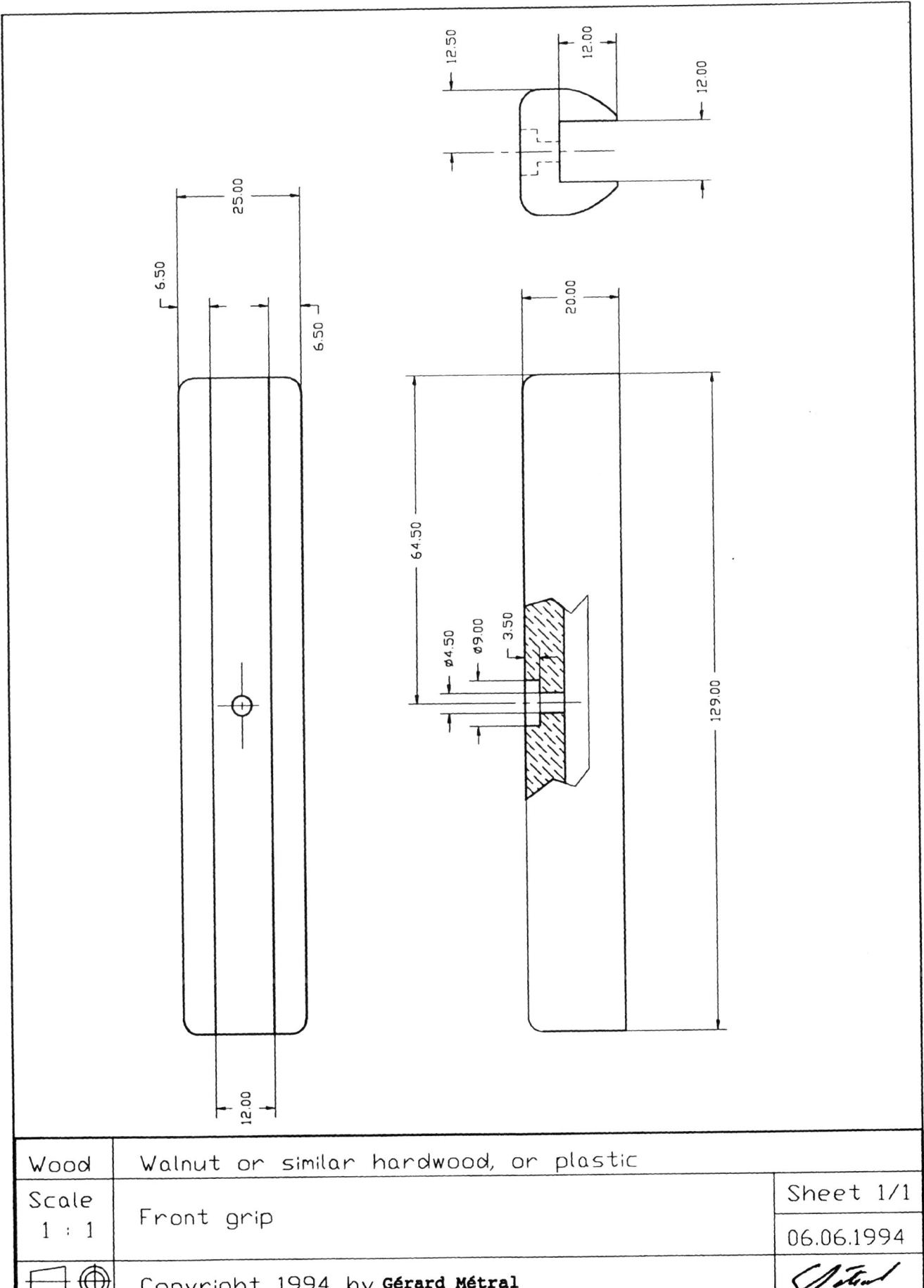

Wood	Walnut or similar hardwood, or plastic		
Scale 1 : 1	Front grip		Sheet 1/1
			06.06.1994
⊟ ⊕	Copyright 1994 by **Gérard Métral**		
Metric	Drawing No. 045	Part No. W3	

Dimensions shown on drawing: 12.50, 12.00, 12.00, 25.00, 6.50, 6.50, 20.00, 64.50, 129.00, ⌀4.50, ⌀9.00, 3.50, 12.00

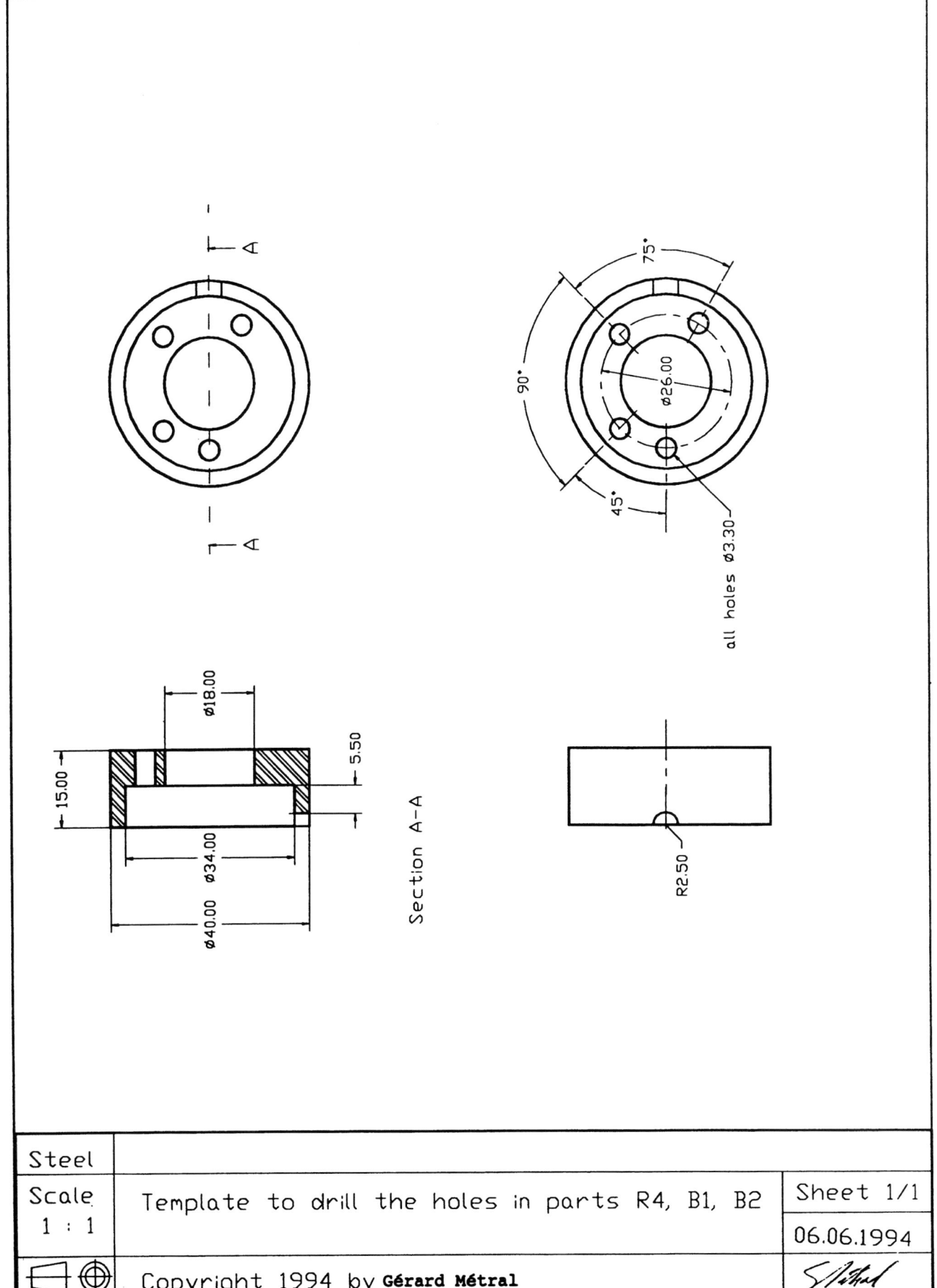

A — A

Section A-A

∅18.00

15.00

5.50

∅34.00

∅40.00

75°

90°

45°

∅26.00

all holes ∅3.30

R2.50

Steel		
Scale 1 : 1	Template to drill the holes in parts R4, B1, B2	Sheet 1/1
		06.06.1994
⊟⊕	Copyright 1994 by **Gérard Métral**	
Metric	Drawing No. 046	Tool 1

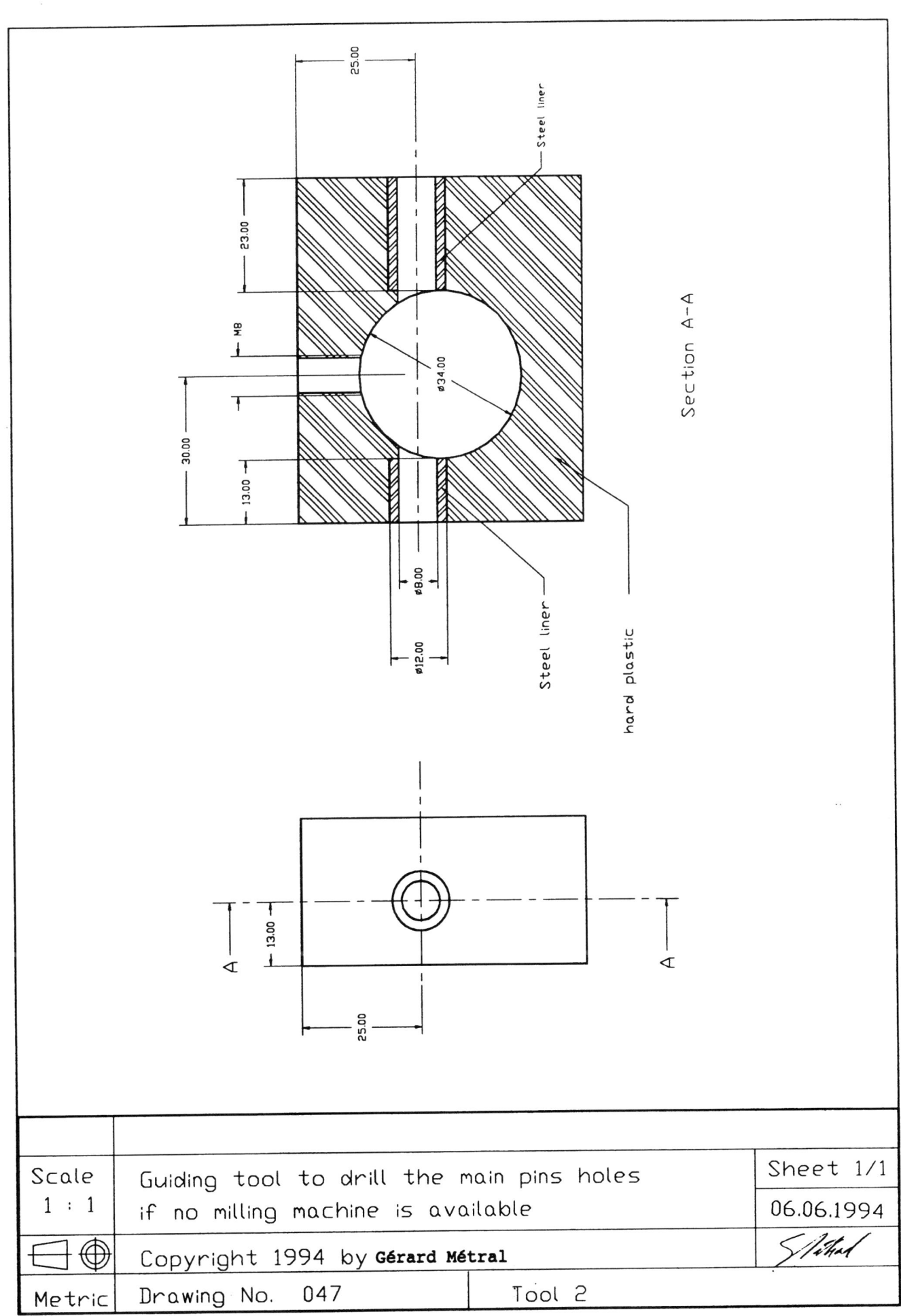

25.00

23.00

M8

30.00

13.00

Ø34.00

Steel liner

Ø8.00

12.00

Steel liner

hard plastic

Section A-A

13.00

A

A

25.00

Scale 1 : 1	Guiding tool to drill the main pins holes if no milling machine is available	Sheet 1/1
		06.06.1994
	Copyright 1994 by **Gérard Métral**	
Metric	Drawing No. 047	Tool 2

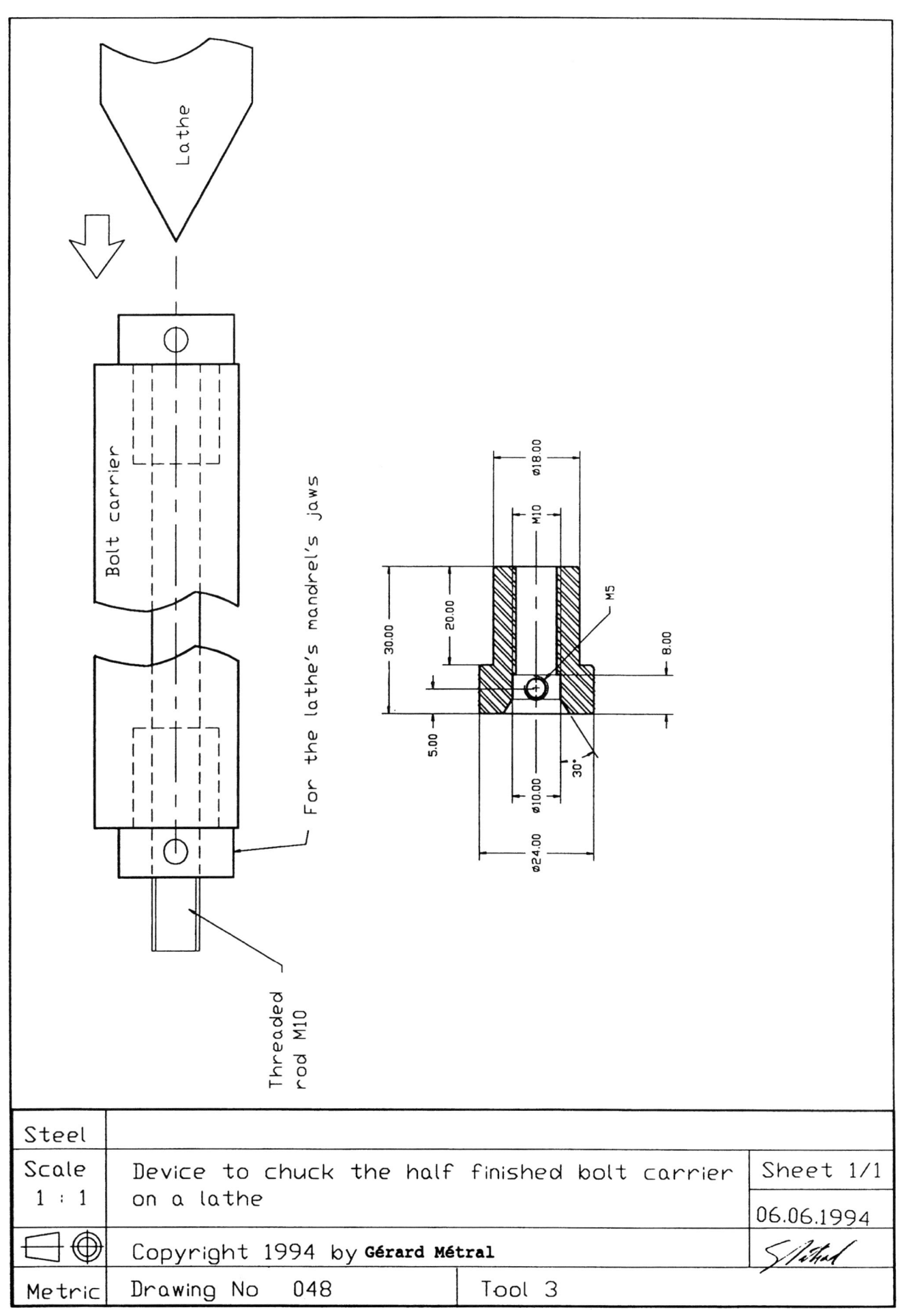

Lathe

Bolt carrier

For the lathe's mandrel's jaws

Threaded rod M10

Ø18.00
M10
20.00
30.00
M5
8.00
5.00
Ø10.00
30°
Ø24.00

Steel		
Scale 1 : 1	Device to chuck the half finished bolt carrier on a lathe	Sheet 1/1
		06.06.1994
⊟ ⊕	Copyright 1994 by **Gérard Métral**	
Metric	Drawing No 048	Tool 3

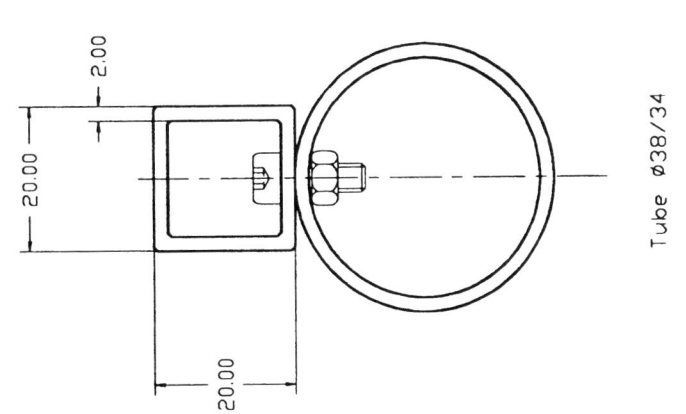

2.00
20.00
20.00
Tube Ø38/34

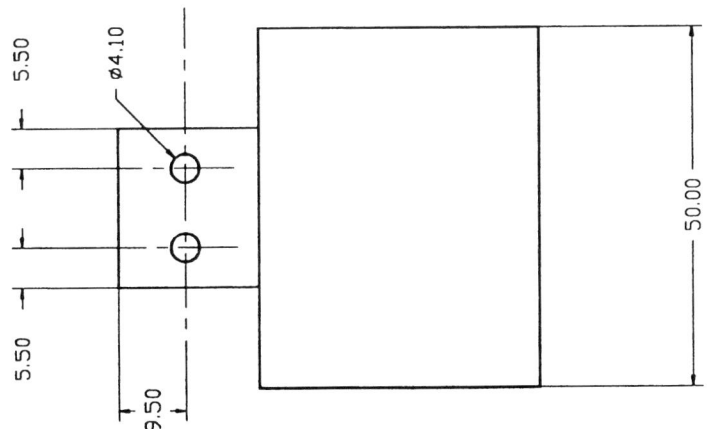

5.50
Ø4.10
5.50
9.50
50.00

Steel		
Scale 1 : 1	Device to help the forming operation of the sights' collars	Sheet 1/1
		06.06.1994
	Copyright 1994 by **Gérard Métral**	
Metric	Drawing No. 049	Tool 4

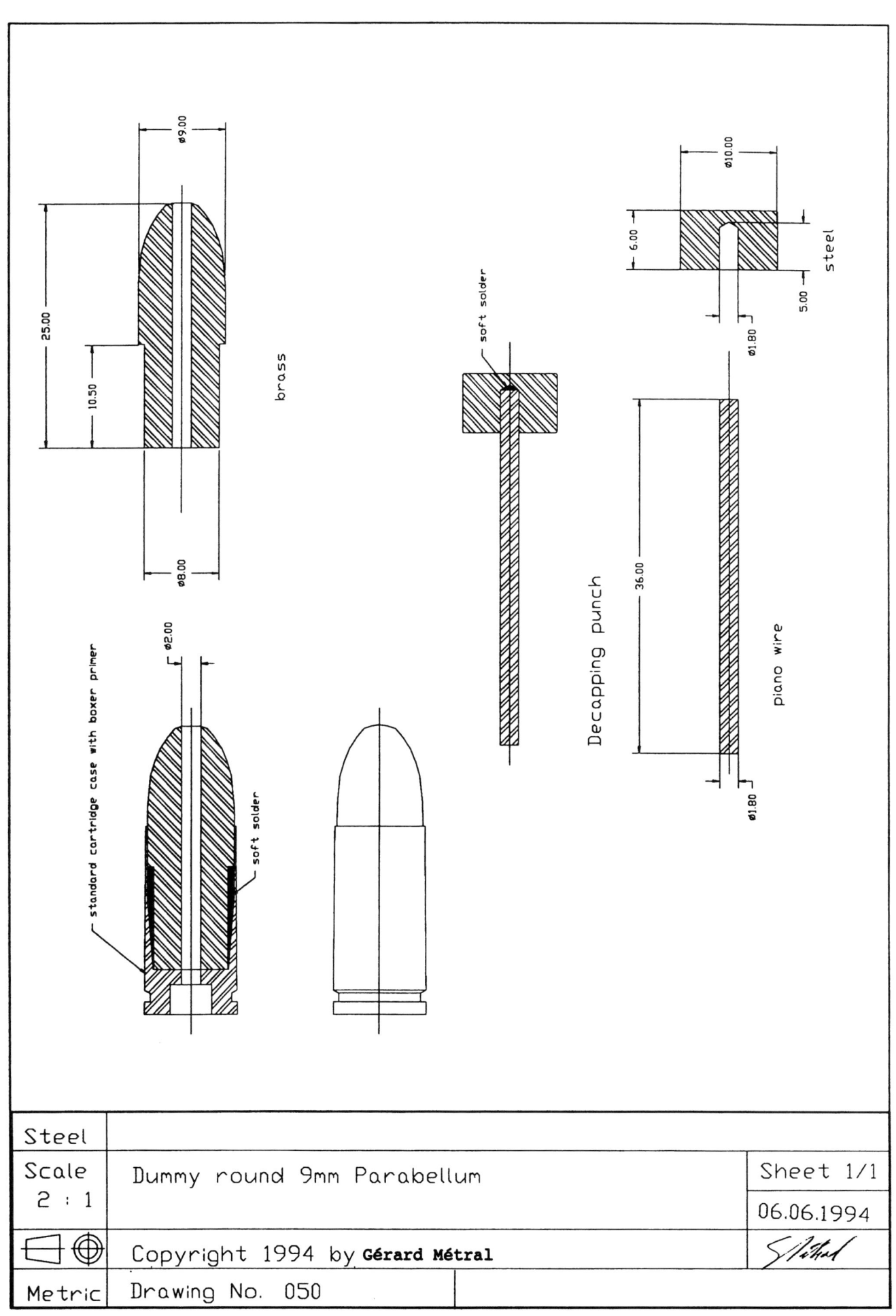

Ø9.00

25.00

10.50

Ø8.00

brass

Ø2.00

standard cartridge case with boxer primer

soft solder

soft solder

Decapping punch

Ø10.00

6.00

5.00

Ø1.80

steel

36.00

Ø1.80

piano wire

Steel		
Scale 2 : 1	Dummy round 9mm Parabellum	Sheet 1/1
		06.06.1994
	Copyright 1994 by Gérard Métral	
Metric	Drawing No. 050	

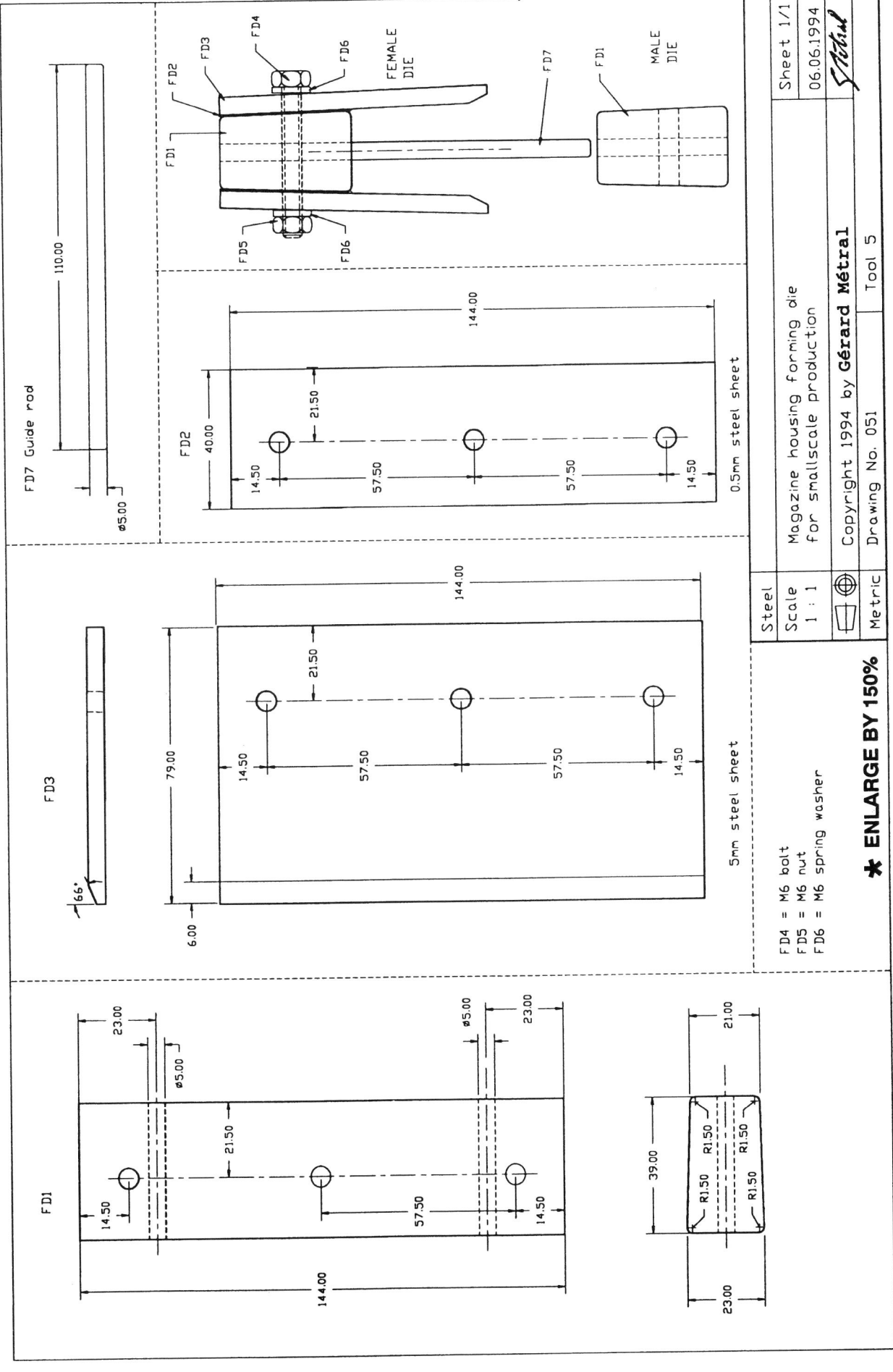

FD7 Guide rod

110.00

Ø5.00

FD2

144.00

40.00

21.50

14.50   57.50   57.50   14.50

0.5mm steel sheet

FD3

66°

6.00

144.00

79.00

21.50

14.50   57.50   57.50   14.50

5mm steel sheet

FD4

FD3

FD2

FD6

FEMALE
DIE

FD1

FD7

FD1

MALE
DIE

FD5   FD6

FD1

23.00

Ø5.00

21.50

14.50   57.50   14.50

Ø5.00

23.00

144.00

39.00

21.00

R1.50   R1.50

R1.50   R1.50

23.00

FD4 = M6 bolt
FD5 = M6 nut
FD6 = M6 spring washer

✳ ENLARGE BY 150%

Steel

Scale
1 : 1

Metric

Magazine housing forming die
for smallscale production

Copyright 1994 by Gérard Métral

Drawing No. 051   Tool 5

Sheet 1/1

06.06.1994

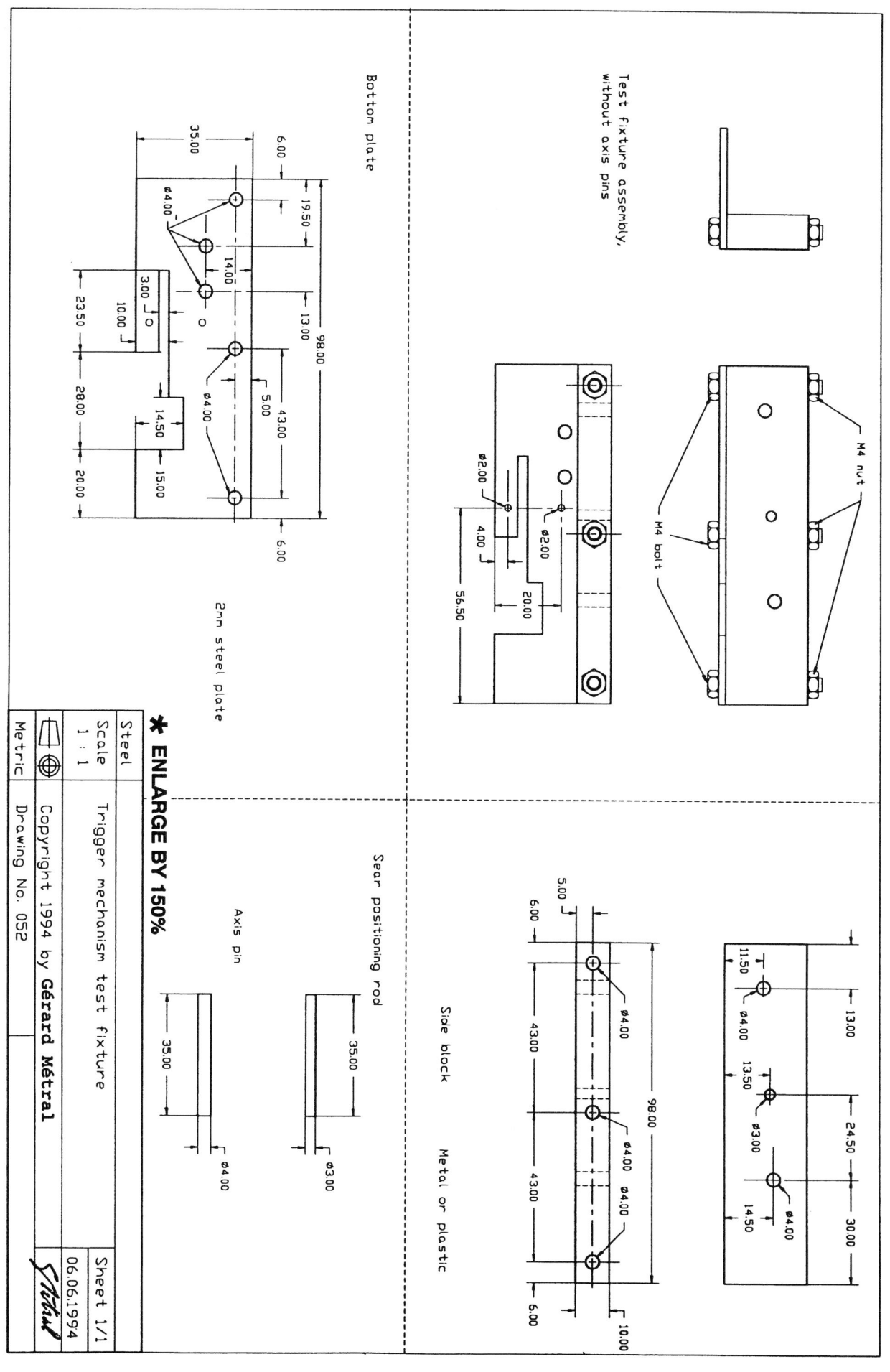

Test fixture assembly,
without axis pins

Bottom plate

2mm steel plate

Side block   Metal or plastic

Sear positioning rod

Axis pin

M4 nut
M4 bolt

✱ ENLARGE BY 150%

Steel	
Scale	1 : 1
Metric	Trigger mechanism test fixture
Copyright 1994 by **Gérard Métral**	Sheet 1/1
Drawing No. 052	06.06.1994

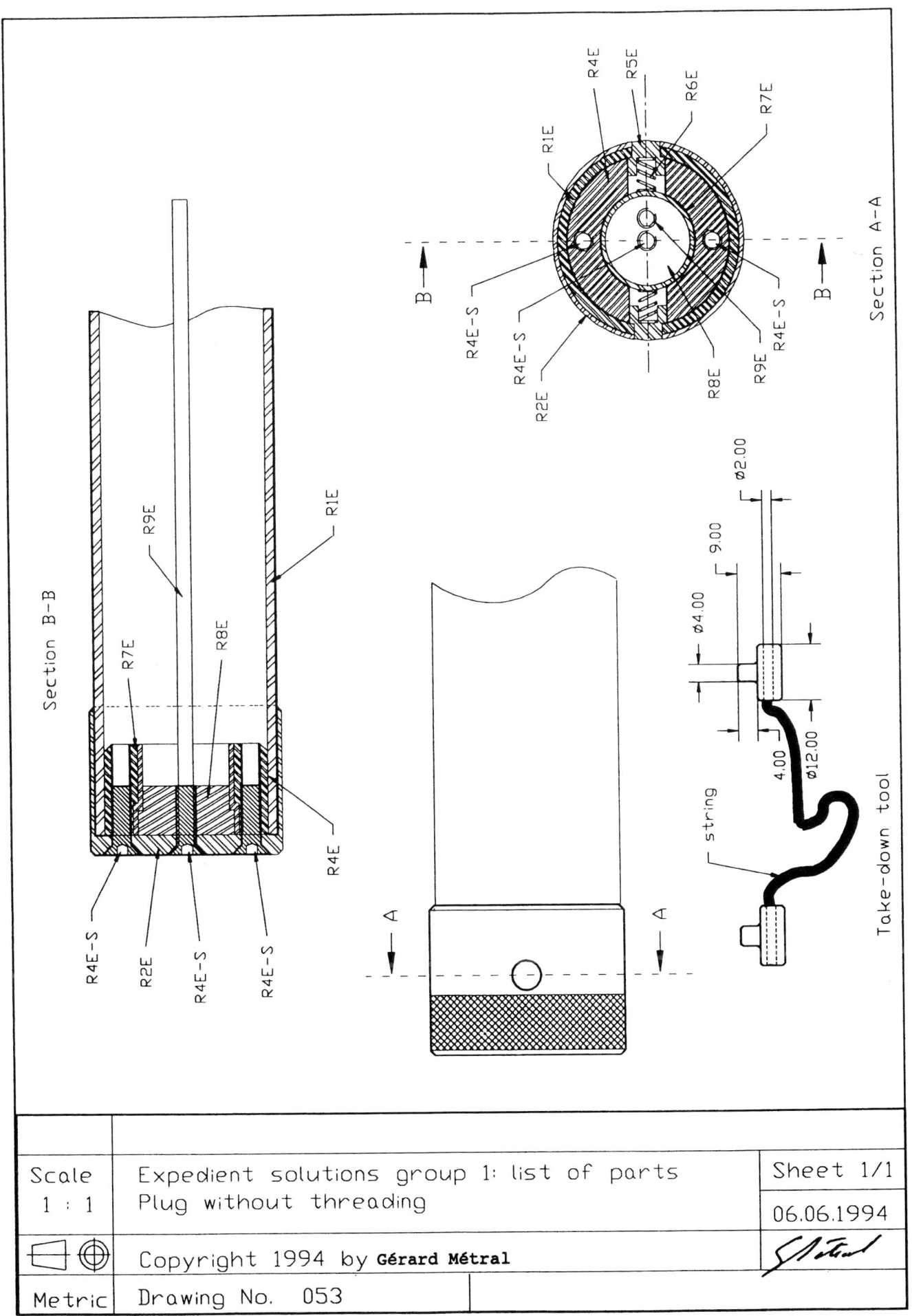

Section B-B

Section A-A

R1E

R9E

R7E

R8E

R4E

R4E-S

R2E

R4E-S

R4E-S

R1E

R4E

R5E

R6E

R7E

R4E-S

R4E-S

R2E

R4E

R8E

R9E

R4E-S

A

A

B

B

string

Take-down tool

⌀2.00

9.00

⌀4.00

4.00

⌀12.00

Scale 1 : 1	Expedient solutions group 1: list of parts	Sheet 1/1
	Plug without threading	06.06.1994
Metric	Copyright 1994 by **Gérard Métral**	
	Drawing No. 053	

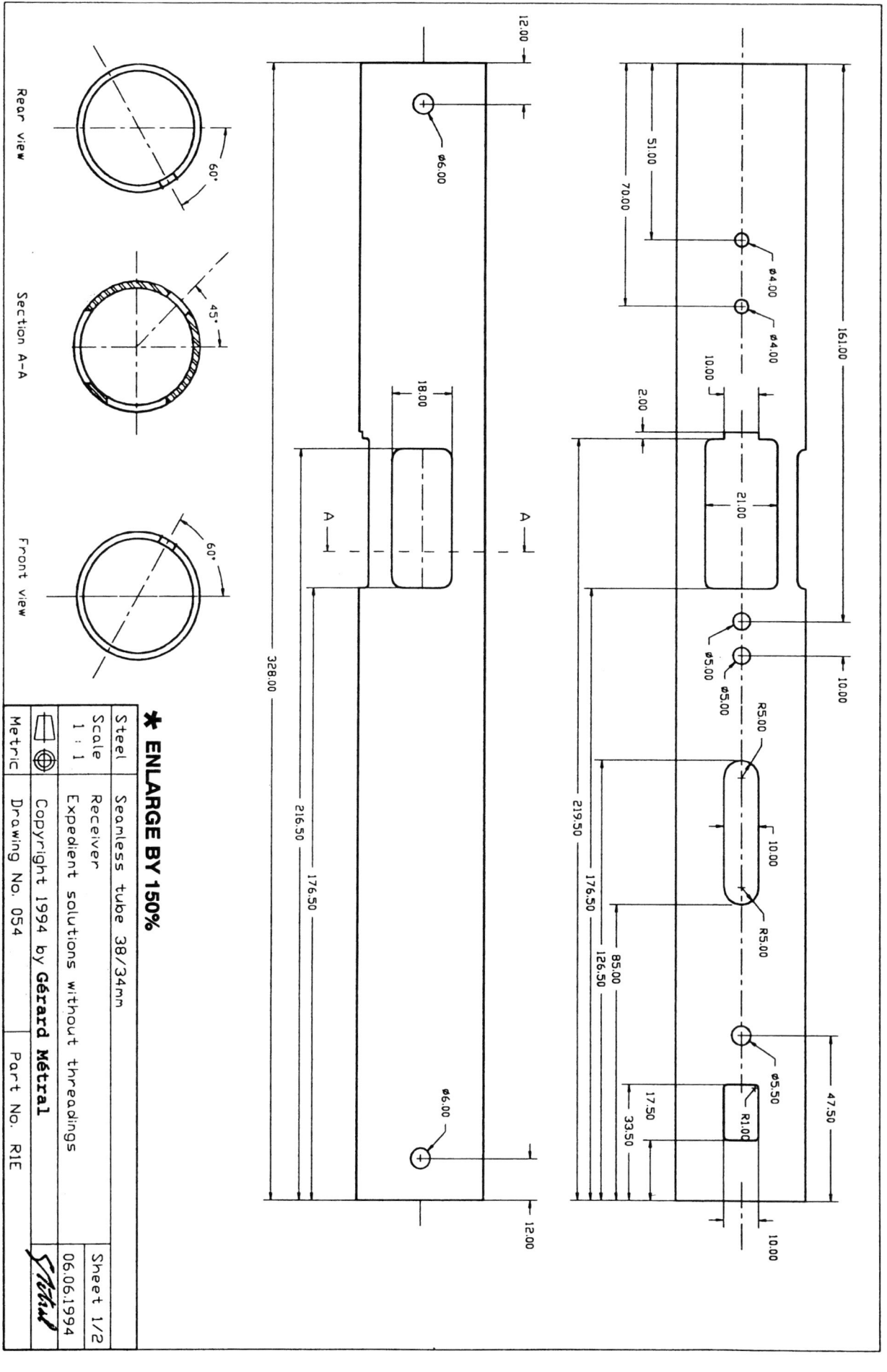

Rear view

Section A-A

Front view

60°

45°

60°

Ø6.00

Ø4.00

Ø4.00

Ø5.00

Ø5.00

Ø5.50

R5.00

R5.00

R1.00

Ø6.00

12.00

51.00

70.00

10.00

2.00

21.00

10.00

10.00

161.00

219.50

176.50

126.50

85.00

47.50

17.50

33.50

10.00

18.00

A

A

A

328.00

216.50

176.50

12.00

✱ ENLARGE BY 150%

Steel	Seamless tube 38/34mm	
Scale	Receiver	
1 : 1	Expedient solutions without threadings	
Metric		

Drawing No. 054

Part No. R1E

Sheet 1/2

06.06.1994

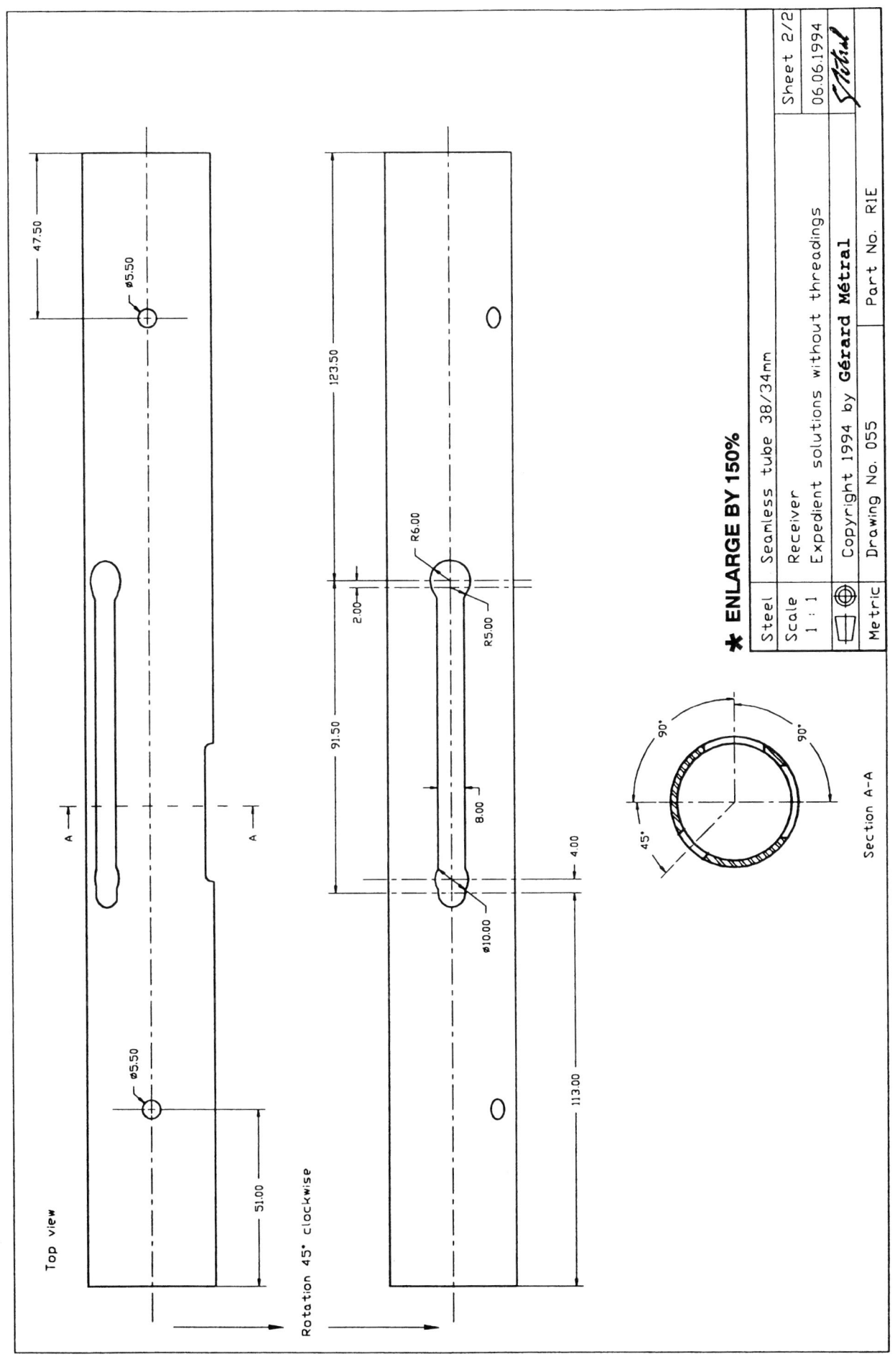

Top view

Rotation 45° clockwise

47.50

ø5.50

123.50

R6.00

R5.00

2.00

91.50

8.00

ø10.00

4.00

113.00

51.00

ø5.50

90°

45°

90°

Section A-A

✳ ENLARGE BY 150%

Steel	Seamless tube 38/34mm		Sheet 2/2
Scale 1 : 1	Receiver Expedient solutions without threadings		06.06.1994
	Copyright 1994 by **Gérard Métral**		
Metric	Drawing No. 055	Part No. R1E	

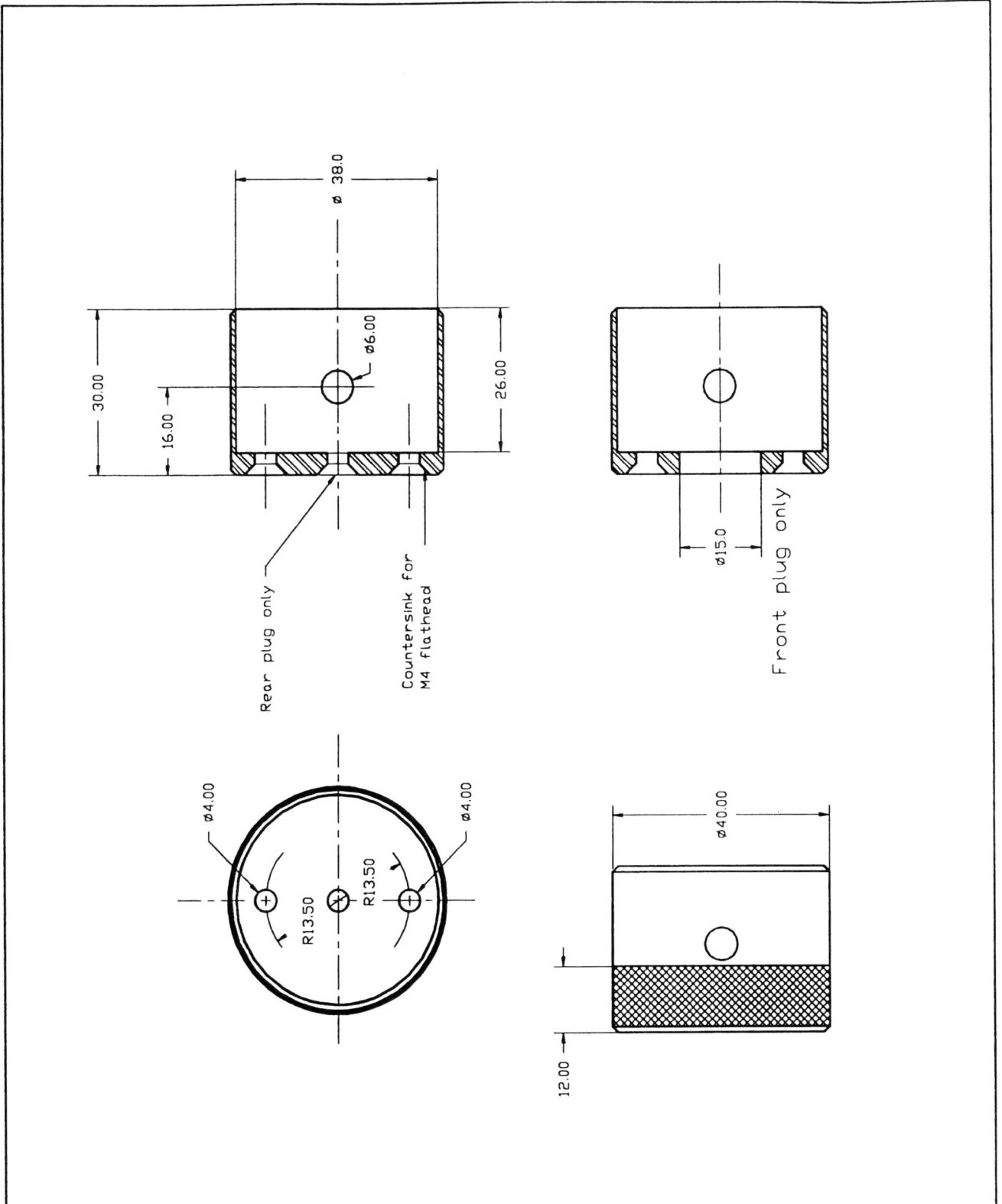

Ø 38.0

30.00

16.00

26.00

Ø6.00

Rear plug only

Countersink for
M4 flathead

Front plug only

Ø15.0

Ø4.00

Ø4.00

R13.50

R13.50

Ø40.00

12.00

Steel		
Scale 1 : 1	Rear and front plugs	Sheet 1/1
	Expedient solutions without threadings	06.06.1994
⊟ ⊕	Copyright 1994 by **Gérard Métral**	
Metric	Drawing No. 056	Parts No. R2E and R3E

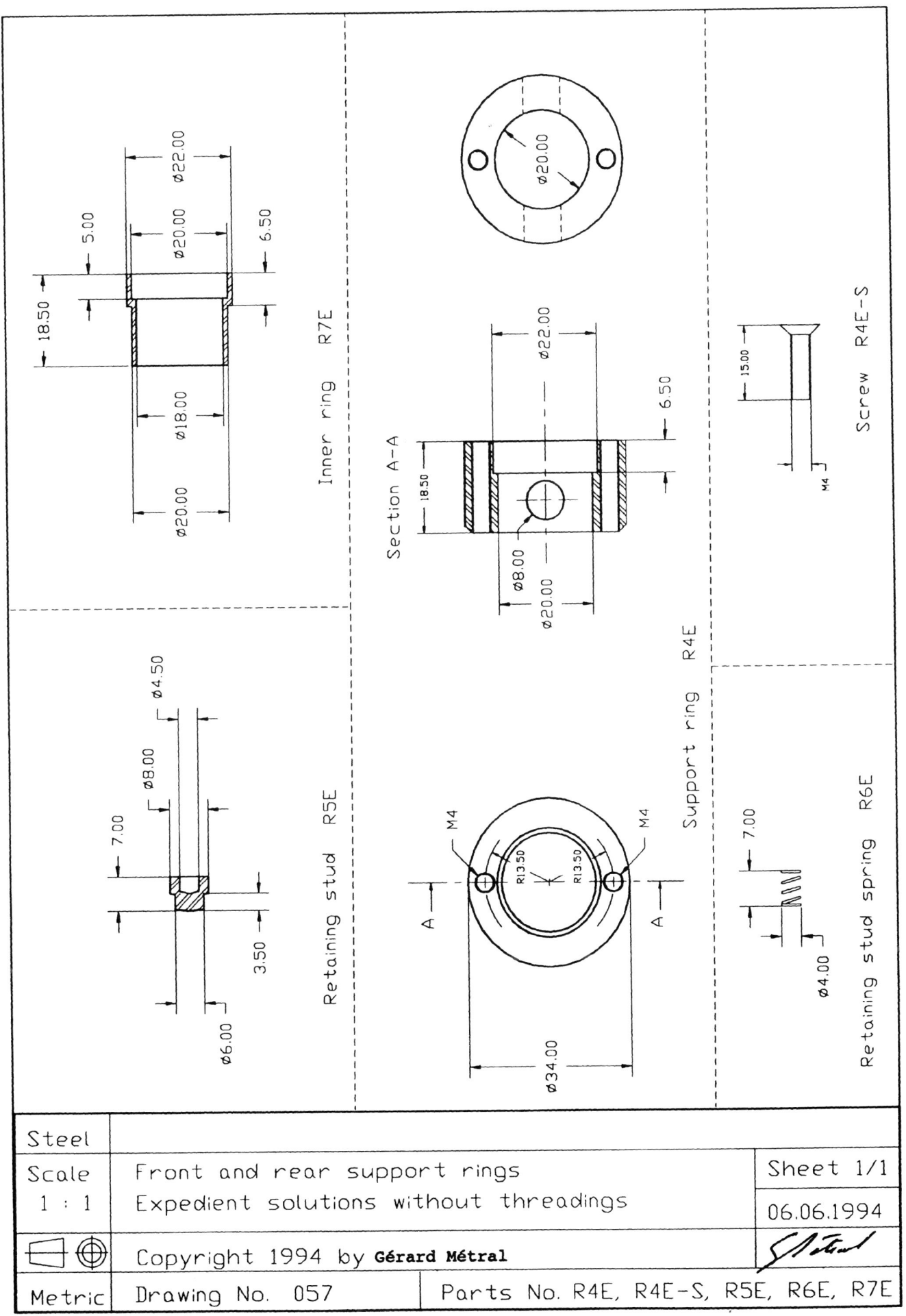

Ø22.00
Ø20.00
5.00
6.50
18.50
Ø18.00
Ø20.00

Inner ring R7E

Ø20.00

Ø22.00
6.50
18.50
Ø8.00
Ø20.00

Section A-A

15.00
M4

Screw R4E-S

Ø4.50
Ø8.00
7.00
3.50
Ø6.00

Retaining stud R5E

Support ring R4E

M4
R13.50
R13.50
M4
A
A
Ø34.00

7.00
Ø4.00

Retaining stud spring R6E

Steel		
Scale	Front and rear support rings	Sheet 1/1
1 : 1	Expedient solutions without threadings	06.06.1994
⬡ ⊕	Copyright 1994 by **Gérard Métral**	
Metric	Drawing No. 057	Parts No. R4E, R4E-S, R5E, R6E, R7E

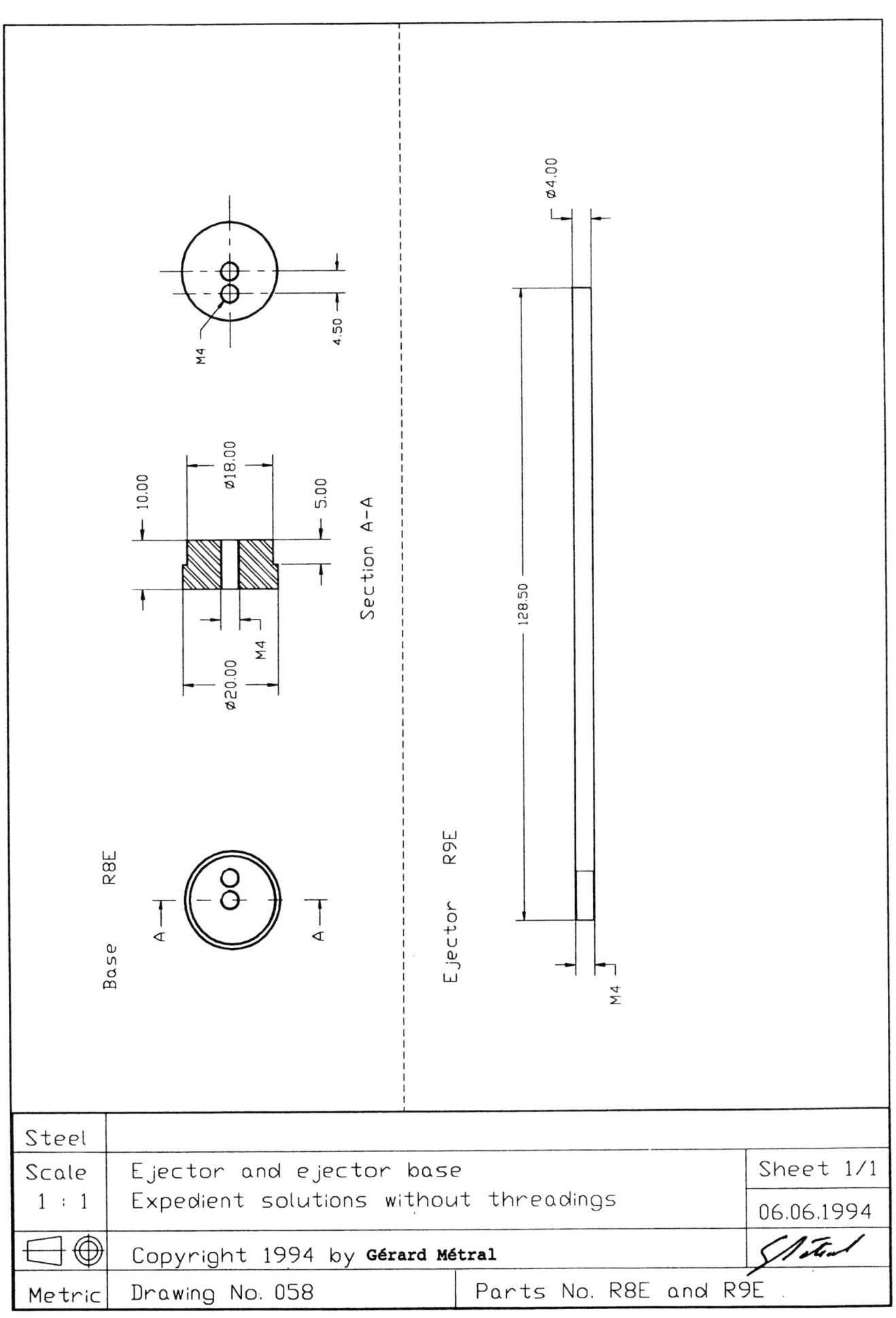

Base   R8E

Section A-A

Ø18.00

10.00

5.00

M4

Ø20.00

M4

4.50

Ejector   R9E

Ø4.00

128.50

M4

Steel		
Scale	Ejector and ejector base	Sheet 1/1
1 : 1	Expedient solutions without threadings	06.06.1994
⊟ ⊕	Copyright 1994 by **Gérard Métral**	
Metric	Drawing No. 058	Parts No. R8E and R9E

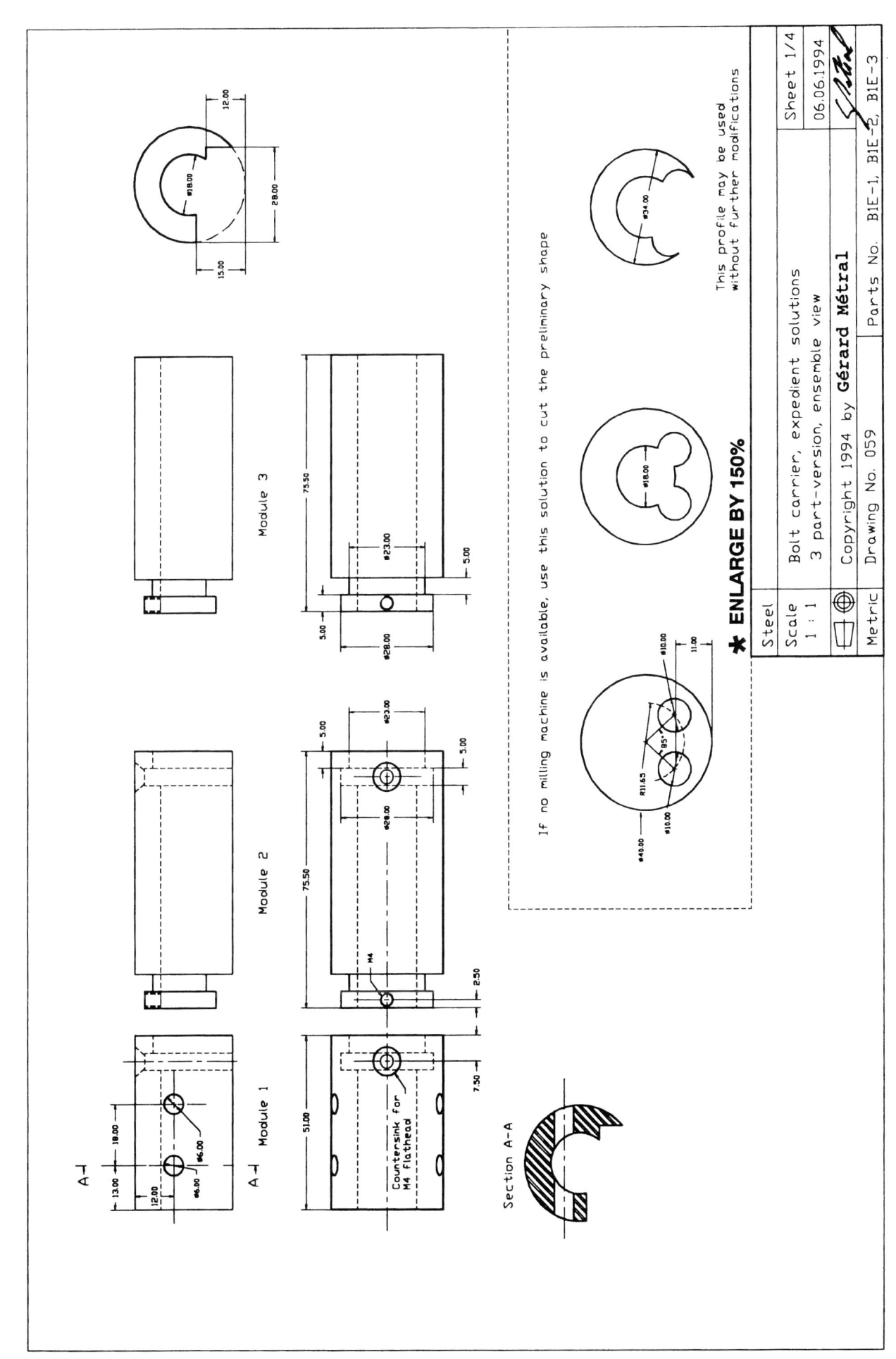

Module 3

Module 2

Module 1

Section A-A

If no milling machine is available, use this solution to cut the preliminary shape

Countersink for M4 Flathead

★ ENLARGE BY 150%

This profile may be used
without further modifications

Steel		Sheet 1/4
Scale 1 : 1	Bolt carrier, expedient solutions 3 part-version, ensemble view	06.06.1994
⊕	Copyright 1994 by **Gérard Métral**	
Metric	Drawing No. 059	Parts No. B1E-1, B1E-2, B1E-3

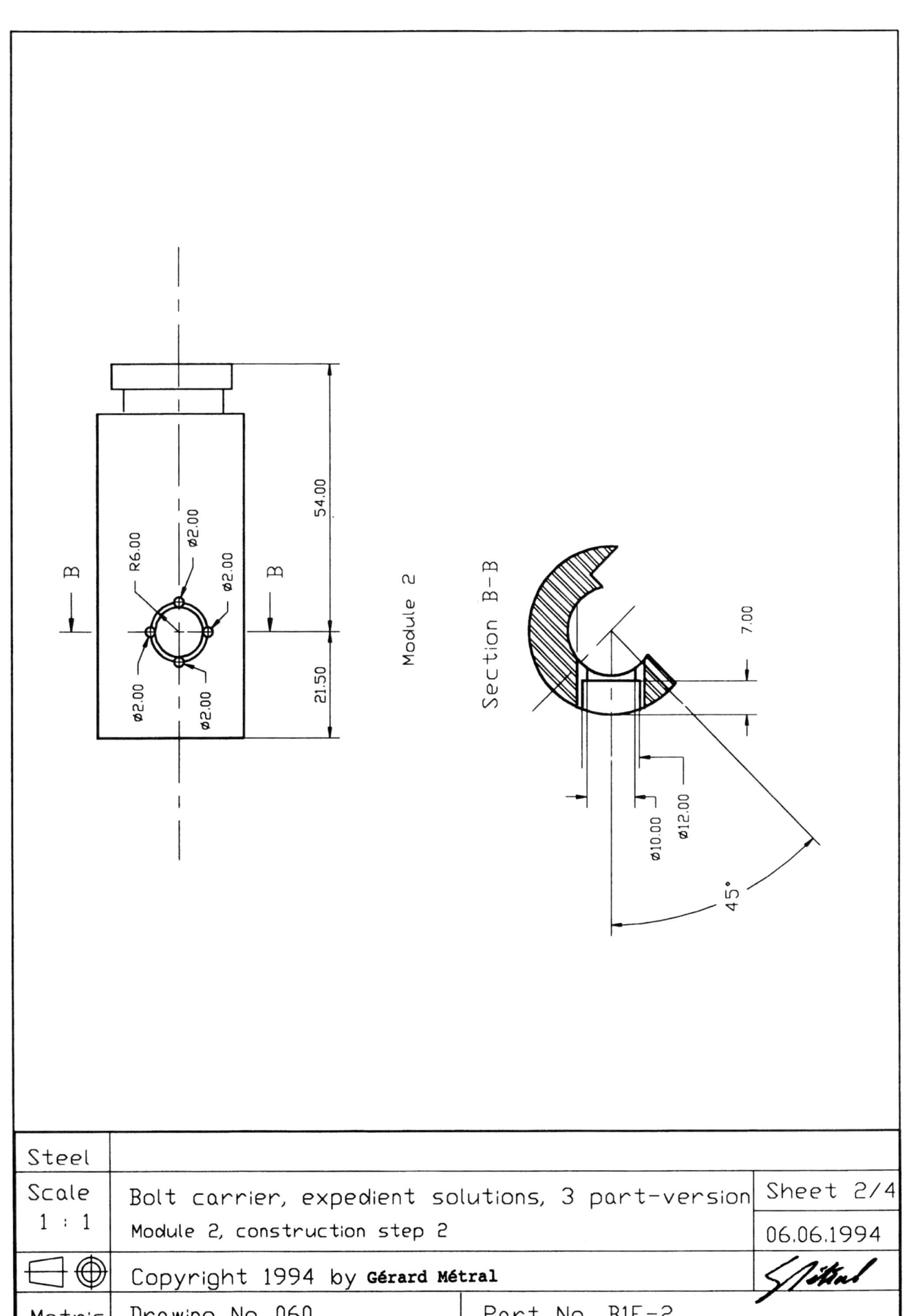

B

R6.00
Ø2.00
Ø2.00
Ø2.00
Ø2.00

B

54.00

21.50

Module 2

Section B-B

7.00

Ø10.00
Ø12.00

45°

Steel		
Scale 1 : 1	Bolt carrier, expedient solutions, 3 part-version	Sheet 2/4
	Module 2, construction step 2	06.06.1994
⊟ ⊕	Copyright 1994 by Gérard Métral	
Metric	Drawing No. 060	Part No. B1E-2

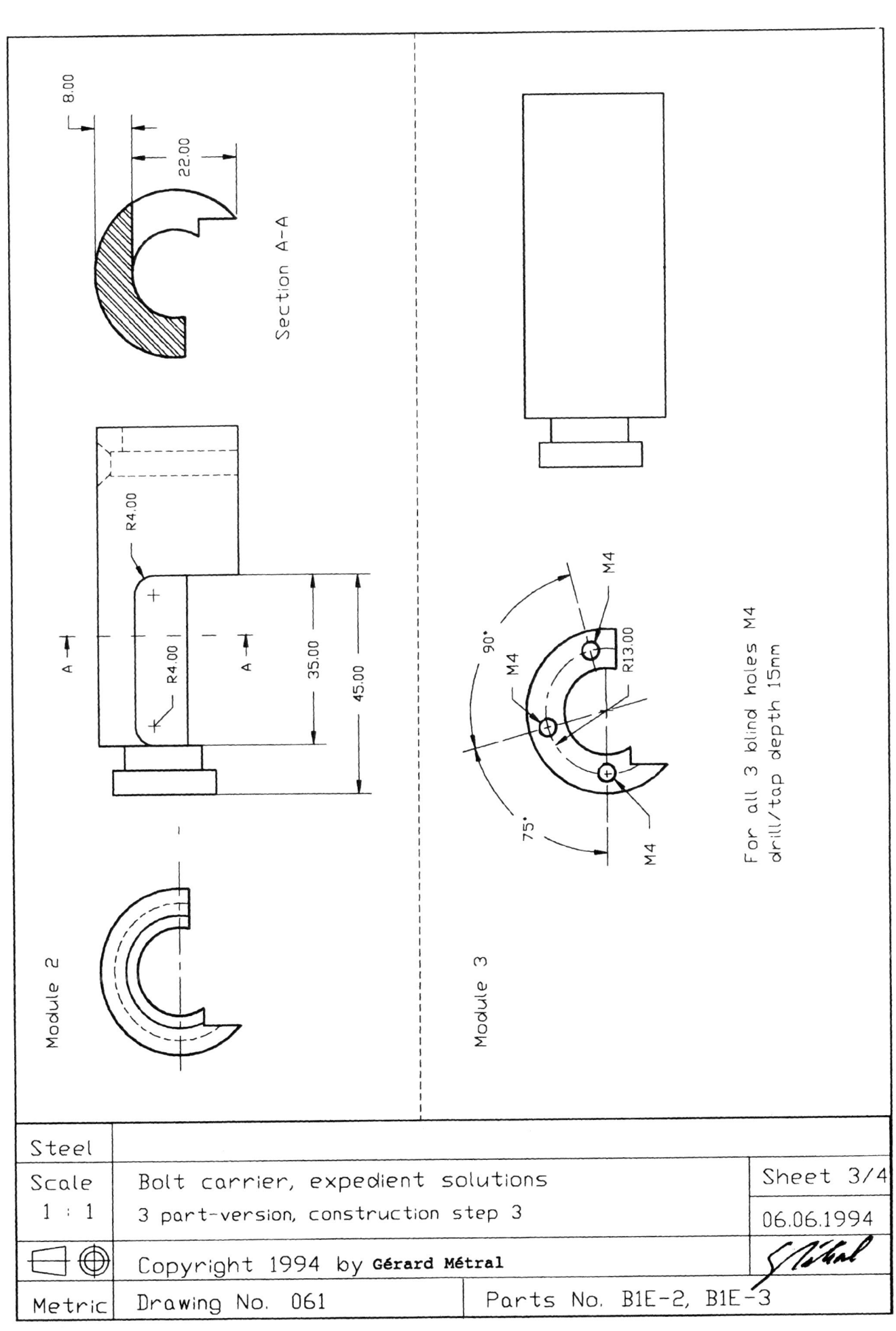

8.00

22.00

Section A-A

R4.00

R4.00

A

A

35.00

45.00

Module 2

M4

90°

M4

75°

R13.00

M4

For all 3 blind holes M4
drill/tap depth 15mm

Module 3

Steel		
Scale	Bolt carrier, expedient solutions	Sheet 3/4
1 : 1	3 part-version, construction step 3	06.06.1994
	Copyright 1994 by **Gérard Métral**	
Metric	Drawing No. 061	Parts No. B1E-2, B1E-3

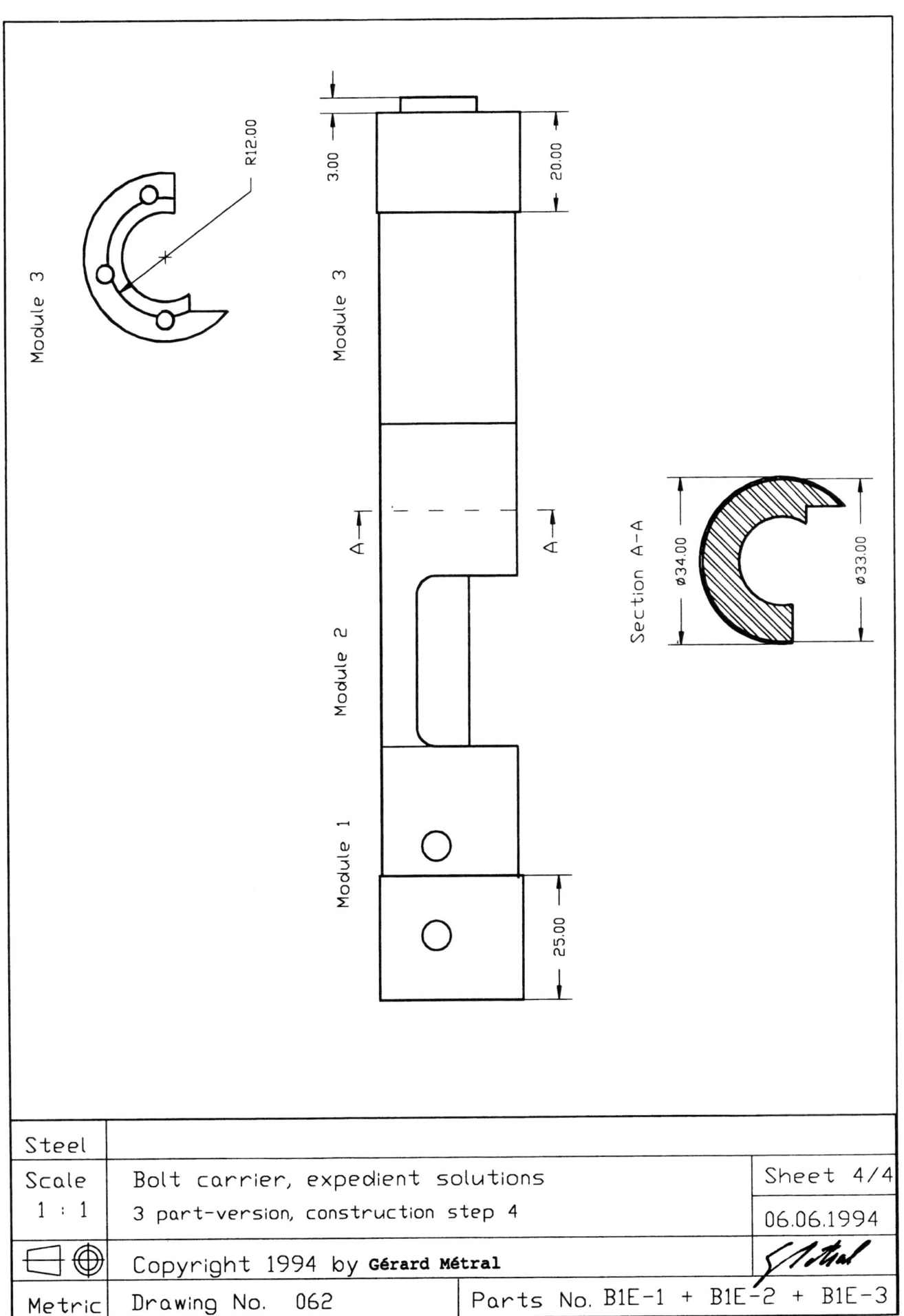

Module 3

R12.00

Module 3

3.00

20.00

Module 3

A —

A —

Module 2

Section A-A

Ø34.00

Ø33.00

Module 1

25.00

Steel			
Scale	Bolt carrier, expedient solutions		Sheet 4/4
1 : 1	3 part-version, construction step 4		06.06.1994
	Copyright 1994 by **Gérard Métral**		
Metric	Drawing No. 062	Parts No. B1E-1 + B1E-2 + B1E-3	

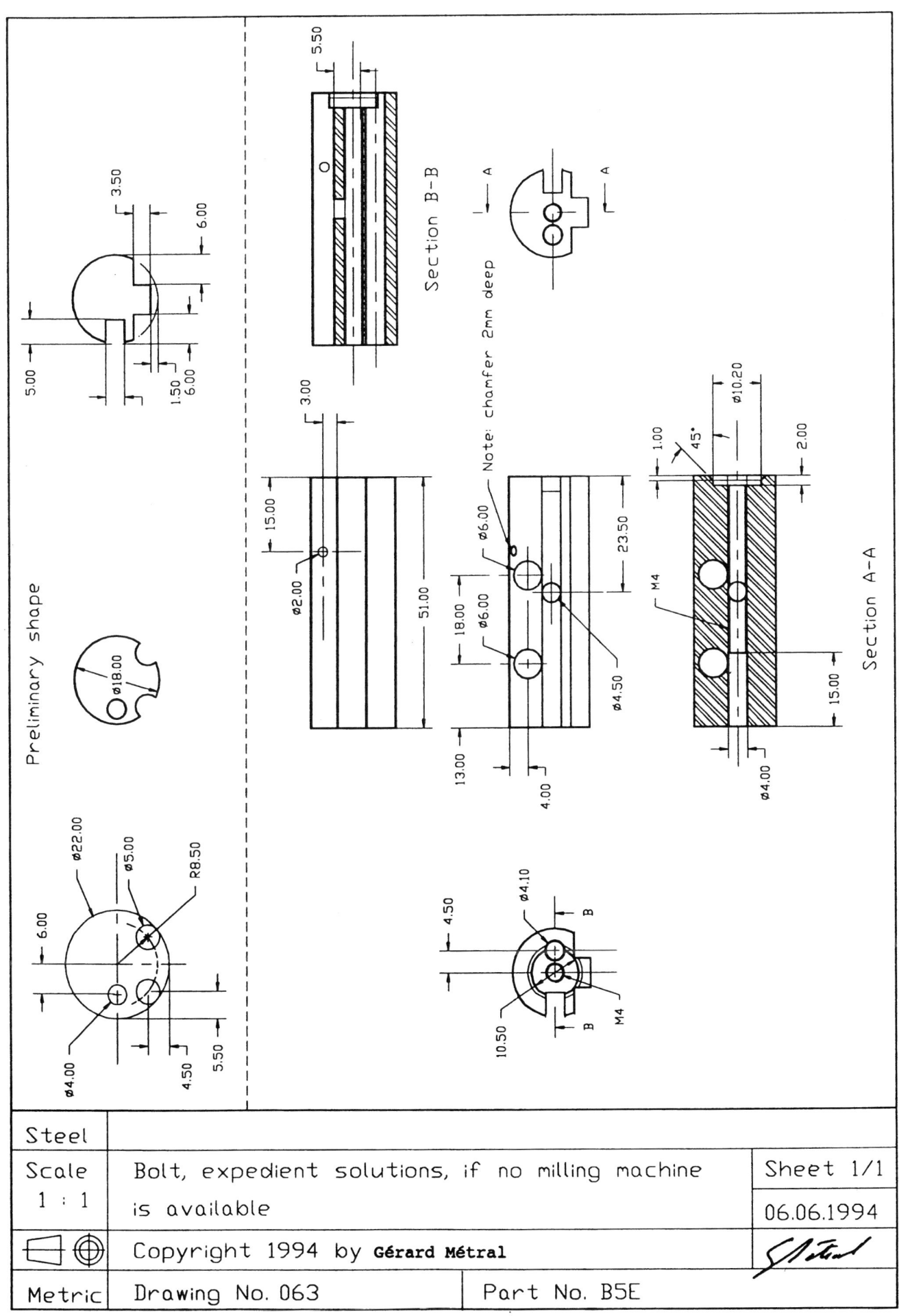

Preliminary shape

Section B-B

Section A-A

Note: chamfer 2mm deep

Steel		
Scale 1 : 1	Bolt, expedient solutions, if no milling machine is available	Sheet 1/1
		06.06.1994
⬖ ⊕	Copyright 1994 by **Gérard Métral**	
Metric	Drawing No. 063	Part No. B5E

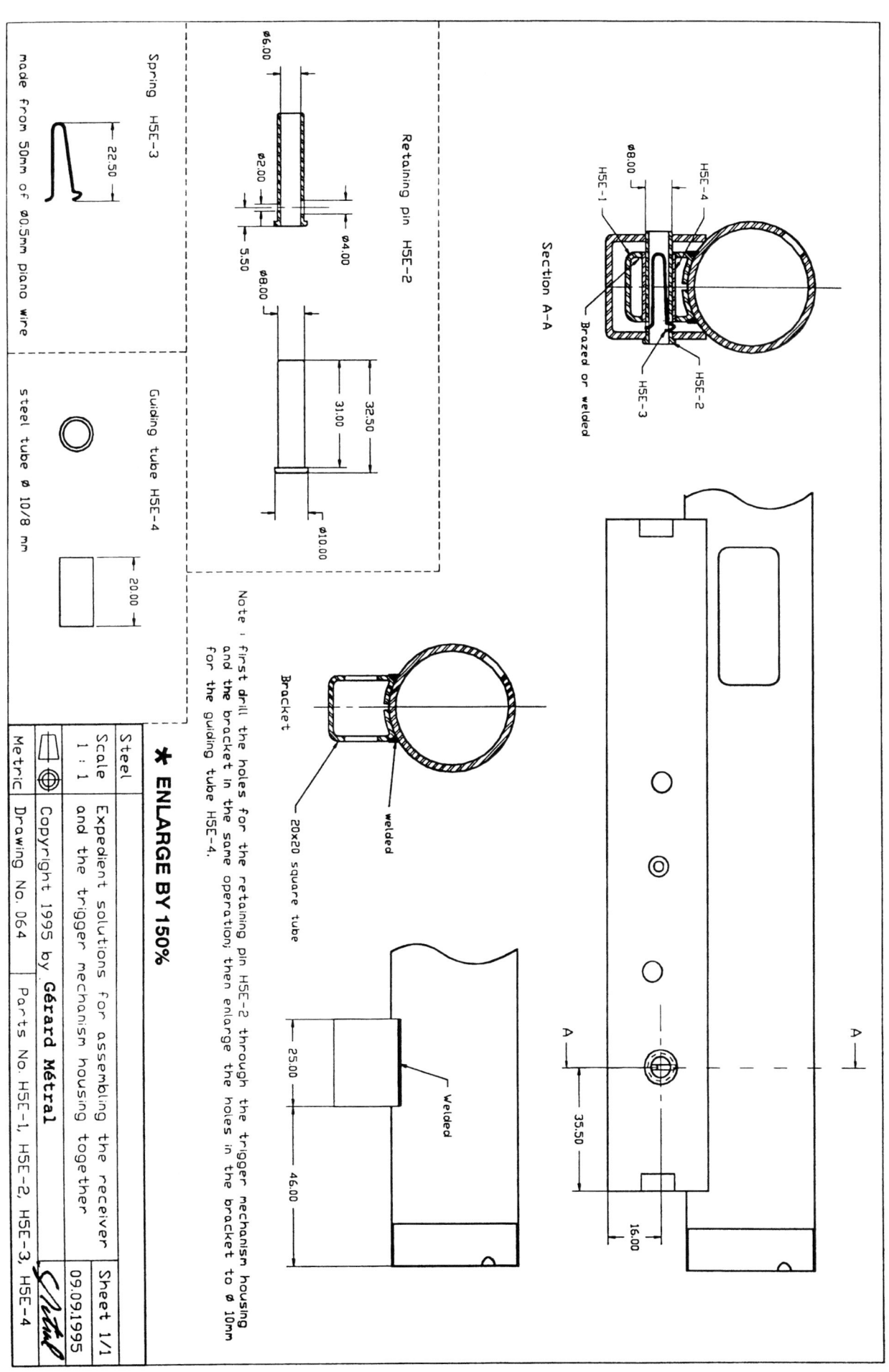

Retaining pin H5E-2

ø6.00
ø2.00
ø4.00
5.50

Guiding tube H5E-4

ø8.00
32.50
31.00
ø10.00

20.00

Spring H5E-3

22.50

made from 50mm of ø0.5mm piano wire
steel tube ø 10/8 mm

Section A-A

ø8.00
H5E-1
H5E-4
Brazed or welded
H5E-3
H5E-2

Note : first drill the holes for the retaining pin H5E-2 through the trigger mechanism housing and the bracket in the same operation; then enlarge the holes in the bracket to ø 10mm for the guiding tube H5E-4.

Bracket

20x20 square tube
welded

welded
25.00
46.00

A
35.50
16.00
A

✱ ENLARGE BY 150%

Steel		
Scale 1 : 1	Expedient solutions for assembling the receiver and the trigger mechanism housing together	Sheet 1/1
Metric	Drawing No. 064	Parts No. H5E-1, H5E-2, H5E-3, H5E-4

09.09.1995

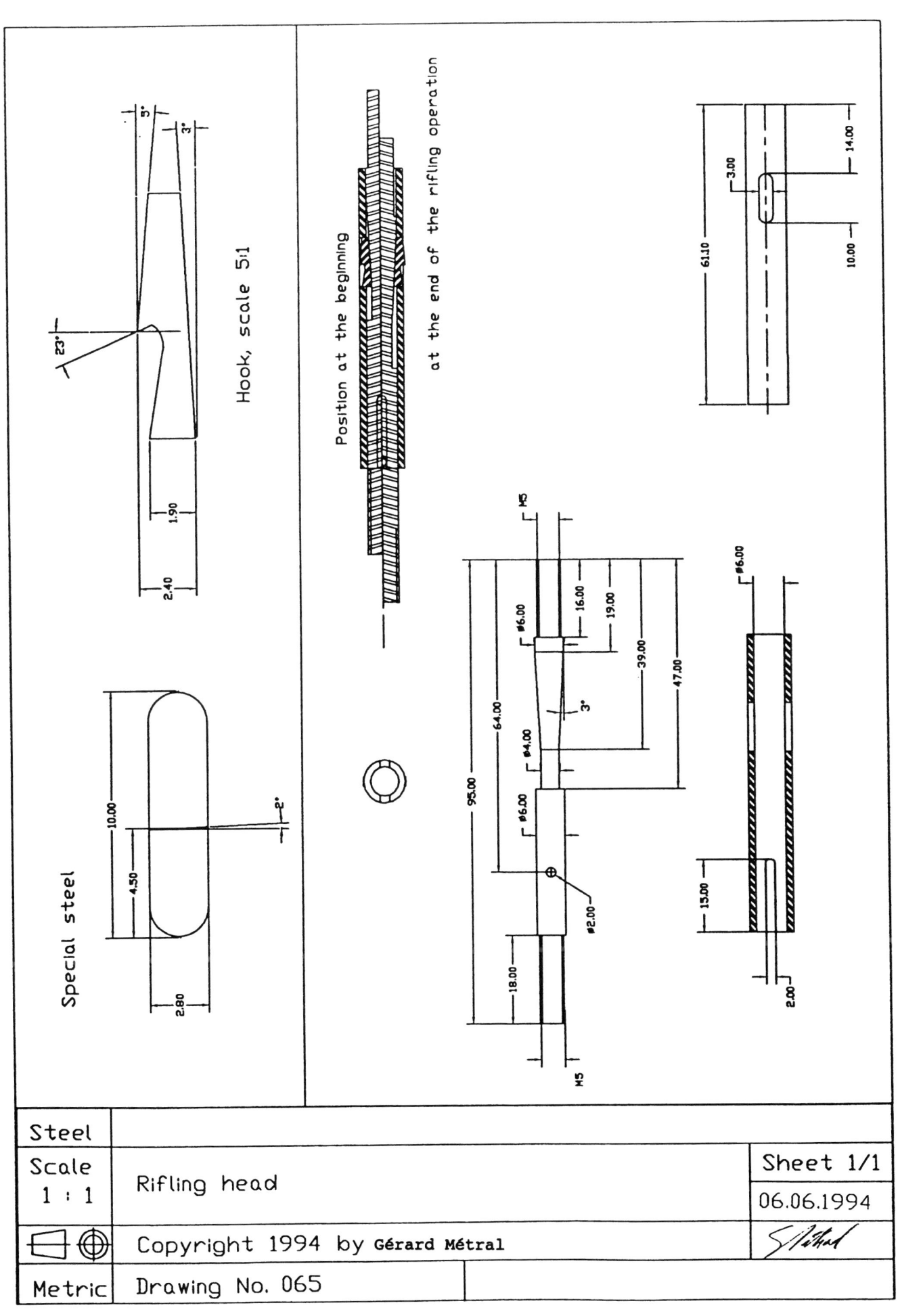

Hook, scale 5:1

Position at the beginning

at the end of the rifling operation

Special steel

Steel	
Scale 1 : 1	Rifling head
	Copyright 1994 by Gérard Métral
Metric	Drawing No. 065

Sheet 1/1

06.06.1994

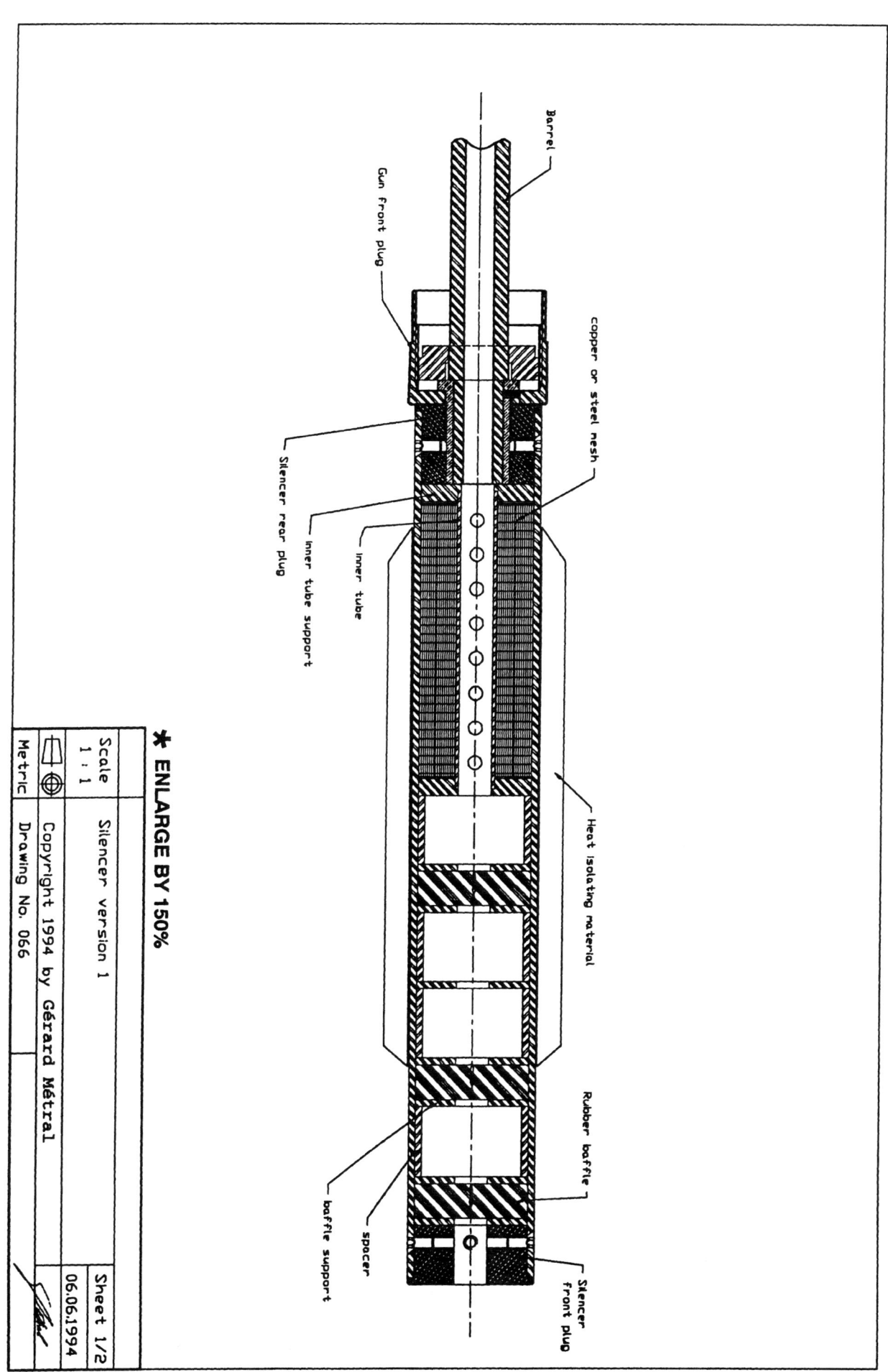

Barrel

Gun front plug

copper or steel mesh

Silencer rear plug

inner tube support

inner tube

Heat isolating material

Rubber baffle

baffle support

spacer

Silencer front plug

✱ ENLARGE BY 150%

Scale 1 : 1	Silencer version 1		Sheet 1/2
Metric	Copyright 1994 by Gérard Métral		06.06.1994
	Drawing No. 066		

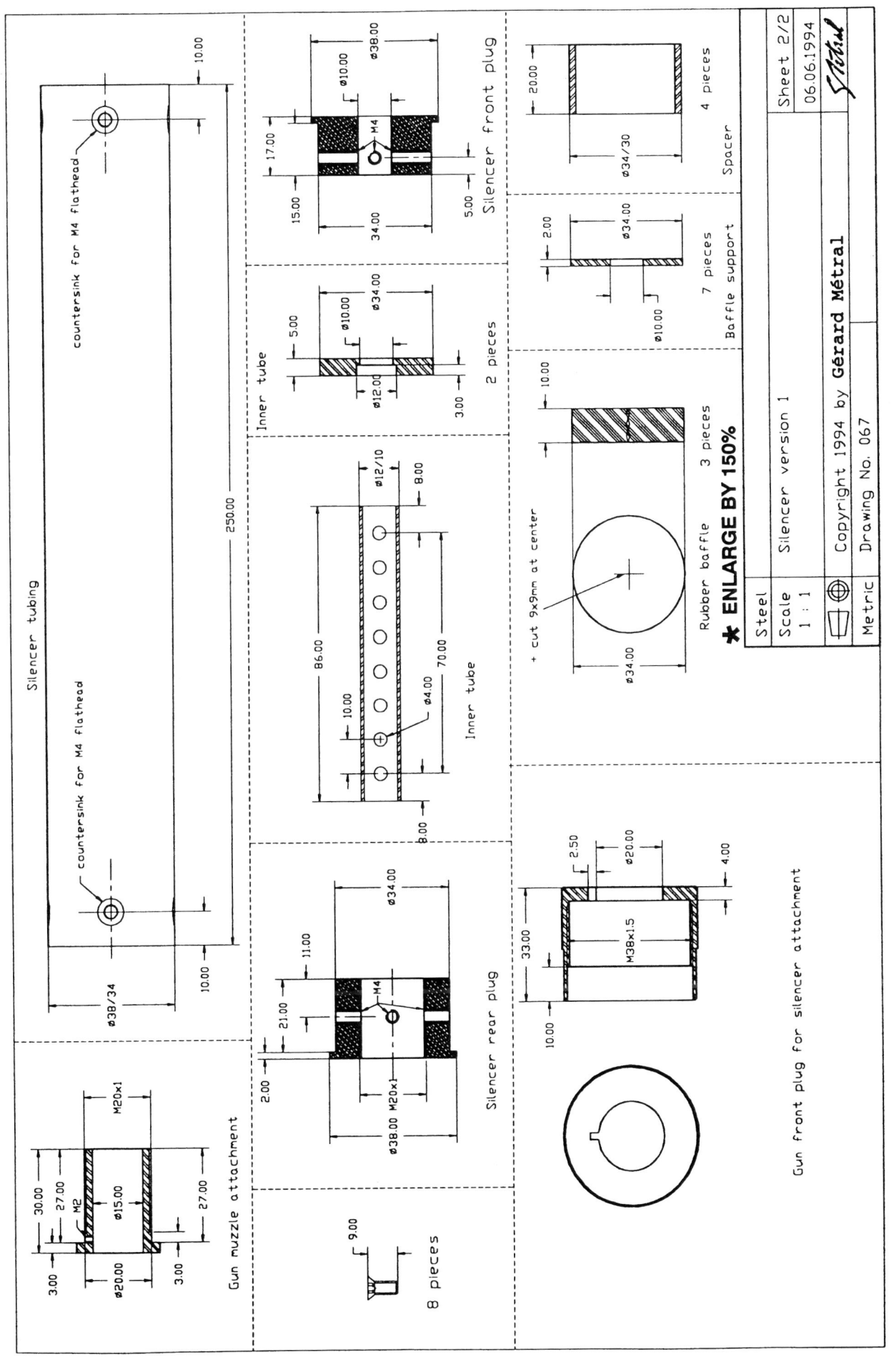

Silencer tubing

countersink for M4 flathead

countersink for M4 flathead

Ø38/34

10.00

250.00

Gun muzzle attachment

M20x1

30.00
27.00
M2
Ø15.00
27.00

3.00
Ø20.00
3.00

Silencer front plug

Ø38.00
Ø10.00
M4
17.00
15.00
34.00
5.00

Inner tube

Ø34.00
Ø10.00
5.00
Ø12.00
3.00

2 pieces

Inner tube

Ø12/10
8.00
86.00
10.00
Ø4.00
70.00
8.00

Silencer rear plug

Ø34.00
11.00
M4
21.00
2.00
Ø38.00 M20x1

Spacer

20.00
Ø34/30

4 pieces

Baffle support

2.00
Ø34.00
Ø10.00

7 pieces

Rubber baffle   3 pieces

10.00
+ cut 9x9mm at center
Ø34.00

Gun front plug for silencer attachment

2.50
Ø20.00
33.00
M38x1.5
10.00
4.00

9.00

8 pieces

★ ENLARGE BY 150%

Steel		
Scale 1:1	Silencer version 1	Sheet 2/2
		06.06.1994
⊕	Copyright 1994 by Gérard Métral	S.Métral
Metric	Drawing No. 067	

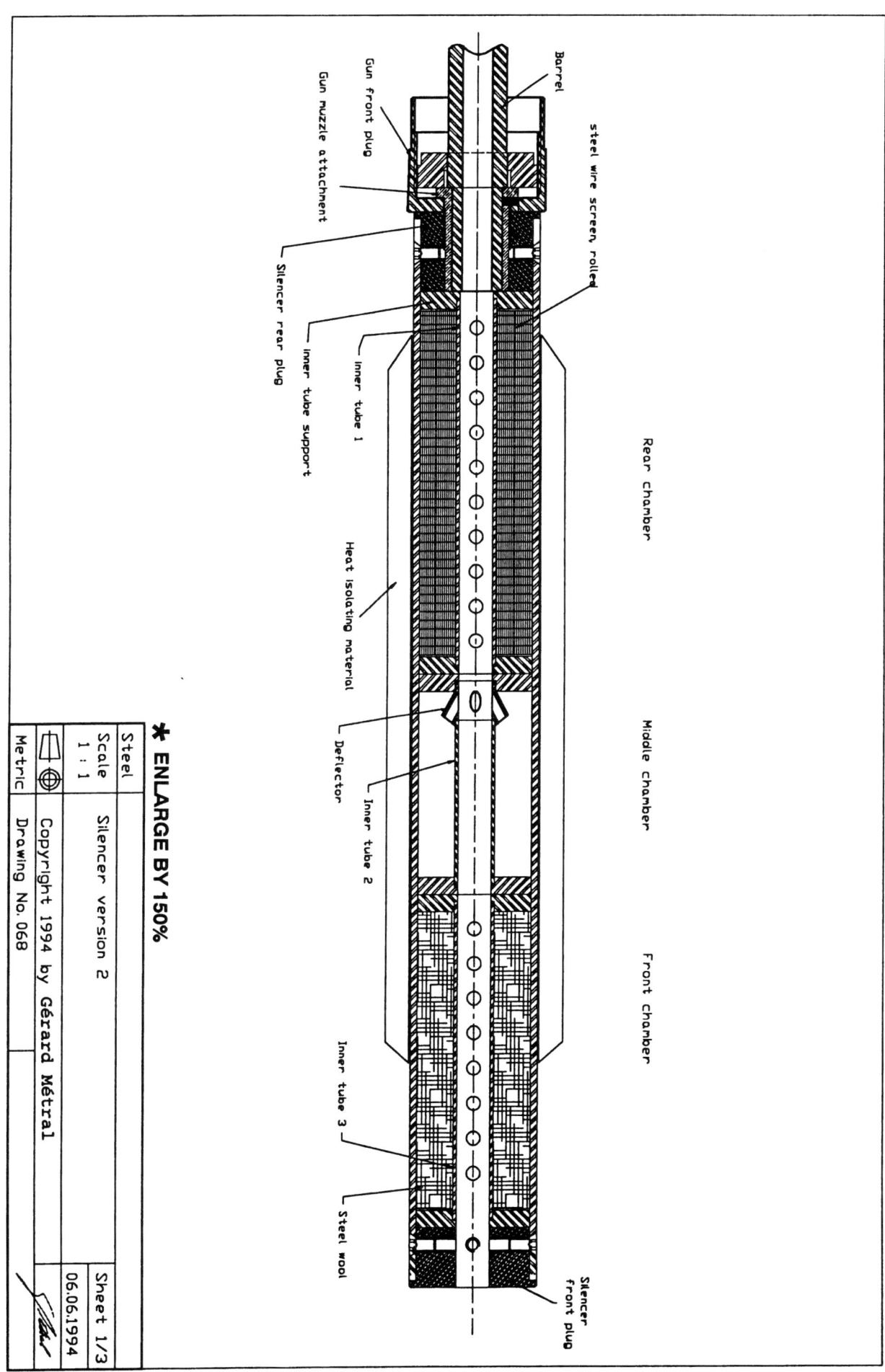

Barrel

steel wire screen, rolled

Gun front plug

Gun muzzle attachment

Silencer rear plug

Inner tube support

Inner tube 1

Rear chamber

Middle chamber

Front chamber

Heat isolating material

Deflector

Inner tube 2

Inner tube 3

Steel wool

Silencer front plug

✱ ENLARGE BY 150%

Steel	
Scale 1 : 1	Silencer version 2
⬚ ⊕	Copyright 1994 by Gérard Métral
Metric	Drawing No. 068

Sheet 1/3
06.06.1994

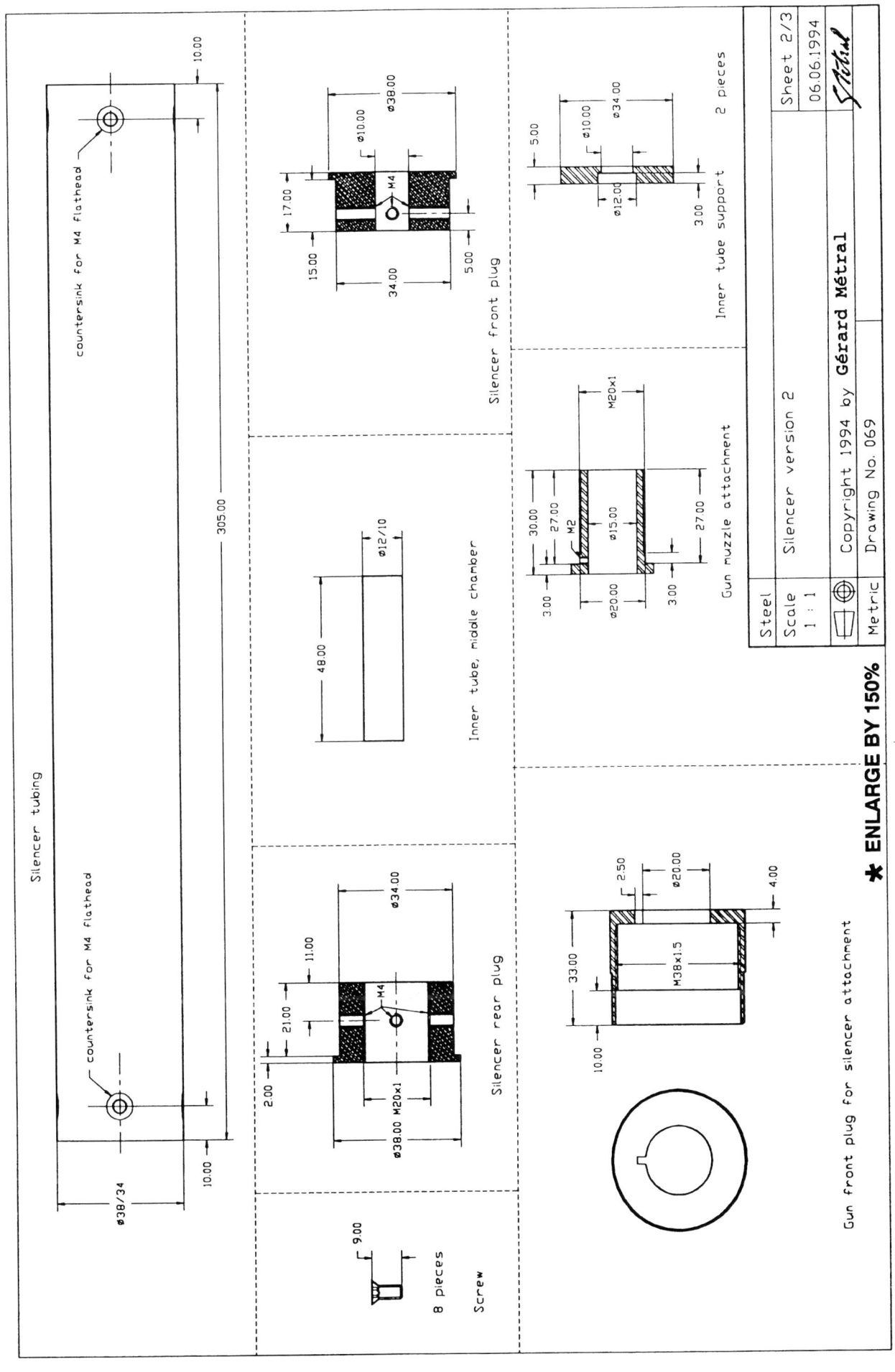

Silencer tubing

countersink for M4 flathead

countersink for M4 flathead

Ø38/34

Silencer front plug

Inner tube support
2 pieces

Inner tube, middle chamber

Gun muzzle attachment

Silencer rear plug

Screw
8 pieces

Gun front plug for silencer attachment

* ENLARGE BY 150%

Steel		
Scale 1:1		Silencer version 2
		Copyright 1994 by **Gérard Métral**
	Metric	Drawing No. 069

Sheet 2/3

06.06.1994

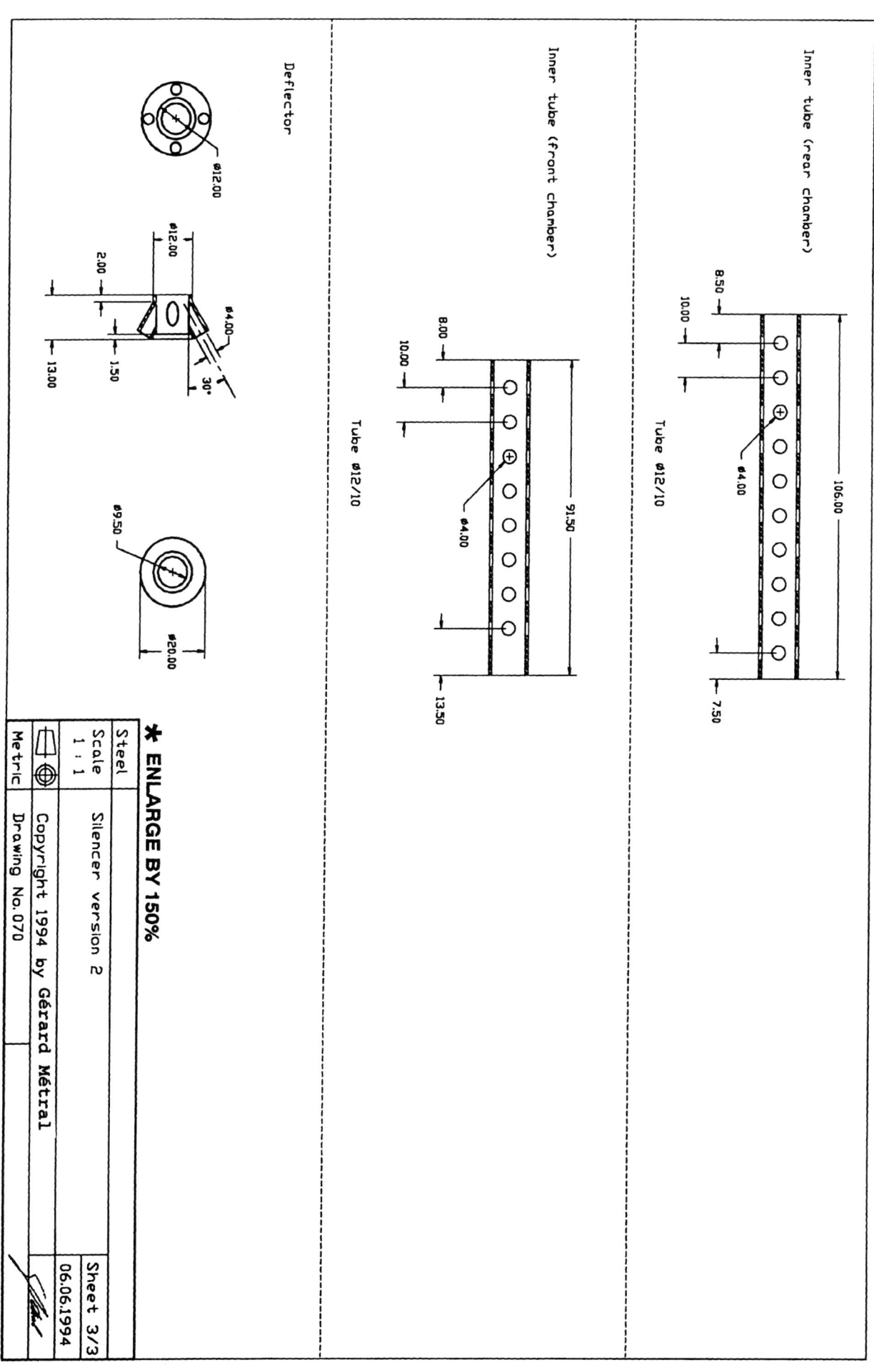

Inner tube (rear chamber)

Tube ø12/10

Inner tube (front chamber)

Tube ø12/10

Deflector

✱ ENLARGE BY 150%

Steel		
Scale	Silencer version 2	
1 : 1		
Metric	Copyright 1994 by Gérard Métral	Sheet 3/3
	Drawing No. 070	06.06.1994

LIST OF STANDARD
INDUSTRIAL COMPONENTS

Designation System
Example: M4x15 = M4 is the threading (metric 4mm); 15 is the length of the threaded part, in millimeters.

Standard Screws

	Parts #	Quantity
Headless Allen screw M4x5	R10, B10	2
Flathead M4x15	B3	3
Allen screw M4x5	H6	2
Allen screw M4x10	H11	2
Allen screw M3x30	G6	1
Flathead M4x5	F8	2
Flathead M4x20	F9	1
Flathead M4x25	F13	1
Flathead M4x30	F14	2
Self-tapping screw CL S, ST 4.8 - 13	W2	1
Self-tapping screw CL S, ST 4.2 - 13	W4	1

Modified Standard Screws (Original Dimensions, Modifications Given in the Drawings)

Parts #		Quantity
Hexagonal head M4x15 mm	R16	2
Allen screw M4x5	B9, B14	2
Allen screw M4x10	H4	2
Flathead M5x10	H8	1
Flathead M3x30	T15	1
Cylindrical head M3x10	S5	2
Flathead M3x10	F3	1

Standard Nuts

M3 self-locking nuts	T16, G7, S6, F17	4
M4 self-locking nuts	F10	4

BIBLIOGRAPHY

Ezell, E.C. *Small Arms of the World* (revised 12th edition). New York: Barnes & Noble, 1983.

Hobbart, F.W.A. *Jane's Infantry Weapons 1975*. London: Jane's Yearbooks, 1974.

_____. *Pictorial History of the Sub-Machine Gun*. London: Ian Allan Ltd., 1973.

Hogg, Ian V. *Jane's Infantry Weapons 1987–1988* and *1991–1992*. London: Jane's Publishing Company Ltd.

Holmes, Bill. *Home Workshop Guns for Defense and Resistance Vol. 1: The Submachine Gun*. Boulder, CO: Paladin Press, 1977.

_____. *Home Workshop Guns for Defense and Resistance Vol. 2: The Handgun*. Boulder, CO: Paladin Press, 1979.

Jane's Yearbook 1987 and *1991*. London: Jane's Publishing Company Ltd.

MacFarland, H.E. *Introduction to Modern Gunsmithing*. Harrisburg, PA: Stackpole Books, 1971.

Machu, Willi. *Die Phosphatierung*. Weinhein: Verlag Chemie, 1950.

Paladin Press. *Home Workshop Silencers I*. Boulder, CO: Paladin Press, 1980.

Skochko, L.W. and H.A. Greveris. *Silencers, Principles, and Evaluation, Report R-1896*. American Ordnance Publications, 1971.

Smith, W.H.B. and J.E. Smith. *Small Arms of the World*. Harrisburg, PA: Stackpole Books, 1966.

ABOUT THE AUTHOR

Gérard Métral has a Ph.D. in biology and teaches at a Swiss university. He is a captain in the Swiss army reserves, where his specialty is artillery. He also has extensive training in mechanics and computer science, which prepared him to create the machinist's drawings that accompany this text. Métral has been a gun collector since the age of 18, and, as such, he has carefully studied all types of small arms to find the best design for a reliable resistance gun. This book is the result of these studies. Métral lives with his family in Geneva.